RELIGIOUS EDUCATION IN THE
AFRICAN AMERICAN TRADITION

RELIGIOUS EDUCATION IN THE AFRICAN AMERICAN TRADITION

A COMPREHENSIVE INTRODUCTION

KENNETH H. HILL

CHALICE
PRESS

ST. LOUIS, MISSOURI

Biblical quotations, unless otherwise noted, are from the *New Revised Standard Version Bible,* copyright 1989, Division of Christian Education of the National Council of the Churches of Christ in the United States of America. Used by permission. All rights reserved.

Cover art: *The Coming of the Holy Spirit,* Soichi Watanabe, Japan, from ACAA
web site: http://www.asianchristianart.org
Cover and interior design: Elizabeth Wright

www.chalicepress.com

10   9   8   7   6   5   4   3   2   12   13   14   15   16   17

Print: 9780827208209
EPUB: 9780827232846   EPDF: 9780827232853

Library of Congress Cataloging–in–Publication Data

Hill, Kenneth H.
  Religious education in the African American church : a comprehensive introduction / Kenneth H. Hill.
     p. cm.
  Includes bibliographical references.
  ISBN-13: 978-0-8272-0820-9
  1. African American theological seminaries. 2. African American clergy–Training of. 3. Theology–Study and teaching. 4. African American churches. 5. Christian education. 6. African Americans–Education. I. Title.

BV4080.H55 2007
268'.08996073–dc22
                                                        2006033389

Printed in the United States of America

Contents

Acknowledgments

Many persons and institutions helped in the development of *Religious Education in the African American Tradition: A Comprehensive Introduction*. I am grateful to the Louisville Institute for the research grant to pursue this project and Emory University Candler School of Theology/Pitts Theological Library for allowing me to serve as a visiting fellow to conduct research and write.

I would like to express my sincere appreciation to Mary Elizabeth Moore, for your patience, insightful guidance, and for encouraging me to reflect more deeply and think more critically upon the educational legacy of my heritage.

Thank you J. Deotis Roberts and Charles Foster for challenging me to think theologically about African American Christian religious education. Thank you Roberta, my wife, who journeyed with me throughout and supported me during the writing of this project.

Thank you Kamasi, my son, for your insightful comments. Your mind and intellect have been a special gift. Gratitude is extended to my administrative assistant, Loretta Matthews, for your editorial work.

Appreciation goes to the students at Payne Theological Seminary in Xenia, Ohio, the Divinity School at Vanderbilt University in Nashville, Tennessee, and Ecumenical Theological Seminary in Detroit, Michigan, who learned with and taught me as we explored issues of Christian education in African American congregations. Thank you colaborers and educators for your friendship, fellowship, and for working with me throughout my journey in ministry. The experiences have been rich and rewarding.

Preface

Dr. Kenneth H. Hill has spent several years as the main religious educator of the African Methodist Episcopal Church. It is a privilege to know Dr. Hill and to have served with him in ecumenical endeavors. As a Baptist minister and theologian, I served with Hill on the Lenten Booklet Committee of the Consultation on Church Union. During this period of dialogue with him, I came to appreciate his spirit of outreach as well as his scholarship.

Hill has witnessed as a Christian religious educator during a unique period of the history of the African American Church Tradition. During the period of Black consciousness and Black power he made a powerful witness for social justice. This was a period of "Black ecumenism" represented by the National Committee of Black Christians. This period gave birth to Black church studies and Black theology as well as many action and social service agencies.

The A.M.E. Church was an important partner with those who sought liberation from oppression due to racism in American society. The A.M.E. Church has a history of prophetic witness that began more than two hundred years ago when Richard Allen walked out of the White Methodist church in Philadelphia. In fact, the A.M.E. Church became a lightening rod for the African American Church Tradition both in the search for roots and the quest for social justice. Nevertheless, this denomination has been a source for comfort and healing for a long-suffering people.

The period of African American history, just described, followed upon the heels of the civil rights movement. This period (1954–68) was represented by the Brown legal decision for the desegregation of education and the nonviolent protest efforts of Dr. Martin Luther King Jr.

More recently, the Afrocentric Cultural Movement has emerged to complement the work done during earlier periods of the African American quest for social justice. This latter movement is more cultural than political or theological, but it has had a significant impact on African American family, community, and church life.

The ministry of Kenneth Hill reflects significant involvement in all these movements that have surfaced over several decades. This forty-plus years of African American history with its search for heritage and social relevance is reflected in the educative thought and life of Kenneth Hill.

I am impressed with the outline of his project, the range of his interest, and the substance of his thought development. His educative work provides this book with a note of authority. His involvement in thought and action makes it so.

The book is much needed. It brings the educational ministry of African American churches in contact with the best academic work in the field of Christian religious education. Due to the quality of his reflection, experiences, and sources, the book will be valuable for all who educate believers in the Church of Jesus Christ.

Hill makes a good case for this study. It is unique in his discussion of Christian religious education in the African American Church Tradition. It has a cultural relevance and meets the practical needs for the educative role of churches in the context of the African and African American roots of believers in the community of Christians.

I was, of course, impressed as he takes seriously the contribution of theology, in the Black tradition, to religious education. As one of the founders of Black theology, I am always pleased to know that the efforts of Black theologians have the recognition of, and importance for the ongoing ministry to African American people.

Hill injects the theme of liberation from oppression into his vision for the field of Christian religious education. This is especially important for African Americans who have had to struggle for a condition of dignity in a society that has constantly denied their true worth. Hill shows competence in biblical thought as well as a profound appreciation for the same. Nevertheless, he provides an openness for dialogue with other religions, i.e., Islam and Judaism, as well.

The author reminds us of the importance of the teaching ministry of the Christian Church. We must address the mind as well as the heart if we are to anticipate a living faith. The entire personality of each one must be addressed.

Jesus admonishes us to teach "everything I have commanded you" (Mt. 28:20a). This follows the summons to love God "with all thy mind" (Mt. 22:37, KJV). This is to say that the whole person is to be involved in a total commitment to the gospel.

It follows that the Christian community needs a teaching ministry. In fact, there should be a teaching and learning dimension in all aspects of worship: music, prayer, preaching, etc. This work stresses the comprehensive nature of the educative task in the life, ministry, and witness of all churches.

Finally, I am delighted to write this preface and to witness the release of this important book. Dr. Kenneth Hill and the editors of Chalice Press have prepared for us a "moveable feast" for our minds, spirits, and Christian witness. The rest is up to those who read and understand this vital message.

J. Deotis Roberts
Distinguished Professor of Philosophical Theology
Emeritus, Eastern Baptist Theological Seminary

Foreword

Reflection on African American Christian education has come of age, and Kenneth Hill is an ideal person to document the history, biblical and theological influences, and educational philosophies that undergird it. Christian education, indeed religious education in the many traditions of African people, has flourished in African and Pan-African communities for centuries, nourished through rituals, communal relationships, stories, spirituals and other music, prayer and praise, critical reflection, and ethical teaching. What is new is the burgeoning literature on African American Christian education—a literature that raises up the importance of elders and youth in the community (Anne Wimberly, Okechukwu Ogbonnaya, Fred Smith, and Evelyn Parker); biblical teaching (Joseph Crockett); stories and story-linking (Wimberly); music (Yolanda Smith); small groups and community life (Lynne Westfield and Grant Shockley); ritual and worship (Wimberly and Melva Wilson Costen); liberation and justice (Shockley and Fred Smith). This literature is rich with insight and pedagogical diversity, and Kenneth Hill presents a thorough and complex picture of that literature and the educational practices upon which it reflects.

Unlike other religious education literature, the emerging Pan-African genre did not need critiques of schooling models of Christian education to point in new directions. African American Christian education, as most African education, has been grounded in community life from the beginning. For Christians, it has also been grounded in God as the Creator and Deliverer of a hurting creation. Further, this education did not need to toss out schooling models as if they were irrelevant. African Americans have valued intellect—as they have valued worship, dance, and song—from the beginning. It is no surprise that many Christian seminaries are finding a generation of eager African American students in Christian education. These are people who have been nourished in the Black church or have discovered the church in their youth and young adult years; they want to preserve their precious heritage. These are the very people who need and hunger for Kenneth Hill's book.

Engaging in Public, Full-Bodied Dialogue

Hill has responded to the hunger for dialogue on Christian education with diligent research. He early on recognized that the literature on African American Christian education needed to be reviewed and expanded. He realized that he and others had no basic introduction to education in the Black church, so introductory courses were impaired by lack of adequate resources. Further, he recognized that exciting and substantive work had been done in recent years—work that needed to be discussed in a public forum and embraced ever more fully in the Black church and scholarly community. Some might think that one or two good books are adequate, but that is not the case. What is needed is a full-bodied discourse with diverse perspectives, approaches, emphases, and agendas. What is further needed is conversation among these various authors and perspectives so that public discourse deepens and develops a common language.

The need for shared discourse and language is a serious issue in the larger field of religious education, both within religious communities (such as Jewish, Christian, and Islamic communities) and across these communities. Many years ago, Dwayne Huebner bemoaned the lack of a common language in religious education. I suggest that this problem is reflected in a tendency of religious educators to quote theologians and philosophers, or icons of popular culture, and to ignore the work of other educators, save for an occasional mention of one or two common sources. We educators rarely build on the work of one another; nor do we engage in active critique and collaborative construction. This may well be caused by our inferiority complex, thinking that no source within religious education is worthy of conversation, while the ideas of authors and leaders in other fields are considered worthy of discussion, even worthy to be called "foundations."

This peculiar issue of non-dialogue is not so rampant in the African American community of scholars and educators. Consider the opportunities created for Evelyn Parker, Yolanda Smith, and Lynne Westfield to present their work in the American Academy of Religion, an organization that has not traditionally welcomed the scholarship of religious educators. Consider also the recent collaborations among African American religious educators and the lively interdisciplinary dialogues among African American scholars in theology and religion. These reveal a collaborative spirit and interdisciplinary discourse that nourish the African American community and challenge the more isolated and isolating approaches of many other religious and scholarly communities. Indeed, the collaborative approach among Black scholars represents a countermovement, which has often been neglected by others. Kenneth Hill's book contributes to this countermovement, as he reviews work in Christian education and offers it back to the community as a gift upon which to build in the future. His book reveals the interweaving threads of Christian education practices in church communities, philosophical discussions in the Black community, biblical and theological scholarship, and developments in educational theory. Thus, he offers a dialogical book reflecting on a dialogical community and encouraging even more active dialogue in the future.

I have raised the non-dialogical oddity in the field of religious education because the work of Kenneth Hill moves the public conversation and common language of the field to new levels. His approach challenges the field of religious education by his example, reflecting on many sources by African American educators. Further, he draws on historical, contemporary, theoretical, and praxis-based sources in relation to one another. His comprehensive approach models a dialogical direction for other educators, which can be emulated by others in a multitude of ways. Even more explicitly, Hill claims a prominent place for African American Christian education within the field of religious education and within African American Christian communities. He offers an introduction to Christian education in African American communities that invites people to see its vitality, learn from its practical wisdom, engage with its theories, observe its grounding in living communities and existential issues, and contribute to the larger interreligious educational dialogue.

Drawing from Deep Wells

What Hill discovered as he began this work is that the riches of African American Christian education arise from a bottomless well, yielding cool waters to nourish many generations to come. In reflecting on the waters in this well, Hill identifies many streams of influence, arising from Africa itself and from life in the Americas during the colonial period and before, and during and after the Civil War. One of Hill's particular contributions is his presentation of African American contributions in the civil rights and "Black Power" movements. Hill does not focus on one denomination, though his own experience in the African Methodist Episcopal Church is worthy of note. Even with his denominational leadership in Christian education for many years, Hill does not have a narrow sectarian or denominational view of education. In fact, he draws widely from different parts of the Black church, including, for example, the Church of the Black Madonna, and he discovers wisdom in each, whether in their theology, philosophy, or active practice of education.

Sociologically, Hill recognizes multiple teachers in the Black church, including clergy and laity, elders and peers, women and men. He also recognizes diverse ways African American communities read the Bible and the complex theologies that generally undergird educational theology and practice. Of practical interest is Hill's description of how a complex of theologies can exist within a single congregation or denomination, allowing for diverse theologies to respond to diverse issues among the people. Hill not only values these multiple voices, but also draws upon them to inform and reflect on Christian education. He does not assume only one way of linking educational practice with theology, but recognizes diversities in pedagogy, in theology, and in their relation with one another. This very diversity is a strength commonly found in African American communities, which have tended less toward homogeneity than toward the kind of dialogue that Hill promotes in his book.

Kenneth Hill has walked through many of the movements described in his book, having spent some decades in pastoral ministry, general superintendency, and denominational leadership in Christian education. He has also researched this work with care, and is now able to offer a thorough, informative, and engaging book. Not only will this book be read in theological schools—both African American and ethnically diverse schools; it will also be read by church leaders and others who care for education. People actually want to learn. Education thus holds promise to challenge, nourish, and guide people in living their daily lives. It is vital to equip people to ask significant questions, live fully and faithfully, care for their communities, and work for the spread of justice and love in this world. No community has been more courageous or creative in developing educational philosophies and practices than the African American community. This is a legacy to celebrate, probe, share with the larger human community, and reconstruct for each new generation. Thank you, Kenneth!

Gratefully,
Mary Elizabeth Moore

Introduction

With the passing of time, I have become more grateful for the gift of teaching, for my membership in the African Methodist Episcopal Church, for being able to participate in theological discourse, and for the opportunity to serve as chief Christian Educator.

This conviction will help the reader understand the origin and nature of this book. The project stems from an invitation to conduct a workshop at the Ecumenical Church Educators Event, sponsored by the National Council of Churches, on "The Theology and Practice of Christian Religious Education in the Black Church."

Another motivation occurred while walking through the stacks at Colgate-Rochester Divinity School library the summer of 1999. The smell of the books brought back memories of my theological wanderings in the stacks during my seminary days at Harvard Divinity School. A spark ignited within me to return to the stacks. During twenty-five years of a ministry of Word through education, I have experienced various beliefs and practices of Christian religious education. Invariably, stirred by these experiences, I began earnestly seeking a better understanding of the dynamics of Christian religious education.

This book has grown out of a long-standing interest in African American Christian religious education (AACRE). In teaching Christian Education at Vanderbilt Divinity School, I found there was no one volume that explained the basics of the contemporary views about AACRE. At present there is no single text encompassing all of the theological, philosophical, and educational imperatives that underpin our theological and practical notions of Christian education.

I began to read the writings of those creative individuals who have been at the forefront of Black church educational endeavors. I discovered Grant Shockley, with his keen sense of history; James Cone, with his awe-inspiring capacity to organize theological data; C. Eric Lincoln, with his incredible creativity in applying old ideas to new situations; Joe Crockett, with his ability to create new Bible teaching methods; and Jacquelyn Grant and Anne Wimberly, with their constructive contributions of Black church educational practices.

The writings of these thinkers, together with many others, constitute the intellectual milieu in which this project had its birth. This is the book I had been hoping someone would write. I didn't think I would be that person. I recall a conversation with Charles Foster about the need for such a book. Foster said, "Take your research and develop it into book form for publication. It would be something I would want to use with all my students." As I considered this, Jack Seymour and Donald Miller's work, *Contemporary Approaches to Christian Education,* helped clarify a method of approaching this topic and outlined certain trajectories of thought. Thus the book *Religious Education in the African American Tradition* was born.

PART ONE

CHAPTER ONE

Understanding the Discipline

The Rise of African American Christian Religious Education

Prior to 1974, African American Christian religious education (AACRE) was relatively unsystematized in whatever forms in which it was expressed. Grant Shockley's research in 1974 contributed significantly to the liberation of Black Christian religious education history and consciousness.[1] Moreover, his research contributed to the development of AACRE as an academic discipline. His research brought to the attention of theological educators, Black and White, the relevance of the academic study of African American religion and education. The term "African American Christian religious education" should not be taken to mean that no scholarly works by African Americans were produced before 1974. To name a few, scholars such as W. E. B. Dubois, Carter G. Woodson, E. Franklin, and Benjamin E. Mays attest to the presence of scholarly interest in the study and interpretation of African American religion well before the 1960s.

What kind of research and scholarship has been done on AACRE? What can be said about the general state of the literature? Research on AACRE prior to the 1880s is part of the history of White Christian religious education. White scholarship on the history of religious instruction of enslaved Blacks tells more about White Christianity and the White religious mission than about the religion of the slaves. From the beginning of the Atlantic slave trade, conversion of the African to Christianity was used as a justification for enslavement of Africans. Gomes Eannes De Azurara, a chronicler of the fifteenth century, observed, "The greater benefit belonged not to the Portuguese adventurers but to the captive Africans, for though their bodies were now brought into some subjection, that was a small matter in comparison of their souls, which would now possess true freedom for evermore."[2] Azurara's mid-fifteenth century observation was to be repeated for four centuries by successive generations of White scholars, intellectuals, and researchers of slavery–a very "White Christianity" view of the situation. In addition, despite the widely held justification of slavery as a means of spreading the gospel, religious instruction of slaves was blocked by major obstacles, not the least of which was antipathy of the slavers and colonists themselves. Therefore, one of the tasks of Christian education is revision. The task of revision is construed primarily as a corrective of the omissions made by "White Christian education."

The earliest account of efforts to instruct Blacks in the Christian faith was published in 1842, The Religious Instruction of the Negroes in the United States, by Charles C. Jones. His work, like other early research on the Black religious experience, assumed that Blacks were culturally uncivilized, religiously heathen, and biologically subhuman. Unfortunately, Jones's examination of slaves' lives and thoughts about Christianity failed to appreciate the religion of the slaves (e.g., African Traditional Religion). He wrote, "The superstitions brought from Africa have not been wholly laid aside…A plain and faithful presentation of the Gospel usually weakens if not destroys these superstitions."[3] Shockley reminds us that research in AACRE had a history. He documented the extent to which religious education among Blacks before the Civil War accommodated the interests of slaveholders, and later in the nineteenth century seldom related itself to the experience of racism that dominated the lives of African Americans.[4]

Origins of the Discipline

African American religious studies, as an academic discipline, began as a political demand that had its origin in both the Black studies and "Black Power" movements of the 1960s. However, it was not until the Black studies movement erupted on seminary campuses in the 1970s, when there were critical masses of Black students, that we began to hear of Black church studies, or African American religious studies programs.[5] The initial thrust of the Black student movement on seminary campuses was to organize Black seminarians into a self-conscious organization capable of defining and advocating their interests.

Prior to the contemporary Black theological movement in seminaries and divinity schools, African Americans could not study and concentrate on African American religion as a legitimate academic subject area. Black theology made the study and interpretation of African American religious thought a genuine possibility in institutions of higher learning. For example, one of my classmates at Harvard Divinity School was studying to earn a Ph.D. in Old Testament. However, a dissertation proposal on comparing sacrifice in the Old Testament with African Traditional Religion was rejected by the chair of the dissertation committee as an illegitimate area of study.

The second thrust of the Black student movement on seminary campuses began with the demand for African American religious studies. For example, I served as the leader of this movement at Harvard Divinity School in 1975. The Black seminarian organization "Harambee," which I served as the first president, held a demonstration at the divinity school that changed the way the school related to Black seminary students, hired Black faculty, and established courses on the African American religious experience. Today many of these former classmates have become premier preachers, theologians, and educators worldwide. I think of Temba L. Mafico, Cornell West, Robert Franklin, Elliott Mgogo, Frank Madison Reid, Fred Lucas, Sunday Mbang, Kathy Gatson, Samuel Hogan, Eugene Rivers, Melvin Brown, Eleanor Ivory, Andy Cleo Lewter, Dexter Wise, Rita Dixon, Thomas Scott, and Simon Maimela.

The third thrust focused on the task of legitimization. Grant Shockley's thinking and writing provided legitimacy for the academic study of AACRE. Shockley might be considered the architect of the new discipline of AACRE. He was certainly steeped in the subject that would come to be a source for the new discipline. Shockley has been the most influential and prolific Black religious education theorist and writer of the past twenty-five years. As an academic he drew heavily on the scholarship and writings of Black Power, theology, and liberation. Shockley's engagement with the interplay of religious education and Black theology contributed to our understanding of AACRE as a distinct academic discipline within Christian religious education.

Shockley was typically the only Black person writing on Black Christian education and lacked the resources, sources, and colleagues needed to articulate indigenous Black religious and educational traditions. Nonetheless, his research brought to the attention of religious scholars and church educators the history of Black religious education. His articles in the 1970s were the beginning for the emerging Black Christian religious education consciousness. In more recent times, other writers and educators have continued the legacy of Shockley.

Relevance of the Discipline

One of the most important concepts in the Black student movement was relevance. It emanated from Christian education's contribution to liberation. Thus, Shockley would contribute to providing quality and relevant scholarship, teaching the African American religious experience, and helping us to understand Christian education within the African American context. His research efforts resulted in assembling and creating a body of knowledge, which was contributive to religious and intellectual liberation.

Shockley's scholarship linked the seminary and the church and was enhanced by his unique position as churchman and scholar. This relationship was best posed in his statement, "Christian educators in the Black church are beginning to recognize...the new questions for Christian education are essentially contextual. From goal-setting to evaluating, Black educators...are viewing the educational process in relation to the kind of learning and teaching that considers the Black experience as central and the liberation of Black people as its focal point."[6] The intent here was to serve and elevate the life conditions and consciousness of Blacks and reinforce the student's relationship with the church through theological and educational discourse. Thus the classic alienation between the religious intellectual/academy and the church is thwarted where knowledge is shared and applied in the service of liberation.

Finally, the current thrust is to establish AACRE as a legitimate, respected, and permanent discipline. This remains both an academic and political problem. The political problem is to win the battle of acceptance with administrators and other departments that question its relevance and viability. The academic problem is to answer the critics of African American religious studies with counterarguments, critical research, solid intellectual production, and effective teaching.

The criticism, however, does not really hold weight given African American religious studies history of teaching, research, and service to students and the university. The relevance of AACRE is its contribution to Christian religious education in general. AACRE poses a more inclusive view of religious education in the United States. It provides an essential theoretical and critical corrective to religious education. It has also demonstrated its relevance as a contribution to the reconstruction of Black history and religion, rejecting the racists myths assembled to deny them.

A final expression of the relevance of AACRE is its contribution to the development of an intellectual/professional stratum where knowledge and social competence translate as a vital contribution to the liberation of the Black church and community. It is at this point that the academy and church benefit from AACRE and become an expression of knowledge placed in the service of community. It is also reflected in the educational philosophy of African American universities, colleges, and seminaries, which have historically structured curricula and instruction to produce the leaders, educators, and pastors society needs.

Scope of the Discipline

The scope of AACRE is interdisciplinary, with its own particular focus on the interplay between theology and education. The scope of the discipline is the totality of theological, historical, and religious thought and practice, even as it allows for and encourages an integrative approach to subject areas within the discipline. As interdisciplinary, AACRE becomes a paradigm for the multidimensional approach to Black religious reality. It is a model of a holistic approach, not simply focusing on Blacks, but including third-world peoples, women, and Whites. It is critical and corrective of the inadequacies and omissions of Eurocentric approaches. Moreover, as a new discipline it is not restricted by the old paradigms, methodologies, and theories of earlier research.

My contention is that in the history of AACRE there have been a number of classic works.[7] These works of Christian education have not received the attention of religious educators, mainly because of the need to establish the legitimacy of AACRE as an academic discipline. AACRE brings theory and practice together to make academic study and religious education praxis an experience of both personal formation and transformation in the quest for human liberation. Thus, AACRE becomes the discipline for praxis between the Black church and the academy.

Reflections on the Status of Research

What is the state of current research on the theory and practice of AACRE? To set that question in its broader context in contemporary graduate theological education, I will venture some observations on the challenges of AACRE as an educational enterprise. As previously stated, AACRE has suffered a dearth of scholarship, which exacerbates the situation for researchers, professors, and scholars interested in the topic. A cursory survey of the literature in the field of religious education from the Black perspective indicates relatively few books but numerous articles.

The literature of AACRE is diverse and limited: diverse when considered within the broader discussions and literature of Christian religious education before the 1960s, and limited when considered as the product of our own scholastic communities. However, a breakthrough is noticed in the literature beginning with the post-civil rights movement period. The 1960s marked the rise of research on AACRE. E. Franklin Frazier's The Negro Church in America became the seminal book on the educative role of the Black church. What theoretical, methodological, and research directions have occurred in the development of AACRE?

Substantive methodological changes occurred in the 1970s, which broaden our understanding of AACRE. These books include Olli Alho's The Religion of the Slaves: A Study of the Religious Tradition and Behavior of Plantation Slaves in the United States 1830–1865, and Albert J. Raboteau's Slave Religion. The importance of these studies is that they rely on slave narratives, spirituals, Black autobiographies, folk tradition, and African tradition religion as sources for the study of religious instruction. Alho and Raboteau focused on the communal role of the slave family and ritual as the primary structures of education.

In the genesis of AACRE as a distinct field, a number of important essays by such leaders as Grant Shockley and Olivia Pearl Stokes established the agenda to which a later generation of scholars has contributed. These authors provide an important analysis of the theological and cultural factors that have shaped AACRE.

Grant Shockley's essay, "Christian Education and The Black Church: A Contextual Approach," frames the thinking about the Black religious education experience.[8] His attention was drawn to the institutional and socio-cultural experience of Blacks in America.

Olivia Pearl Stokes's "The Educational Role of Black Churches in the 70's and 80's" was both clearer and more cultural. Stokes was aware of both the potentials and limitations of Black religious education. In relating Christian education to the Black religious experience, Stokes states, "We must have a curriculum that reflects the values of the Black experience and develops techniques for liberation."[9] For her, research in religious education was clearly a theological and cultural search for understanding. The understanding that these formative figures had of Black religious education as a discipline is significant to our search for identity. They did not understand their task as simply borrowing insights from the other disciplines. Although they were deeply informed by philosophy, history, theology, and the other sciences of education, they saw this discipline as providing only raw data to be reconstructed into new theoretical concepts.

AACRE is coming into its own as a distinct field. Intensified efforts in recent years provide a new self-understanding of the richness of the educational dimensions of the African American religious education experience. The new additions to the corpus of literature include a socio-cultural perspective on AACRE. The Black Church in the African American Experience offered a sociological examination of the influence of Black consciousness on the educational content of the Black church and to the provision of Black role models in Sunday school materials. This study revealed that Christian religious education needs to be sensitive to the cultural world and worldview created by African Americans.[10]

Other important studies by Joseph V. Crockett and Anne S. Wimberly broaden the field to increase awareness of the hermeneutical and pedagogical concerns.[11] There are signs that research in AACRE is passing from childhood into adulthood, which had been envisioned by our progenitors. The twenty-first century has accumulated a growing body of literature about the "discipline in search of an identity." AACRE as a body of knowledge and field of study is still in progress. There is a self-conscious community of scholars who study, practice, and teach this body of knowledge.

Presently the discipline of AACRE is developing in three directions. Each of these directions is rooted in the history of the discipline and is represented by major thinkers. The first direction centers on the attempt to formulate a Black theology of education. Religious education scholars agree that an intimate relationship exists between theology and Christian education. The work of James Evans, James H. Harris, Grant Shockley, Olivia Stokes, and Okechukwu Ogbonnaya provides major representation of this direction. These scholars affirm Black theology as the primary focus for African Americans. A close look raises a number of issues about the role of theology. The issues are: Black theology as the content for Christian education theory and practice; contemporary Christian education theory and practice in African and Christian communal understanding of God and humanity; the use of Black theology by educators/pastors to train clergy and laity and other leaders who in turn explain and defend it; the necessity of Christian education and Black theology to engage in dialogue to bridge the gap between theory and practice; and collaboration between Black theologians and Black church intellectuals to enlarge Black religious thought.

The second direction focuses on the theory and practice of religious education. How do we educate? What approaches have found their way into Christian education? Here, education is the central focus and the task is to describe religious education activity. The research seeks to explore the relationship between the theory and practice of Christian education in the African American church. A cursory examination of the literature suggests that Black religious scholars have placed more emphasis on practice and less on theory. In recent decades perennial efforts of Black religious thinkers to provide models regarding the nature and processes of religious education have emerged. The works of Yolanda Smith, Grant Shockley, Okechukwu Ogbonnaya, Lynne Westfield, and Anne S. Wimberly have focused on these matters.

The third direction of the discipline is spiritual education. Here the focus is on spiritual formation, nurture, and development. The spiritual education of Black believers calls for the practice of the spiritual disciplines. The creation of such works as Reclaiming the Spirituals: New Possibilities for African American Christian Education, Nurturing Faith and Hope: Black Worship as a Model for Christian Education, and Joy Unspeakable: Contemplative Practices of the Black Church reveal how Negro spirituals, worship, and spirituality educate the faithful in the faith.[12]

Recent decades have witnessed a renaissance in scholarly interest in the subject. The new generation of scholars—Fred Smith, Evelyn Parker, Yolanda Smith, Lynne Westfield, and Lora-Ellen McKinney—has a sense of indebtedness to the contribution of our ancestors in faith. AACRE has a rich heritage. Indeed new dimensions and directions on AACRE have emerged. However, much of what our ancestors in the field have wrestled with still makes a claim on us today. *Religious Education in the African American Tradition* responds to this claim.

CHAPTER TWO

Reconnecting with Our History

Black religion in African American life has been substantial and enduring since its inception. From its earliest days in Africa, and as an invisible spiritual community in North America, the Black church obviously was a sanctuary against the violent and destructive character of the slave world. Historically, African American churches have always been educational institutions. The church educated enslaved Africans and engaged in both public and denominational educational projects, setting up schools and training clergy and teachers in the struggle for Black liberation and a truly higher spiritual level of human life. In the early African Methodist Episcopal Church, for example, "the church leaders were not educated people, but they had a clear perception of what education would mean to the interests of the church and the advancement of the African people then held in abject slavery. Bishop Daniel A. Payne, who had been a schoolmaster in Baltimore, set the educational goals for the fledgling institution by insisting upon a trained ministry, and by encouraging AME pastors to organize schools in their communities as an aspect of their ministries."[1] Seen as a tool for removing the social and political shackles of bondage, educational opportunity in its Christian forms provides for African Americans something that cannot be stolen: our minds. The church has most often been supportive of education as a desirable goal for the liberation of Black people.

The church, as the central institution in the Black community, has carried forth its educational ministry to form, inform, and transform people in Christ. Education in the Black church takes a shape quite distinctive from education in White Protestant churches. What does this mean? The Black church historically created an environment of spiritual awareness in which one could experience "faith in freedom" and know faith by participating in the life of the church. This task has largely focused on *forming* communal identity. The Black church has its antecedents in the "invisible institution," the secret religious meeting and praise houses during slavery.[2] At these meetings, slaves celebrated life under their own vine and fig tree and affirmed their personhood in a country where Blacks were sold as property. Black Christian character has thus been shaped through the guidance of the religious community.

For *formation* to be effective, it must go hand-in-hand with *information*. Every succeeding generation of Black believers has learned of the struggles of their forebears from slavery to freedom in the Black church. Religious education in the Black church has focused on passing on the beliefs, values, and confessions of faith. This task makes it possible for persons to enter into the life of the community. It is imperative that religious educators of the third millennium are well informed in their faith. If this is to happen, there must be no flaw at the foundation. A clear presentation of Black religious worldviews, tailored to the present age, is essential. The ministry of religious education in the Black church is not only to form and inform, but also to *transform* people in Christ. Enslaved Black folk discovered themselves free before God in the only place that they controlled. When they met they experienced "faith in freedom."[3] Faith in freedom, as the ultimate concern in the African American experience, originated in Africa. Though enslaved, the people did not retain the identical faith structure of the African ancestors. They did, however, maintain the belief in freedom. Thus, from slavery until today, faith in freedom has blanketed African American life. Blacks experienced such faith in freedom upon conversion. When Jesus entered their lives for the first time, Blacks sensed a profound turning away from sin and toward freedom. Conversion sets a person on a new direction of salvation. This new journey, or way, provides certainty about future liberation. Even whippings could not deter the proclamation of hope for good news to come. The following testimony confirms this assertion:

I'se saved. De Lord done tell me I'se saved.
Now I know de Lord will show me dee way, I ain't
gwine to grieve no more. No matter how much you all done
beat me and my chillen de Lord will show me de way.
And some day we never be slaves.[4]

Being conformed to Christ implies such transformation. Transformation is a changing of persons. For Blacks, transformation is the slow and painful process by which they have experienced the liberation of mind, body, and soul. Howard Thurman calls this the "Inward Journey" to the center of one's being.[5] Conversion has enabled Blacks to turn away from the sinful system of slavery, segregation, and racial discrimination. These educational tasks are crucial, and they take on a particular urgency at this point in history. Stories and histories of the church contain and carry the teaching and learning of Christian education. The historical experience of African Americans in the United States illustrates how their cultural distinctiveness emerged. How did Black Christians effectively relate their faith to their culture? How did they educate for this living faith? A careful consideration of historical foundations provides an awareness of both the possibilities and complexities of education. This chapter traces historical underpinnings of AACRE and suggests some implications it may have for the theory and practice of Christian education in America.

Christianity and Education in Africa

Africans did not come to America devoid of all culture and education, but brought with them a rich and dynamic heritage, which they tried to preserve. A part of that heritage included an elaborate system of religious beliefs and oral tradition based on ancient African traditions. Black religion, like Black people, began in Africa and thus it is important to discuss its historical forms before turning to its current expressions. In searching for the starting point of Black Christian education, many scholars note that it can be found in the pages of the New Testament. In Acts 8, the Ethiopian who will become the first African convert has an encounter with this new religious phenomenon called Christianity. Noted African American religious scholar, Gayraud Wilmore highlighted this story in his book *Black Religion and Black Radicalism:* "The gospel made its first appearance in Africa not in the Delta region, but in the Upper Nile Valley through the Ethiopian eunuch who was baptized at an oasis on a desert road between Jerusalem and Gaza by Phillip [*sic*] the Evangelist."[6] The Ethiopian also asked Philip to guide him through the scriptures.

Although this narrative does not exhaust the full scope of this encounter, it is safe to say that the intersection of Christian education and African people runs deep within the well waters of history. This era of Christian history and its relationship to Blacks was void of the exploitative and oppressive activity that would take place in other "visits." After this encounter came the establishment of the first Christian church in Africa, around 42 C.E., by John Mark, the noted writer of the gospel. Mark's disciples and converts, early Black Christian educators, further propagated the gospel message and spawned the spread of early Christianity through the Delta and Upper Egypt. Thus, Africans were converted to Christianity before they arrived in the United States.

Africa's contribution to Black religion is now well documented. Historian Yosef Ben-Jochannon (1970) and John Jackson (1972) are well-known advocates of this position. Ben-Jochannon has argued at length, as the title of his book demonstrates: *African Origins of the Major Western Religions.* His work stresses heavily the Egyptian-African contribution. Ben-Jochannon argues that Horus is the model for Jesus, pointing out the similarities: both Horus and Jesus had two mothers, one who conceived them (Isis, Mary) and one who raised them (Nephthysis, Mary, Wife of Cleophas); both had an earthly father (Seb, Joseph); both were the only child in one family and one of five in the second family; from twelve to thirty there is no record of Horus' or Jesus' life; John baptized Jesus at thirty, and Anep baptized Horus. Horus, when baptized, was transformed into the beloved and only begotten son of the Father or Holy Spirit represented by a bird; Jesus underwent the same with Holy Spirit represented by a dove.[7]

John Jackson cited several legacies of Egypt to Christianity. First, he argued that the concept of the Virgin and Child in Christianity is clearly based on the Virgin Isis and Child Horus of Egypt. Jackson stated that, "Gods, heroes, born of virgins, were quite common in olden times and the sources of most, if not all of these divinities seem to have been Egypt."[8] Upon their arrival in America, African slaves already possessed beliefs about God and the capacity to develop a new form of religious expression. The power of the spoken word transported these beliefs and made up the religious and spiritual consciousness of Africans. The African American church was a fuller development of the African traditions still alive in the memories and instinctive desires of the slave. African people brought with them the following: a belief in a high–God who was both immanent and transcendent; experiences of engaging in daily interaction with divinities who were seen as God's intermediaries; veneration of ancestors as guardians of family traditions and ethics; and a belief that a person was defined by the community to which he or she belonged.[9] John Mbiti states, "I am because we are, and since we are, therefore I am."[10] Traditional African religion did not separate the sacred and secular. The spiritual importance of life merged into everyday experiences.

Education in Africa was a communal experience that required full participation of each person in the tribal community. To be human was to belong to the community, and to do so involved participating in the beliefs, ceremonies, rituals, and festivals of that community. The community to which one belonged and in which one found identity and relevance defined what it meant to be human. The African worldview was based on the extended family. Africans related to one another in family terms and feelings. Primary among the African family features is the primacy given to extended families versus nuclear families. Although scholars do not agree on the degree of African influence on African American culture and family, there is agreement that slavery did not destroy all.[11] Another important aspect of African education was the oral instruction that emerged through music, dance, poetry, folk tales, rituals, proverbs, stories, and historical accounts. These cultural vehicles served as viable tools of instruction. For example, storytelling was often used to transmit historical information, to teach the values of society, to guide the administration of government, and to teach religious beliefs and practices. Priests, chiefs, the elders of the community, and clan leaders conducted this.

Yolanda Smith states, "This aspect of African education was so deeply rooted in African customs and traditions that African slaves continued this form of education even after their arrival in the new world. Since African slaves were not allowed to teach their children, they often taught their children through the oral tradition."[12] She further explains, "African education consisted not only of vocational training and oral instruction, but also of higher education. Such education was available in West Africa and the Near East through the University of Sankore in Timbuktu."[13] The oral tradition of Africans survived the middle passage and contributed to the process of religious syncretism in the new world.

Colonial Period

The religious history of Christian-colonial expansion (1492–1780) provided the context of the mission history of the United States. Columbus and other explorers from Spain, Portugal, France, and England came to these shores with a "divine" mission. Conquest and conversion were expansionist partners. Christian churches aided and abetted the conquest by providing a religious legitimation for such actions. Notions of cultural, racial, intellectual, and moral superiority grounded colonial expansion. Africans were victims of overt, direct, and social violence arising from the conflict of expansion and nation building. At the time when the colonization of North America was beginning, it was not unusual for enslaved Blacks to be taught reading and religion. The teaching of religion to slaves, however, soon became problematic. The difficulty hinged on the question of baptism. Some slaveholders believed that baptism made the slaves free, while others felt that this was not the case. The matter was resolved in colonial courts. Between 1664 and 1706 six colonies passed acts stating that slaves were not freed by baptism.[14] During the early 1700s, the Society for the Propagation of the Gospel (SPG) figured prominently in the call for religious instruction among Blacks. White settlers in antebellum America exhibited ambivalence in their attitude toward regular formal religious instructions and the prospect of what might occur if the slaves became Christian. The goal of religious instruction during this period was to introduce enslaved Africans to Christianity, which would lead to conversion.

Antebellum Period

Attempts to proselytize and give religious instruction were unsuccessful during this period. However, a series of revivals known as the Great Awakening, beginning around 1740 and lasting almost fifty years, somewhat changed this situation. Blacks joined churches in significant numbers, especially Methodists and Baptists. According to Alho, the egalitarian element in the Awakening influenced enslaved and free Blacks in their choice of those denominations.[15] During the later eighteenth century, there were some efforts among White Christian denominations to educate enslaved Africans, but most activities were handled by missionary societies. Nonetheless, there was evidence that those of the slave communities were well aware that their evangelization was being used to keep the noose of slavery tight. The slaves formulated new ideas and practices on their own that specifically colored their religious principles with a pronounced longing for freedom. The meetings in the brush harbors and praise houses were coined the "invisible church."

The meetings of the invisible church could not have gone on without the instrumentality of the oral tradition. Story and song became the major structures of education in the preliterate era of slavery. The religious expression of Black people could not have developed or survived without constant reinforcement of this oral tradition. Thus, the oral tradition as an education structure was indispensable to forming and preserving communal identity. Despite obstacles, education of the African continued–education that would be conducted by newly established independent African churches. The first established African churches, such as the African Baptist church that emerged at Silver Bluffs, South Carolina, in 1773 and Mother Bethel African Methodist Episcopal church, which began in 1787 in Philadelphia. Like other African churches of its period, the pulpit and Sunday school addressed the spiritual and educational needs of African people.

At the dawn of the nineteenth century, education for Africans was available in the North and restricted in the South. In the South there was a prohibition of all forms of education for the African. Slave revolts, such as those led by Gabriel Prosser (1801), Denmark Vessey (1822), and Nat Turner (1831) contributed to White fears that education of the African would result in the rebellion of African slaves. The Nat Turner rebellion almost brought a halt to instruction of Blacks. Daniel A. Payne, who later became a bishop in the African Methodist Episcopal Church, operated a small school in South Carolina and was forced to abandon this venture because White Southerners made it a crime for Blacks to learn to read, or to congregate for religious instruction. Throughout this period, however, free Northern Blacks under the African Methodist Episcopal Church carried forth religious education activities through the medium of preaching and teaching.

Post-bellum Period and the Evolution of Sunday School

It is important to note that during this era, the Black church served as the primary institutional response against racism, segregation, and other oppressive devices perpetuated by external forces. Education was the principal weapon used to fight against outside aggression as well as internal strife. The latter half of the nineteenth century saw the rapid growth and expansion of Black churches and denominations. The development of religious education quickly took the form of Sunday school. Robert Raikes, a printer in Gloucester, England, founded the Sunday school movement in the year 1780. American Sunday schools were started in the 1790s modeled on British experiments. They aimed at offering the illiterate, urban poor a basic education–reading and writing–with the Bible as the textbook. Bishop Asbury organized a Sunday school in 1786 in Virginia. In 1787, knowing nothing of Raikes or Sunday schools elsewhere, a poor African woman, Katy Ferguson, started a Sunday school in New York City for the benefit of the poor street children of the humble quarters in which she lived.

Richard Allen, founder of the African Methodist Episcopal Church and first African American bishop, organized Mother Bethel AME church in Philadelphia, and included a school where adults and children were instructed in the faith, as well as in reading and writing. The African Methodist Episcopal Zion Church, founded in New York in the early 1800s, also included a school in their first church building.[16] The evolution of Sunday school within the Black church is an important page in the history of Black Christian education. Although in many respects contemporary Sunday schools serve to reinforce the ideals, doctrines, and principles of Christianity, Sunday schools in the early Black church emerged primarily as a response to the lack of literacy in the Black community. Publicly funded schools during the 1810s and 1820s systematically discriminated against women and Blacks; hence, Sunday schools became an alternative institution to gain access to basic education. In the early 1800s many evangelical churches formed Sunday schools. They attracted scores of Blacks in the North and South, particularly Black women.[17]

The Sunday school movement in the United States played a significant role in the education of African Americans from the mid-1820s to the Civil War. Carter Woodson commented on the value of the Sunday school of this time:

> The "Sabbath-school" constituted an important factor in Negro education. Although cloaked with the purpose of bringing the Blacks to God by giving them religious instruction, the institution permitted its workers to teach them reading and writing when they were not allowed to study such in other institutions.
>
> Even the radical was slow to object to a policy which was intended to facilitate the conversion of men's souls. All friends, especially interested in the mental and spiritual uplift of the race, hailed this movement as marking an epoch in the elevation of the colored people.[18]

In her description of the early Sunday school movement, Anne Boylan notes, "Adult Blacks in particular sought out Sunday schooling opportunities and exhibited a disposition for receiving instruction...In 1819 about two-thirds of the almost eleven hundred adults in Philadelphia Sunday and Adult School Union schools were Black."[19]

This was short-lived because of the spread of tax-based funding for public schools. This proliferation of funding began in 1823, resulting in Sunday schools' abandoning the emphasis on literacy education. As Sunday schools began to emphasize religious education, the latter half of the nineteenth century saw the rapid growth and expansion of Black churches and denominations. Christian religious education of Blacks by Whites had left a great deal to be desired. Blacks were taught to admire the traditions of Whites while disclaiming their own traditions.

After years of feeling dejected and discouraged, the Black Baptists decided to foster a publishing effort of their own. In 1894, Dr. E.C. Morris, elected president of the National Baptist Convention, USA, took a firm stand that the Black man possessed the capacity to own and operate his own educational printing business, as exemplified by other Black publishers of the era. On January 1, 1897, the first curriculum came off the press. Movement was made that launched the beginning of what is now known as the Sunday School Publishing Board (SSPB). In 1925 construction of the SSPB building was completed.

In the Church of God in Christ, the Sunday school program was started in Lexington, Mississippi, in 1908. In 1924, Bishop Mason appointed Elder F.C. Christmas as National Superintendent of the Sunday school program. In 1951, the denomination's first National Sunday School Convention convened in Kansas City, Missouri. In 1968, under the direction of Roy Winbush, the Publishing House in Memphis, Tennessee, was established.

Twentieth Century

What was the response, if any, of the Sunday school in the Black church to the issues of racism, segregation, and racial discrimination; cultural pride; self-help; and racial identity in the twentieth century? The self-determinative focus that had sustained the early Black church's educational efforts during the nineteenth century, when it was freed from the evil of slavery, began to shift during the dawn of the twentieth century. Powerful new forces of segregation, coupled with urbanization and industrialization, contributed to a kind of de-radicalization of Black church education. Much of the curriculum, especially among Black Methodists, was reserved for preparing clergy rather than educating Black Christians generally.

By the beginning of the twentieth century a Sunday school system was operational in at least the large urban church settings. The Sunday school served as a means of integrating new converts into the life of the church. The Sunday school was clearly not intended to provide academic training. Its goal was to provide religious instruction in the biblical and doctrinal content of the Christian faith. When I sifted through samples of the Sunday school materials written in the twentieth century by African Methodist Episcopal, African Methodist Episcopal Zion, and National Baptist Publishing Board, I discovered the literature failed to address social justice issues such as war, hunger, racism, and Black Power until the 1960s. Much of the Sunday school literature prior to the 1960s focused on knowledge of scripture, self-help, and a place of warmth and acceptance in which the love of God could be experienced. The Black church Sunday school appeared only concerned with cultivating a personal piety to the neglect of issues of civil rights and Black Power. How did Black Christians effectively relate their faith to their culture? How did they educate for this living faith? A careful consideration of historical foundations provides an awareness of both the possibilities and complexities of education.

As Sunday school in the Black church began to expand and evolve, writers of curriculum materials created a portrait of a world engaged in an immense cosmic struggle of good versus evil. It is quite remarkable that curriculum materials continued to present Jesus as the one who changes the hearts and lives of people and lead them in the way of justice, but did not engage in liberation. Nonetheless, Black denominations at the turn of the century tended to see racism and segregation as an entrance door, with more converts coming into their churches than ever before.

In my reading, I discovered that many Black Protestant publishing houses used the Uniform Series texts in preparing their material for use in their denominations. In April 1872, the Fifth National Sunday School Convention, meeting at the Second Presbyterian Church in Indianapolis, Indiana, took the historic step which set in motion the cooperation of Protestant churches on curriculum for the Sunday School–Uniform Lessons. Sunday schools all over the country, Black and White congregations, united on the same course of Bible lessons, but each school taught the lessons in its own way, and each denomination provided the best helps for its students. The remark is often made that the most segregated hour for America is at 11 a.m. Sunday, during worship, but, in contrast all Protestant Christians are united in Scripture during the Sunday school hour when they share and study the same Bible lesson.

To date, the Committee on Uniform Series (CUS) develops the outlines on the basis of a six-year cycle of the entire Bible. With the development of the cycle 2004–2010, the committee moved to a new concept of biblical scope, organized around major themes such as: creation, call, covenant, community, and commitment. CUS works in age-group subcommittees to prepare topics and short descriptions of the context the writers may use in the development sessions. CUS is one of the Ministries in Christian Education of the National Council of the Churches of Christ in the United States. Several African Americans have chaired this committee.

Rise of Christian Education Institutions

The late nineteenth and early twentieth centuries witnessed the Black church establishing Black colleges for training clergy and teachers. These institutions represented the broad range of Black Christian thought. The seminaries represented the more liberal to moderate theology, while the Bible schools were more fundamentalist in their approaches. Black Christian higher education (colleges, seminaries, and universities) grew out of another form of church education. Because Whites had denied education, overall there was a high regard for education together with a legitimate concern that Black Christians might be advanced to a more competitive relationship with other educated Christians. In the mid-1800s Daniel A. Payne helped establish Wilberforce University and then Payne Seminary for the African Methodist Episcopal Church. In 1863, Payne became the first Black college president in America.[20] By 1926, more than one hundred schools were owned and operated by the Black church. Again, these institutions represented a form of Christian higher education that reinforced Black cultural and religious values.

By the turn of the twentieth century, the Black church became the main school, community center, and political organization of African Americans. As such, it educated. The task of religious education was relating the faith to a new historical context and reconstructing it in light of the historic period. Religious education in the twentieth century was marked by the formation of structures and processes that supported the activity of teaching in the church. Pastors and religious educators recognized that the Sunday school did not offer enough time or continuity of participation to deal with issues in great depth, especially those involving sustained intellectual discussion or personal self-disclosure.

As a result, Black denominations in the late nineteenth and early twentieth centuries established publishing houses and Christian education departments as alternative centers for teaching and learning to assist local congregations in carrying forth the teaching ministry. The African Methodist Episcopal Church established one of the first Black religious publishing houses in 1882. Charles S. Smith, a bishop in the African Methodist Episcopal Church, founded the denomination's Sunday School Union. Smith viewed publishing and writing as a component of educational ministry. He constantly sought to promote the idea of religious education through the publication of Sunday school material. He built a distinguished publishing tradition. Smith utilized the publishing house as a very effective literary vehicle to educate a wider community.

Between Reconstruction and World War I, the African Methodist Episcopal Sunday School Union produced literary works and provided a channel for Blacks' continued participation in the national and global conversation about the intellectual, cultural, and social issues of the day. About these literary contributions, Smith commented:

> They are of inestimable worth, providing the groundwork of future similar performances on a more enlarged scale. It is true, however, that in proportion to what we need, ought to have, and must have,

if we would continue our existence as a distinct Christian force, that they are but as a drop in the bucket…Our literature is yet to be produced.[21]

Overall, his contribution improved tremendously the quality of religious education in the Black church. The other well-known denominational curriculum publishers were established by the African Methodist Episcopal Zion Sunday School Union in 1872; Christian Methodist Episcopal Church Sunday School Union in 1918; National Baptist Convention USA Sunday School Board in 1897; and Church of God in Christ Publishing Board in 1912. Again, most Black denominations utilize the Uniform Lesson Series.

Black denominations established Christian education departments to serve the educational needs of their local churches. Elected (Methodists) and appointed (Baptists) officers headed these departments, which were staffed by trained persons involved in Christian education. The African Methodist Episcopal Zion Church department of education, established in 1892, was incorporated into its Christian education department at the General Conference of 1932.[22] The Christian Methodist Episcopal Church General Conference of 1914 established a department of education.[23] The African Methodist Episcopal Church Christian Education Department was established in 1936. The National Baptist Convention USA Christian education department was established in 1937.

Black Methodists conducted Christian education teaching and training in districts or in connection with annual Christian education and connectional meetings. Black Baptists and Pentecostals held events at state and national Christian education conferences and conventions. Support for Christian educators in Black churches by denominational educational organizations is slowly growing. A tangible expression of increased interest in Christian education organizations was the establishment of the Assembly of Christian Educators in 1988 by the African Methodist Episcopal Zion Church. The African Methodist Episcopal Church established in 1997 its Fellowship of Church Educators out of a concern for upgrading and certifying teachers in the local church. Thus, denominational involvement advanced Christian education in the following ways: establishing Christian education departments and publishing houses; developing and distributing denominational literature and curriculum; and implementing training programs for pastors, church leaders, and Sunday school teachers.

Christian Education During the Civil Rights and Black Power Movements

When I attended Sunday school during the 1950s and 60s, I understood it to be a place where I would learn the stories of the Bible, sing, participate in Christmas and Easter programs, and each February celebrate Negro history. I do not recall ever having a problem with attending my classes, nor do I recall discussing Martin L. King Jr. and the civil rights movement. For me, Sunday school was a warm, accepting, and pleasant place to be. However, on a Sunday morning in May 1963, a bomb exploded in a Birmingham, Alabama, Black church. It killed four girls attending Sunday school. The chaos of racism erupted in the institution the girls loved–the Sunday school. This explosion was the turning point when Black Power eclipsed civil rights as the major concern for the liberation movement. In addition, it led me to seek a church that was involved in social-political struggle for the liberation of Blacks.

The Shrine of the Black Madonna, Black Christian Nationalist Church led by Albert Cleage, taught, preached, and engaged in the struggle for the liberation of Blacks. I joined this church to live out my convictions for Black liberation. During the mid-1960s and 1970s the Black Nationalist movement experienced a revival. Because of its widespread appeal across many facets of the Black community, it influenced the Black church and Christian education. The emergence of Black theology in the 1970s can be considered a demarcation point signaling the shift from a Christian religious education paradigm of European cultural universalism in biblical interpretation and curriculum resources to one of cultural pluralism that presented an Afrocentric cultural perspective.

During the 1960s and 1970s, Black nationalists and theologians began to critique Black church education, especially the Sunday school literature, for not being relevant to the Black community. Issues of Black Power, cultural pride, and self-determination were neglected issues of discussion. The hypocrisy of religious institutions inevitably made them logical targets for attack. Black theologians and nationalists condemned them for failing to act on the principles they affirmed to be true. My involvement in the Shrine of the Black Madonna exposed me to radical Black Christian education. The Black nationalists' critique of Black church education was that Black church education was more "other worldly" than "this worldly," more a goal of integration than liberation, and more of social gospel than social justice. Black Christian Nationalism (BCN) viewed integration as neither desirable, nor likely, as a means of achieving Black liberation in the United States.

The essential function of BCN was the restructuring of society to bring Black liberation. Cleage believed that BCN must first restructure the minds of Black people. BCN developed an educational process that included a new theology based on the revolutionary teachings of Jesus, and developed a school of Black studies that replaced the traditional church school. A critical element in Black Christian nationalist education is pride in culture and its Black consciousness. As Mark Chapman observed, it was pastors such as Cleage whose "ministry demonstrates that the Black theology of the late sixties emerged in the churches as pastors sought to respond to the challenges of Black Power."[24] Everyone who joined the Shrine had to go through a twelve-month training program before formal invitation into full membership. The total BCN program is founded upon teaching. This is our basic contribution to the Black struggle.[25]

In Cleage's view, Blacks have accepted the White man's declaration of Black inferiority and, seeing ourselves through the White man's eyes, we have come to hate ourselves and identify with the oppressor. Therefore, BCN must restructure the minds of Black people. Nothing can be accomplished until Black people's minds are transformed. This means Christian education as liberation. This was my view of Black church education until I attended seminary and realized that my view was sectarian. The exposure to new intellectual and theological thinking while at Harvard Divinity school caused me to wrestle with this Black nationalist ethic. My exposure to other forms of Black religious thought enabled me to transcend my thinking, allowing me to embrace a more inclusive vision of Christian education. Still, BCN instilled within me a pride and consciousness of our cultural heritage that continues with me today.

Although BCN gained adherents throughout the country in the 1970s and 1980s, it was no longer effective in attracting substantial numbers of young Blacks by the close of the twentieth century. During the late 1970s and through the 1980s, the Sunday school curriculum began to change. Pre–civil rights Sunday school curriculum's primary emphasis was on the universality of the Christian faith. Post–Black Power Sunday school literature began to place emphasis on the significance of "Blackness." The issue of Black rights was a concern for the Black church and a legitimate part of the content for the Sunday school curriculum. Writers began to convince persons within the church to be about the work of social justice. In more than fifty lessons between 1975–85, the *Adult Quarterly* of the African Methodist Episcopal church dealt with racism and prejudice. Those in the Sunday school were reminded over and over again that Blacks were its victims in the United States and were asked to do what they could to bring changes. For example, in a lesson for adults on June 22, 1975, *The Gospel of Social Concern (Lk. 4:16–17)* states:

> When those who have the name of Christians and ought to be followers of their Lord fail to show that they are in any real sense bringing good news to the poor and setting at liberty those who are oppressed, the deepest reason may be that the springs of their emotions have been stifled by too much dust of indifferent things. Nobody can strive passionately for justice who has not first suffered in his sympathy. No one can have a flame of indignation against the cruel callousness of powers of wealth or devote himself with his whole-soul power to the bringing in of a social order of more equal opportunity unless he first has that compassion for the poor which Jesus expressed in what he said in Nazareth.[26]

And so, the writer continued, "Every AME member should at one time or another serve on the Social Action Commission of his local church. The Jesus whom we worship from Sunday to Sunday proclaims a social gospel."[27]

Bible Study

Bible study has played an important role in Black church education. Next to sermon preparation, Bible study by Black pastors is a vital teachable moment for pastors. However, little to no data exist that document the role that Bible study has played in the lives of people within the church. Every week, usually Tuesday or Wednesday, scores of Black Christians flock to their local churches to participate in midweek services (usually referred to as Bible studies). Bible studies have also served to help facilitate and emphasize themes from the Sunday sermon. However, while in most mainline Black denominations the Sunday sermon serves to proclaim the gospel, the Bible study seeks to reinforce Christian values. The values taught in Bible studies center around stewardship, ethics, personal and family responsibility, and social and church relationships.

The format for many Bible studies usually includes elements in addition to studying the Bible, such as testimonials, the singing of hymns of praise and worship, and prayer. While the Bible studies have historically centered on adults, contemporary Bible studies have expanded to include instruction for all members of the church. There are Bible studies for youth, children, singles, married couples, and seniors. These Bible studies address the primary issues and needs that are particular to the aforementioned groups by employing traditional teaching methods such as discussions and lectures.

Conclusion

In summary, the religious instruction among Black people began in the pre-Emancipation era in the history of the Black church. During the period from Emancipation to World War II, the Black church grew into a national and racially separate religious institution. Its programs of religious education likewise became institutionalized. Further, most of the programs of religious education in Black churches going on between the 1920s and the 1960s evidenced replication of White Protestant church designs. The radicalizing events of the 1960s and 1970s, together with the birth of the new Black church, challenged religious education to consolidate its mission with the Black community in order to liberate the oppressed and empower them. To be Black and Christian in the twenty-first century represents African Americans' defining, defending, and developing their own understandings of identity, which place the African person at the center of analysis.

Blacks have always had their own ideas about Christian religious education and its relevance for their own people. When Blacks began to take control of the process of religious education, they asserted the principles of liberation, emphasizing racial self-help, self-pride, and self-reliance as necessary to that process. Certainly, a fundamental challenge facing the Black church's work of teaching and learning in any age is that of immersing people in their special heritage as Black Christians. In the ministry of teaching we must help people remember who they are, help them make the common stories and symbols of faith their own, and help them enrich their heritage with special meaning for their own lives and times.

As Black Christians, we claim a common ancestry. We belong to a family with roots in the praise houses and bush arbors of slavery. We are heirs of the faith of Richard Allen, Jarena Lee, Anna Julia Cooper, Daniel A. Payne, Benjamin Mays, Howard Thurman, Adam Clayton Powell, Isaac Lane, William Miles, Joseph Lane, and James Varick, and we participate in the new Black church. We believe that our ancestral faith is living still in us. The kinship ties that bind an extended family together give the members an identity that sets them apart. So too are the ties that link us to the faith of our forebears. But not only does our heritage shape us; we also take part in shaping it. Through the repetition of certain stories, the recollection of important events, and the reenactment of traditions and rituals, we appropriate our heritage. We make it our own, and, in so doing, we enrich it, adding our own distinctive emphases, stories, symbols, and rituals. Thus, the past serves as an ever-present tutor for present and future AACRE. Beyond the insights of history, Christian educators are also called to consider the larger story of the unfolding view and vision of religious education emerging from African American religious thinkers, educators, and leaders.

CHAPTER THREE

Reading, Interpreting, and Teaching the Bible in the African American Church

Black people have had a unique and peculiar experience in relation to the biblical text. Their introduction to it, its varied influence on their existence, and the issue of its continuing relevance in their struggles for freedom and wholeness all signal the need to ask critical questions of the Bible. What is the relationship between the Bible and Black experience? What is the context in which African Americans have had to read, interpret, and study the Bible? What role has the Bible played in the history of African Americans? The Black church has always been committed to biblical foundations in Christian education. There can be no Black church without the Bible. Black Christians regard the Bible as sacred and holy, the revelation of God's nature and will, and the record of God's action in history with and on behalf of a chosen people. The Bible has always stood at the center of teaching, preaching, and worship. The Bible serves as the chief source of teaching. Primers, catechisms, uniform lessons, quarterlies, and many other teaching aids supplement it.

Among African American Christians, there has never been any doubt that the Bible is the basis of Christian belief and practice. Our sermons are preached from the texts of scripture. Our responsive readings are from the Bible. Our creedal statements are great affirmations summarizing the central themes of the Bible. Our spirituals, gospels, and hymns restate and exalt the biblical view of God's liberating power. Our imagination is awakened and shaped by the stories and images from the Bible. Our church materials are drawn from the Bible. Our deeds of love and service come out of God's commands and Jesus' example. All of these together are used by the Holy Spirit to form us into Christians. Thus, the vital role the Bible has played in the life of African Americans is attested on every hand. The Bible, as a teaching source, illuminates the mind, moves the heart, and stirs the soul. The Bible permeates every aspect of the Black church's life.

For example, Stephen Reid states in his book *Experience and Tradition: A Primer in Black Biblical Hermeneutics*:

> It is no secret that the Bible occupies a central place in the religious life of Black Americans. Depicted in the Bible are the experiences of many Black people, from slavery onward: Egyptian bondage and oppression of the Israelites, deportation into Babylonian captivity, the request of their captors to sing "their songs" in a strange land, a mocked and crucified Jesus, and the bedevilment by principalities and powers of the present age. It was from the Bible that many Black slaves learned to read and it was to the Bible that so many of them went to find guidance, comfort, a word of hope, and the promise of their deliverance from sin and slavery.[1]

Further building on a similar point, Anne Wimberly shares, "The Bible has historically held special importance for the approach of African Americans to freedom from oppression and struggles. During slavery, African Americans found in the Bible a liberation pathway."[2]

African American engagement with the Bible can be best understood as stories for freedom and vocation. This chapter explores the educative role of the Bible in the religious life of African Americans. The first section summarizes the role of the Bible in the periods of the early invisible and later institutional Black church. The second section concentrates on the study and interpretation of the Bible. The last section offers what are and/or should be some distinctively African American features of biblical study and teaching.

Reading the Bible in the African American Church

Since the formation of the African American church in the eighteenth century, the issue of biblical authority has been discussed. The early African American interpretative traditions relied on traditional African and African American folk traditions and scripture as source and criteria of theological authority. The long history of oral tradition in the African American church has rich values, many of which have been only lately addressed and made clear. Practical studies have centered on teaching the Bible to African Americans.[3] Ways of teaching and interpreting scripture have recently become another focus of various writings.[4] However, books on Black theology often fail to address the important place that the Bible has played in AACRE. The approach here is to move through a consideration of the historical background necessary for an adequate understanding of the role of the Bible in African American Christian education today.

For the first two centuries of the Black church's life, most African American Christians would have been puzzled if asked if they had read the Bible. Most did not read it. Yet during much of this time, especially in the eighteenth century, the average believer's knowledge of scripture was not higher than it is today. We must therefore ask two questions. First, why did they not read the Bible? Second, how did they come to learn what the Bible said? This issue of how African American Christians read, study, and interpret the Bible is at the crux of many of the major points of discussion in the academy and the Black church today. In our conversations and disputes, all of us attempt to wrap our views securely in the mantle of selected biblical texts that appear to justify our positions. The truth is that we all recognize "a canon within the canon."

The Journey to the World of the Bible

One useful way in thinking about the educative function of the Bible among African Americans is to think of the Bible as a "language."[5] The experience of being uprooted from their African homeland and forced to labor in a strange land produced in the first African slaves a cultural disorientation. For the great majority of the first enslaved Africans, the first reaction and response to the Bible was shock and awe. On the one hand, they rejected any notion of "book religion," especially because they possessed a strong oral tradition. On the other hand, because the enslaved African people rejected the form of Christianity presented by the slaveholders, an invisible church emerged as a new form of faith. This fresh, new, religious expression retained many elements from the African cultural and religious heritage and then was infused with themes and texts from the Bible that spoke to these social conditions.

Flora Bridges writes, "The early enslaved African in eighteenth century America had no book, nor did they express themselves through written doctrines, creeds, and tenets formulated by a religious hierarchy of elders. Instead, it was written on the tablets of the people's hearts and expressed itself throughout daily African culture to the extent that religion was separate from culture."[6]

In addition, when Africans and their descendants encountered the Bible, their spirituality allowed them the freedom to interpret it as the Whites interpreted it, or in ways that met their own needs. African Americans have a rich history of oral communication that reaches back to their African roots. African literature included tales, proverbs, and stories transmitted from generation to generation by cultural narrators-*griots*. When Africans were uprooted from their homes and brought to America, their oral tradition was preserved. This tradition contributed to the continuity of aspects of African thought and life. The significance of narrative in the life of African people survived the torturous passages from the coasts of Africa to the shores of America. The oral tradition was crucial to psychic survival and sanity. The purposeful singing, drumming, dancing, and narration of African culture never ceased.

Africans were generally forbidden to read and write, but they developed creative symbols and stories communicated through their oral tradition. Most slaveholders misused the Bible to encourage docility and submission in the slave community. Nonetheless, enslaved Africans reinterpreted their religious instruction. As they became more familiar with the Bible, they appropriated it, primarily through storytelling. The Black preacher became the dominant storyteller of God's liberating activity in the lives of God's suffering people. Thus, liberation became a dominant theme of their Bible stories. Many African people enslaved in America, often unable to read the English Bible, began to memorize verses that spoke words of liberation and hope to their life experience. These Bible verses soon became core beliefs that were reinforced by a strong oral tradition of Bible stories that told of people in settings similar to those of the enslaved Africans in America who struggled for liberation.

African people were first exposed to the Bible through public readings or sermons. Once able to read, enslaved Africans began the journey to the world of the Bible. Plantation preachers became the travel guides through the Bible, traveling with Black folk through life and accompanying them with the word throughout their journey. Primarily the preached word served as the cornerstone to teach scripture and convey African American understandings of God, Jesus Christ, and the Holy Spirit.

The Bible and Emancipation

Throughout the history of slavery in the United States, White slaveholders did not want their enslaved Africans to hear about the Bible because they were afraid enslaved African people would understand that Christianity made their masters equals before God. The masters "feared that Christianity would make their slaves not only proud but ungovernable, and even rebellious,"[7] and history showed that they turned out to be right. In the early and mid-nineteenth century, congregations and denominational bodies developed among African Americans that were independent of White control. Religious anti-slavery argument followed this development. The scriptures proved essential in the Black church's battle against slavery. The Bible, the book used by Whites to enslave and dehumanize Africans, is the same book that enslaved Africans used to bring liberation and true salvation to African Americans. Frederick Douglass, Richard Allen, Harriet Tubman, and David Walker employed the Bible's message of freedom for laying the moral and spiritual foundation from which they waged a war on the institution of slavery.

Sermons, spirituals, orations, exhortations, and addresses crafted by converted enslaved Africans and freed persons reflected concern about the evils of slavery. As Vincent Wimbush points out, "What is striking is that both the explanation for the social situation of the Africans and the solution to these problems were cast in biblical language."[8]

Enslaved Africans heard about Moses leading an oppressed people out of slavery and they lifted voices in prayer to God to do the same for them. "Oh Mary, don't you weep, don't you moan," they sang, "Pharaoh's army got drowned." As Frederick Douglass pointed out, many of the slave spirituals were codes with messages about escape to the North.[9] Gabriel Prosser, leader of a major slave revolt, saw himself as a new Samson called to battle with White Philistines and liberate his people. Harriet Tubman was identified as the "Moses of her people" who led over three hundred people to freedom.

As one African American scholar pointed out, "Black freedom fighters waxed biblical about the kinship of all of humanity under the sovereignty of the one God, about slavery as a base evil in opposition to the will of God, about the imperatives of the teaching of Jesus to make all nations a part of God's reign, and about the judgment that is to be leveled against all those—including slaves—who frustrate God's will on earth."[10] Vincent Wimbush has further stated, "Beginning in the nineteenth century and extending into the twentieth, African Americans consistently and systematically attempted to make use of the Bible to force biblical America to honor biblical principles."[11] For example, David Walker denounced slavery in God's name: "All persons who are acquainted with history, and particular the Bible...are willing to admit that God made man to serve Him alone... that God Almighty is the sole proprietor or master of the whole human family...this God will not suffer us always to be oppressed."[12] From early on in the nineteenth century, an entire network of resistance arose to help enslaved Africans in their quest for freedom. The high degree of success of the organized resistance movement associated with the Underground Railroad was viewed as a threat to slaveholders, but as a godsend by the enslaved. Thus, when a runaway African successfully eluded slave catchers and was able to reach a safer place—free states and Canada—they did not forget their brothers and sisters in bondage and sometimes returned to free them. Frederick Douglass and Harriet Tubman were two of the most noted examples of fugitive slaves who joined and led the resistance movement against slavery.

Various Black churches served the Underground Railroad; the most vigorous organizers of networks to freedom were Black churchmen. Richard Allen and other early Black religious leaders were vehemently opposed to slavery. According to biblical scholar Wimbush, "The key passage to Christian moral and social ethical thinking and practice was there is neither Jew nor Greek, there is neither slave nor free, there is neither male or female;

for you are all one in Christ Jesus"[13] (Gal. 3:28). The Bible was their source of strength for much of their resistance. Their understanding of the gospel of Christ motivated Frederick Douglass, Richard Allen, Harriet Tubman, and Sojourner Truth all. Enslaved and freed Africans recognized that the Bible had more to say about Jesus lifting burdens than slaves obeying masters. It is to the credit of our forebears that they could discern real Christianity. The fact that the abolitionists used the Bible as a moral authority to combat slavery suggests that it may be put to similar use for justice today.

The Bible in the Aftermath of Slavery

Our free Black ancestors in the North sacrificed much in the days of slavery and afterward. Though they had little, they put together what they did have and used it to help their people. They lived as simply as they could and formed societies to better their race, to fund schools for their education, and to advance the cause of abolition. Even after slavery, it was faith that sustained our people in the face of segregation and racism. The aftermath of slavery and the early decades of the twentieth century opened new windows of engagement with the Bible.

After Emancipation, White religious bodies were motivated to expose newly liberated Africans to religious education. The Sunday school movement in the United States, for example, originally began as an agency of social betterment to reform society. The Sunday school's use of the Bible as a text was a means of influencing and moralizing the character of African people, and thereby improving the social fabric. The Sunday school movement was developed by Whites and adopted by Blacks in their churches. However, very early after their liberation, Blacks had their own ideas about how the Bible was to be relevant for their people. As early as 1886, Black Christians were beginning to formulate their own goals and objectives of the proper place of the Bible in African American life. Two of these objectives, as reported by James D. Tyms, are, "1. To guide Negroes in adjusting themselves socially, morally, and spiritually, under the influence of Jesus' ideal of God in a complex social order. 2. To exalt the Word of God and proclaim its regenerative power in the heart of men."[14] These objectives speak to the reality that Black Christians expected their faith to assist them in movement toward liberation.

The American Bible Society (ABS) also figured prominently in the call for religious instruction among Blacks. In keeping with their objective to serve those who serve by providing scriptures that meet the needs of African Americans, after Emancipation the ABS stepped up its efforts to get Bibles to African Americans of the South. From the 1900s to the 1930s the ABS distributed nearly a million copies of the scriptures to Black pastors eager for the members of their churches, and everyone else in their community, to have a chance to read the Bible. From the 1930s to today the ABS has been deeply and actively supported by the traditional African American denominations.

What the Black church does now by way of organized religious education is clearly an outcome of the Sunday school movement of the late eighteenth century. With the emergence of independent Black churches in the nineteenth century, the Sunday school became the churches' principal agency for teaching. Eventually lay led, it came to be called the Sunday school department. Beginning about 1920, other structures concerned with or at least related to teaching the Bible emerged: agencies such as women's groups, youth societies, men's groups, and vacation Bible school. In the 1960s, the Black mainline churches began to bring many of these agencies together to form the church school, with the Sunday morning session as the center.

During most of the nineteenth and twentieth centuries the Sunday church school had three purposes: teaching the Bible, conversion, and nurturing persons in faith. Throughout the nineteenth and twentieth centuries a Bible-centered approach to teaching continued its dominance.

Liberating the Bible

Throughout the nineteenth and twentieth centuries, and widely also in the present century, the Bible has been central in the African American church. Is the Bible a source of liberation for Black people? We have already several occasions to show that the Bible has been used as a tool for oppression: slavery, segregation, and racial prejudice have been supported by a selective use of Bible verses. Yet concurrently throughout our history, Black people have been empowered by a biblical faith that instilled in them the resolve to survive injustice. If the central message of the Bible is that God is a God of liberation, then why is this understanding not more widespread? Why do we hear that Christianity is the "White man's religion"? Because the Bible has been used as a tool for oppressing Black people, for many the Bible itself may need to be liberated. The Bible needs to be liberated from being culture-bound. Biblical interpretation has certainly been culture-bound. The message of the Bible needs to be liberated from the shackles of European cultural superiority. This means that we must acknowledge that all biblical interpretation is influenced by culture. The Bible itself must be liberated from these imposed viewpoints so that it can be free to be a source of liberation.

African American Christian educators debate the centrality of biblical content as opposed to that of Afrocentric history and experience. African American Christian education must make provision for including our role in Christian history, the nature of our faith, so that our congregations can be grounded in the true history of their faith. Most African American Christian educators agree about the place of the Bible in the curriculum of the church. However, it appears that we have given little thought to the way the Bible is actually used in the curriculum. It is one thing to assert that the Bible is our textbook. It is quite another to translate that assertion into practice. African American Christian educators and pastors are concerned that, even after years of church membership, the majority of church members lack basic biblical knowledge. Reading and studying the Bible is not an easy task. Biblical ignorance cannot be erased until people are taught how to study God's Word for themselves. One reason for biblical ignorance may be that many persons are unaware of the roles that Africans play in the Bible.

The various concerns related to the Bible as curriculum do not take into account that African American history, culture, and experience have played a significant part in the spiritual development of African Americans. Church leaders, theologians, and educators attest to the Bible's role in spiritual development. In the curriculum, Black church history, African spirituality, and the Bible can never be separated. The events of Black church history are the history of African people's attempt in life and thought to interpret what they have found in the scriptures. The life and thought of Martin Luther King Jr., for instance, lights up in a new way the significance of nonviolence. Or the story of Black religious nationalism in America takes on new meaning when seen against the background of Jewish nationalism in the New Testament. Thus, in the study of Black church history, we are not turning aside from the Christian message to an unbiblical subject. We are trying to see in what way the Black church's past experience enables us the better to grasp and interpret the gospel for our own day.

The late professor Charles B. Copher's writings demonstrated the significance of African people in the Bible. The presence of Africans in the Bible is an important reminder for African Americans who can read about their foremothers and forefathers in the Bible and identify with a heritage that reaches back to the beginning of humankind and continues to the present. Charles B. Copher reminds us of the importance of when our identity as a people begins. He states, "not only does Africa and some of her peoples and places have a place within the biblical context, representing most periods of biblical history, but additionally, topic-wise, the Bible has had a place in the life of African peoples ever since its existence as a body of sacred writing down to the present day."[15] He further comments,

> Even before that portion of the Bible known as the Hebrew Scriptures, the Old Testament of the Christians, had reached its final form around the year A.D. 100, Africans were acquainted with and using them, as is indicated by Luke's account of an Ethiopian eunuch who, as he was returning home to Africa from Jerusalem, was reading from the fifty-third chapter of the book of Isaiah. And what is more, the eunuch was reading from a version of this scripture that had been produced in the African city of Alexandria, Egypt.[16]

The question of identity involves the interpretation of Black culture and the Bible. Identity and interpretation act as partners. The Black preacher, theologian, and educator hold Black culture and tradition in one hand

and the Bible in the other. The close of the twentieth century and the beginning of the twenty-first century marked the recovery of the Black biblical tradition. The recovery of the Black biblical tradition has to do not only with the African experience in the Bible, but also the ways in which they have understood, interpreted, and used it. What is the meaning of this all too brief sketch? To be sure, it reveals the importance of the Bible in experiences and aspirations of African Americans in the past and present. The next section looks at how Blacks today are interpreting the Bible from their own perspective.

Interpreting the Bible in the African American Church

One of the most popular and often quoted of all books is, of course, the Bible. Unfortunately, most of what is popularly known about the Bible stems from ideas and interpretations that are less than accurate. The fact that persons are "sincere" in what they believe the Bible teaches does not make their understanding correct. Understood correctly or not, through the years the Bible has been afforded a place of awe and esteem in the lives of many faithful people. Presently in the Black community there appears to be a growing hunger on the part of faithful people to study the Bible, to learn what it really says, to understand its meaning and message, and to attempt to relate those teachings to present existence.

How do African American Christians think of the Bible? How do scholars, teachers, and people interpret scripture? What methods of interpretation are operative? In recent years, the importance of African American contributors to biblical interpretation has come to be appreciated by an ever-widening group of scholars. What has been the process by which African people have appropriated, narrated, and interpreted the Bible? African Americans have attempted numerous approaches to the study of the Bible. This section seeks only to introduce what is involved in the process of interpretation. Here the interpretative act is comprised of the interpreter, source of interpretation, and scope of interpretation.

Who Interprets?

The Bible is central to Christian education. The Bible is always being interpreted. People inevitably translate what is read to a personal context. For this reason, it is important to explore the ways African American Christians interpret the Bible. Blacks have interpreted the Bible differently than Whites. Who interprets the Bible? Historically, the Black church as a community, particularly the clergy, has determined the boundaries of interpretation. The Black preacher as interpreter is represented by persons such as the late Benjamin E. Mays, Mordecai Johnson, Frederick Sampson, and Howard Thurman, as well as those working today—Renita Weems, Samuel D. Proctor, Gayraud S. Wilmore, Jacquelyn Grant, Charles Adams, Frank Madison Reid, III, John Bryant, Vashti McKenzie, and a host of other well-known and lesser-known heralds of the gospel. In the historic Black denominations, the clergy usually mirrors the interpretations of the denomination that ordains them, and usually the congregation in which they find themselves. But so inconsistent is biblical study within most Black congregations that it is possible for the minister to have one approach to biblical interpretation, the Sunday school teacher(s) another, and church member(s) a third.

Since the 1980s, we have witnessed leaders and groups within historic Black denominations and congregations that differed and split. The divisions, unlike the earlier divisions based on power, publishing rights, polity, and race were based on their interpretation of the Bible and worship style (i.e., Full Gospel Baptist Fellowship and other nondenominational Black congregations). These new religious groups share a more fundamentalist and Pentecostal orientation to the Bible than traditional mainline Black denominations. The late twentieth century is also marked by the ascendancy of Afrocentric scholars (biblical/religious) who have expanded the boundaries of meaning and whose creative thinking and writing often leads to valuable insights. These orientations of the Bible were reflected in their critiques and more radical (Afrocentric) and conservative (Pentecostal/evangelical) interpretation of the established Black Protestant–defined Bible.

Today, who interprets the Bible? The interpretive community entails three constituencies: the academic (educators-theologians), ecclesial (clergy-laity), and cultural communities. We have to say the primary interpreters for African American Christians consist of Black educators, preachers, and scholars. Each generation has interpreted the Bible differently within the life and history of Black Christians. God's Word has been and is heard in many ways. There are a variety of approaches to understanding scripture. For centuries African Americans have know about our liberating ways of reading the Bible. Our presence today as a people is a testimony to our liberating engagements with the Bible. Many different views about the Bible coexist today among African American Christians. Therefore, in constructing an African American hermeneutic there is no *one* appropriate way to interpret scripture but a variety of perspectives in the quest for liberation.

Sources of Biblical Interpretation

What are the sources that influence the interpretative process in the African American believing community? The Bible has long been a source of strength for African American Christians. It is and always has been an essential resource on which African American Christians ceaselessly rely for spiritual nourishment and formation. For this reason it is important to explore the sources that Blacks bring to their interpretation of the Bible. How have African Americans engaged the Bible? Scripture, experience, Black church tradition, and culture have shaped African American biblical understandings. The hermeneutical architects have been primarily but not exclusively members of the African American community: biblical scholars, educators, and theologians. Persons like J. Deotis Roberts, Randall C. Bailey, Renita Weems, Clarice Martin, James Cone, Albert Cleage, Stephen B. Reid, Cain H. Felder, Brad Braxton, Michael Brown, Thomas Hoyt, William Meyers, and Vincent Wimbush have had prominent roles in setting the parameters for a Black biblical hermeneutic, which is developing. Work in scripture reveals a richness of thought unique to individual thinkers in the discipline.

The first source of African American hermeneutic is the Bible. Black people have always seen the Bible as a prophetic book of faith. The authority of the Bible for African Americans is its liberating story. Cone holds that the Bible is an essential witness to God's revelation and is foundational for Christian thinking about God, for the Bible has been a source through which Blacks experience a liberating and sustaining God. The significance of the Bible for African American Christians is that their lives and culture have been influenced by it. The result is an exegesis of freedom. The book of Exodus, as well as the Jesus with whom they have identified as the God of the disinherited, serves as an evaluative standard for contemporary interpretations of God's Word, and the biblical witness is that God unquestionably is a God of liberation.

The second source is experience. God is present and active in human experience. The Black experience is foundational and determinative for a Black biblical hermeneutic. African Americans first clearly experienced God in the dehumanizing experience of slavery in the United States. It was in that experience that they were taught that God favored the slave masters. Yet as they learned to read the Bible for themselves they realized that God so loved the poor and the oppressed that God set them free. God, therefore, served as validation for African Americans of their lives, their humanity, and their hope for freedom from all forms of oppression. The Black experience in America has certainly conditioned Black interpretation of the Bible.

The Black experience is a religious experience in which the forefathers and foremothers reinterpreted the Christian faith in the light of their suffering. They did not just read the Bible. They brought to the text their total experiences—pain and pleasures, hopes and despairs, agonies and ecstasies, and the belief that a better day was coming. They expressed their experience of God in song, story, and prayer. A major part of the Black experience has been and continues to be the Black church.

The third source is the African American church. The focal point of God's liberating activity was and is the Black church. The Black church was not only the place where these oppressed people could be affirmed in their personal worth but also was where they heard stories and sermons about the Lord, who was always at work. The Black church historically has empowered African Americans with a ministry that met spiritual and material needs. It has consistently provided strong models for the struggle against racist oppression. The Black church has a long and influential history dating back to the days of slavery. The African American church is an abundant source for Black hermeneutics. This includes a narrative of the struggle to affirm our culture. Foundational in these stories are the religious faith of our people and the embodiment of this faith in the Black church. The tradition of the church is a source for Black biblical hermeneutic.

African American interpretation of scripture has been guided by Black church tradition or confessional heritage. Tradition is the compilation of theological reflection arising from the history of the Black church from its beginnings in Africa to the present day, and also the critical reflection of African Americans upon that tradition from their own particular faith perspective. Historic Black denominations, the particular form that confessional identity takes in the African American religious experience, frequently reinforce denominational tradition. Black biblical hermeneutics consults church tradition, but from a critical, evaluative position facilitates the interpretation of that which advances liberation.

The fourth source is culture. The cultural life of Blacks is found in their music, art, literature, and folk tales. These cultural expressions serve as forms of cultural resistance to Euro-American cultural domination. When we examine the cultural beliefs and practices that developed among enslaved Africans, we find that the value of community was pervasive. In African American culture, the importance of community cannot be overemphasized. Historically, African American Christians have defined themselves socially and not doctrinally. What has bound us together are not so much strict adherence to confessions or creeds, but rather the community joys and pains. African American Christian communities understood and explained their existence in communal terms. Our cultural distinctiveness was forged in the crucible of slavery and segregation.

The idea of community/communality is deeply rooted in African tradition. African understanding of the world is communal. The goal of religious instruction, as was practiced within the early African American Christian communities, was aimed at developing and enhancing a sense of spiritual and social belonging or "peoplehood." Africans carved out space for themselves and proved that no matter how oppressive the plantation was it was not severe enough to crush the enslaved African creative instincts. The African American church was the cultural womb that taught values of resistance. When seeking to understand the Bible from a cultural perspective, it is important to know that our cultural and social settings shape the rule or methods we use for interpretation. We bring to the text our culture in a liberating perspective. Liberating culture is vital for a constructive African American hermeneutic. Therefore, if the Bible is to have sway in the African American community, it must speak to communal as well as personal needs.

Scope of Biblical Interpretation

The scope of interpretation provides a background against which the distinctive emphases of scripture can be viewed. How do African Americans perceive the nature and function of scripture in the Black Christian tradition? Biblical hermeneutics is the application and interpretation of the biblical text. As noted, African American theologians, educators, and pastors have had prominent roles in setting the parameters for a Black biblical hermeneutic.

What follows tries to show the basic views of major contemporary African American theologians and educators about scripture. The following explanations are not exhaustive treatments. In some cases, representative figures are chosen and citations made from a number of different works. At other times, one main figure is targeted and that person's work made the central concern. Calling the Bible a spiritual tool allows us to focus on several of its most significant functions: *scripture as story, scripture as message, scripture as liberation, scripture as stories of Black women's freedom, and scripture as identity formation.*

SCRIPTURE AS STORY

The Bible is the foundation for Christian education because through its pages Christians learn who God is and how God acts. The Bible is at the center of Christian education. This centrality arises from the Christian church's basis in the story. The story of God's love is made known in creation, in redemption through the people of Israel, and through the life, death, and resurrection of Jesus Christ. Each member participates in that story.[17] Christianity is based on the story—our story. As Christians, everyone participates in this story. God's Word is heard in many ways. African Americans interpret the Bible differently.

What are the stories Black people tell about themselves and those that help structure their world? Anne Wimberly explores the relationship of story to the Black experience. We all have a story. Wimberly notes we are a storied people. She suggests, "Stories reveal persons' yearning for God's liberating presence and activity in their lives. And they reveal persons' yearning for meaning and purpose in life. Stories also reveal God's concrete presence and action in persons' lives and persons' responses to God."[18] Through the vehicle of story, Blacks heard and read the Bible through the reality of their oppression in America. That reality allowed them to identify with the historical oppressions recorded in scripture. Blacks appropriated the Bible mainly through storytelling.

Storytelling is a form of communication among Blacks. Before having been uprooted from West Africa, Africans had a rich history of oral communication. The popular African literature included tales, stories, and proverbs preserved and transmitted from one generation to another by storytellers—the *griots*. The preacher was chiefly responsible for transmitting the stories of how Israel was liberated from the bondage of Egypt to the masses of Black people. The stories found in the Bible tell us how to look at the Black story.

Thomas Hoyt, Black biblical scholar and bishop in the Christian Methodist Episcopal Church, is right: "Blacks can neither properly understand nor appreciate the story found in the Bible without knowledge and understanding of Black history."[19] Bishop Hoyt aptly writes, "In Black culture the story is that which established the authority of the Bible, for in its story, Blacks find the essence of their story in modern life."[20] Blacks are excellent story-communicators. The lyrical rhythms of rap music are a contemporary continuation of this oral tradition. Storytelling has had an important role among African Americans. Joseph Crockett wrote, "Oral tradition of story telling in African American communities is the cultural experience that serves as the basis for teaching scripture as story."[21] Anne Wimberly explains the relationship of narratives to the Black experience. She firmly believed Blacks must reclaim their storytelling tradition, especially interpreting the Christian story from an African American perspective. Wimberly wrote, "Of particular importance are predecessors who interpreted and acted on difficult and oppressive life issues by identifying with stories/texts found in scripture. Our intent is to place their lives in dialogue with Bible stories/texts."[22] She believed that stories of freedom were powerful because they echoed the longings in the hearts of those who suffered injustice of various kinds.

A second important contribution to life stories focuses specifically on the Bible and on the category of narratives in scripture. Biblical scholars like Thomas Hoyt and Delores Williams, who concentrate on this approach, find examples of narrative trends in scripture and seek to answer how these texts function as "authority" in the life of African American Christian communities. As an example, for Delores Williams, God's liberating activity in Black women's lives is inextricably linked to the Hagar wilderness experience, rather than the Exodus model. Dr. Williams's work draws analogies between Hagar's experience in the wilderness and African American women's understanding of their wilderness experience. Williams argues that Hagar's story and African American women's story of survival/quality-of-life tradition are similar. "What that means is to see the Hagar-Sarah text in the Bible from the position of the slave women rather than the perspective of slave owners (Abraham and Sarah) and their culture."[23] As the Bible is read, studied, and proclaimed through preaching in the church, we may locate our own stories in God's story as told in scripture. The story in scripture, told in and through the church, shapes our understanding of reality. The scriptures provide a grid or set of images by which we may come to believe and interpret our own life experiences.

Scripture expresses the Christian story. Scripture itself presents its own means for teaching: parables, poetry, proverbs, prayers, liturgies, symbols, songs, and stories of ordinary people. Christian education is that dimension of the church's ministry that seeks to bring the life story, cultural story, and Christian story into conversation, one with another. The story enables the learner to participate in the lives and situations of those people to whom God was speaking and through whom God was acting. We are Moses, Jeremiah, Ruth, Hagar, and Paul. When the Bible is taught as story, teaching scripture as a story and connecting scripture to African American experiences and traditions make possible the release of God's life-changing power into the lives of persons.

SCRIPTURE AS MESSAGE

At the close of the twentieth century and the beginning of the twenty-first, there has been a growing segment of Black religious life that is part of a new movement of Black evangelicals. Men and women (predominately men) whom I would classify as neo-evangelical lead these congregations. Black neo-evangelicals look to the teachings of White forefathers such as Charles G. Finney (1792–1875) and Dwight L. Moody (1837–1899) as the most faithful historic expositors of the basic gospel message of scripture. Also Black neo-evangelicals look to contemporary and modern-day Black evangelical thinkers and preachers for theological and inspirational guidance, such as: Dwight Perry, Anthony Evans, William Banks, William Bentley, William E. Parnell, John Perkins, and Tom Skinner. Black evangelicalism has varieties and diversities. Beyond the historic continuity of an American evangelical tradition is the theological or doctrinal basis that defines Black evangelicals. Black evangelicals differ with the historic Black church on the significance of scripture. For Black evangelicals, scripture is the inspired word of God that comes to the church through the words of human writers. Scripture contains a divine message in written words. The thrust of scripture is God's active living Word. Through preaching, the message of the gospel is expressed in living form.

Bishop Joseph A. Johnson has offered the most comprehensive theological position on the meaning of scripture as message. For Johnson, the message of scripture is understood through the proclamation of the gospel. As Bishop Johnson puts it, the Black preacher understands hermeneutics as wrestling with the will and word of God.[24] Black preaching throughout its history has been centered in the Bible, especially the gospel message. The Black preacher believes:

> The great subject of all the Bible is the Lord Jesus Christ and his work of redemption for mankind. The person and work of Jesus Christ are promised, prophesied, and pictured in the types and symbols of the Old Testament. In all of his truth and beauty, the Lord Jesus Christ is revealed in the gospels; and the full meanings of his life, his death, and his resurrection are explained in the epistles...the great purpose of the written Word of God, the Bible, is to reveal the living Word of God, the Lord Jesus Christ.[25]

For Black neo-evangelicals, the scripture as message becomes authority when there is faithful adherence to the basic doctrinal beliefs.

Therefore, for Black evangelical theologians and clergy, the purpose of scripture is to bring people to faith and salvation in Jesus Christ. The Bible is a book that presents a gospel that does not come to us as timeless truth, but as a message of salvation received, interpreted, and handed over to humanity. The words of Jesus were focused on salvation (Jn. 20:31) and were intended to equip the believer for every good work. Scripture is the word of God. For Black evangelical interpretation, scripture is to be interpreted in the light of its central message of salvation. Scripture is its own interpreter and is to be interpreted in the light of faith. Scripture is accepted in faith, and then through the use of reason one moves on to a further understanding of the message of scripture.

Scripture is the inspired word of God that comes to the church through the words of human writers. Scripture contains a divine message expressed through a variety of forms. Through preaching, the message of the gospel is expressed in living form. The Black evangelical preacher seeks to help the congregation understand the particulars of their biblical interpretation of God, church, and world. Biblical text "comes alive" in the context of the Black community, particularly in preaching during worship. As the preacher enters the biblical text, embodying it so that the text speaks out of the depths into the community's experience, Black preachers know that when they hear "Amen" they have rightly interpreted the Bible. Evangelicals tend to think that the Bible and the Christian tradition are a fixed deposit of beliefs on which the community can draw. Interpretative conversation in the Black evangelical community focuses on understanding, doing, and living out the message of the gospel.

Scripture as Liberation

The Bible has been traditionally the most important source for the articulation of liberation in the experience of people of African descent in North America. African American biblical interpretation looks for the liberating reading of biblical texts. African American biblical scholars have taken seriously the call of Black theology for intense engagement within the Bible. According to Michael Brown, a New Testament scholar, "Exploring ways they could assist the cause of liberation, many African American scholars of the Hebrew Bible and New Testament begin to pursue the possibilities for a liberated and liberating reading of scripture."[26]

It is clear that in Black communities whatever is said about the nature of scripture is inseparable from the way scripture is interpreted. Black experience has shaped ways of understanding scripture just as scripture has helped to interpret Black experience. Biblical interpretation has always been shaped by historical settings and cultural experiences. African Americans read the Bible with the experience of oppression as a point of departure because this is where most find themselves. The emphasis of scripture as a liberating word is apparent among Black theologians and biblical scholars.

James Cone speaks of the importance of the exodus event as the focus of God's actions with Israel when he writes, "By delivering this people from Egyptian bondage and inaugurating the covenant on the basis of that historical event, God reveals that he is the God of the oppressed, involved in their history, liberating them from human bondage."[27] The most important biblical model of liberation in African American social and religious history is the exodus. Thus it was through the scriptures that enslaved African American people found models of liberation to construct visions of hope.

Like Cone, many other authors—such as James H. Evans, J. Deotis Roberts, Cain Hope Felder, Michael Brown, Vincent Wimbush, Stephen B. Reid, Randall Bailey, as well as womanist theologians such as Delores Williams, Jacquelyn Grant Kelly Brown, Renita Weems, and Katie Cannon—are committed to interpreting the Bible from this perspective. James Evans has indicated how African American experience has made an impact on Black views of scripture and its interpretation. Evans suggests, "Scripture as liberation achieved its status in the heat of a liberation struggle, and...it is only within the contemporary struggle of the Bible can be validated."[28]

Roberts affirms that a Black biblical hermeneutic must be universal in vision and have human rights as its focus.[29] Stephen B. Reid argues that a Black hermeneutic has a twofold task: it must first engage the text in a serious way, and it must show how the text contributes to the fulfillment of human potential.[30] Cain Hope Felder sees Hebrew culture, like African American Christianity, as an infusion of biblical faith and culture. Felder suggests that African Americans give allegiance to biblical faith and witness, primarily because their own experiences seem to be depicted in the Bible. Using the dual sources of the Bible and culture, the task of interpretation for Felder shows how African Americans have engaged the Bible through the symbol of Blackness.[31]

Michael Brown and Vincent Wimbush suggest a few additional approaches that make interpretation more authentically liberative. They argue for new biblical models of biblical interpretation that are Afrocentric and include the multiple struggles, voices, and perspectives of the African American experience.[32] Today these Black biblical scholars are revealing the so long ignored or denied active and central presence of Blacks in scripture, and developing new interpretations that make connections with Black and African history and experience. Black scholars have sought to develop a new hermeneutic, one in alignment with their own consciousness as a people of faith and struggle. If one of the goals of African American interpreters is to tell the truth about history and scripture, then we must tell the entire truth. Clearly one of the critical challenges facing a Black biblical hermeneutic is to identify with the liberative dimensions of historical-biblical Christian doctrine.

Scripture as Source for Black Women's Freedom

It should not be surprising that Black history, a history built upon and by the Black church, also provided female prophets as models of liberation. Harriet Tubman and Sojourner Truth were both dramatically affected by religious beliefs forged in the experience of slavery. These female liberationists shared significant characteristics with contemporary womanists. They had a fierce hatred of racism and sexism and adopted an activist approach to confronting these evils. This activist interpretation of religious faith is grounded in Black women's experiences for freedom in connection with scripture.

Womanist thought is the name chosen by Black women in various fields of religion who claim two things. First, they affirm the experiences of African Americans as a basis for biblical interpretation. Second, African American women are made in God's image, and therefore their values, voices, experiences, looks, and ways of being in the world have divine significance. The definition of womanism given by Alice Walker is best summed up in her phrase, "You acting womanish."[33]

With the emergence of the womanist concept in the African American community, more Black women are claiming their places in the development of Black biblical interpretation. Black womanists believe the Bible to be a record of God's revelation to humankind, a record that shows God dealing with women and men as fully equal. Black women theologians, preachers, and educators see the Bible as containing stories and experiences of Black women's quest for freedom and liberation.

One of the critically important texts published in the 1980s, noted for its contribution to the development of womanist thought in general and biblical interpretation in particular, is *Just a Sister Away: A Womanist Vision of Women's Revelation in the Bible,* by Renita Weems. Weems interprets nine biblical stories featuring women, beginning with Hagar; through her interpretation of this story, Weems relates Black women's oppression and exploitation with that of the slave Hagar.[34] Womanists place their experience and culture first and then attempt to make sense out of the Bible, creating a variety of interpretative possibilities.

The relative recent contributions of Black women scholars have had an important impact on contemporary Black interpretation. Inevitably, the woman's movement that began in the 1970s brought Black women into prominence as biblical scholars. Among the voices in the ongoing development of womanist interpretation of the Bible are Delores Williams, Jacquelyn Grant, Kelly Brown, and Katie Cannon. Their understanding of God's revelation was revealed directly to them and witnessed in the Bible, and read and heard in the context of their experience. For womanists, interpretation of scripture is the story of Black women's freedom.

Scripture as Source for Identity Formation

African American Christian identity is a matter of spiritual formation, of becoming what we sing, the story we tell. We become the living texts of Christianity. Becoming Black and Christian involves a change; a spiritual and cultural conversion takes place in the believer. The Black church provides an organized community that aids in the spiritual/cultural development of those who are in the church. The church has fostered and nourished the self-concept of African Americans.

The Black church has historically been the agency for identity formation. Through storytelling, drawing on images from Black culture, the Black church could interpret their voices for communal identity. However, today the integration of African Americans into the mainstream of American society has led some Blacks to forget, ignore, or choose not to identify with their Blackness, and others are just ignorant of their rich African, African American, and Christian heritage. This kind of attitude represents a clear assault on identity and the right interpretation of social context. Hence we need a rereading of scripture that entails a basic recovery of historic African Christian identity.

As this sense of self comes under attack, African American Christians must reappropriate the biblical witness in a way that restores the Black communal definition of self, rooted in traditional African values, that says, "I am because we are." Efforts are beginning to be made by Black biblical scholars to overcome the omissions and deficits in the treatment given Blacks and their history and experience in scripture. African American biblical scholars and educators like Westfield, Wimbush, Roberts, and Reid provide a communal approach to interpretation, which probes the text for the images of faith that shape identity. In this context, the Bible is interpretive as the source of Black identity formation in Christ. For example, Cleage, Holmes, and Thurman proposed a communal hermeneutic that eventuates changes in self.

Some contemporary Black preachers and scholars are putting more emphasis on the influence of cultural perspectives when reading and understanding scripture. Clearly there are multiple cultural perspectives that shape identity and interpretation of scripture. The Bible had been a primer, culturally speaking, and a sacred authoritative book for Black people. Thomas Hoyt wrote, "Its character as primer relates to the history of slavery in American culture and its practice of restricting slaves from reading and writing."[35] This means for Blacks the Bible attained its authority as that authority conforms to the Black story through experience and culture. In this respect, the Bible was one of the chief components of the Black experience.

According to Stephen B. Reid, the question of identity organized Black biblical interpretation. Reid observed, "Black biblical hermeneutics, like those of any oppressed people, is ultimately the quest for identity as God's believing community. This entails the interpretation of Black experience, which calls for the interpretation of the data, as well as scripture. A Black biblical hermeneutic must interpret both Black experience and biblical text."[36] Here, reading the text required a critical reading of the text, the recovery of the Black interpretation of the text, and the application of the text to the life experience of the Black community.

Cain Hope Felder, in *Stony the Road We Trod,* and J. Deotis Roberts, in *Africentric Christianity: A Theological Appraisal for Ministry,* best highlighted this perspective. Felder's original scholarship, followed later by Roberts's, constructively interprets the Bible with the Black religious and church tradition from an Afrocentric perspective. Roberts believes that the interpretation of scripture from an Afrocentric perspective helps us to improve our sense of self-worth and our somebodiness as a people.

The interpretative history of African Americans has been shaped by their experience. They articulate their interpretations in their own way—in songs, prayers, sermons, testimonies, and folk traditions. With these sources, African American Christians laid the foundation for what can be seen as an emerging "canon." Therefore, given the foundational impact of the Bible in African American life, African Americans are beginning to seize hermeneutical control in their use of the Bible.[37] All of these readings of scripture emerge from the African American social world and historical moment. The challenge facing Black biblical scholars, Christian educators, and teachers is to connect these interpretive perspectives to teaching the Bible in the local church.

Teaching the Bible in the African American Church

These interpretive approaches have direct bearing on teaching. Teaching is interpretation. Here we focus on the interrelationship of biblical interpretation and teaching. H. Edward Everding wrote:

> Teachers regularly and dramatically confront the hermeneutical problem every time they teach the Bible. Each student, as well as the teacher, has his or her own understanding of a text. This often results in multiple and sometimes conflicting interpretations. This phenomenon frequently leaves the teacher with many unanswered questions such as: How do I account for these different interpretations? Are they all correct, or is there one normative meaning of the text? What then should be my goals in teaching the Bible? What can I do to achieve these goals?[38]

What is the aim of teaching? Our teaching must reach far beyond the transmitting of information about the Bible and its contents. We are teaching and training African American Christians to be witnessing disciples and servant leaders. The teacher of the Word requires biblical grounding. Teachers are expected to act and speak in accordance with the faith and life that are manifest in the Bible and that become theirs through the word of the Bible.[39] The teaching ministry of the church equips the people of God to identify their own story with the Bible story. Anne Wimberly calls this process story linking, whereby persons connect their personal stories with Christian faith heritage stories of African Americans. Thus by linking with their faith heritage stories, they relate themselves to spiritual exemplars whose lives and experiences were informed by the gospel.

How can we teach the Bible effectively? Christine Blair wrote, "The art of teaching does more than simply guide the reading and discussion of biblical passages. The teacher recognizes that the Bible and the learner need to connect in a meaningful manner. This connection requires understanding the nature of the biblical texts, their history and shape, and the ways in which they have been interpreted."[40] How do we teach and interpret the Bible in ways that form and transform persons and the church? Too often, the concern in teaching the Bible is only with how to transfer biblical texts into the minds of the students. But to teach the Bible for formation is to have transformation as our goal. This kind of spiritual formation takes place when we allow our word to be shaped by the word of God.

From my experience of teaching the Bible in Black churches, Blacks engage biblical text in a wide variety of ways that reflect unacknowledged but deeply held assumptions about biblical interpretation. For most African American Christians, the Bible is the word of God. The Bible is sacred and holy, the revelation of God's nature and will, and the record of God's action with and on behalf of a chosen people. African American Christians believe that God will bring reconciliation to all humanity.

To you who teach the Bible in the Black church, to teach responsibly you need to be self-aware of the way that you are interpreting biblical texts as you teach. Further, having an awareness of the ways biblical texts are interpreted by biblical scholars can help teachers understand how students are approaching and understanding scripture. Such insight also allows teachers a perspective from which to challenge students to explore new ways of interpreting and understanding the Bible.

In this chapter we have discussed different ways Black scholars interpret the Bible. Here these different ways of reading and interpreting the Bible suggest certain ways each approach may be used in teaching the Bible in the Black church. What are the educational goals that flow from these views? Given the variety of ways in which the Bible is interpreted, we can identify different educational goals. Viewing the Bible differently leads to different educational goals. Our goals in teaching the Bible are determined in large part by our understanding of the Bible. For most African American Christians, the Bible is the word of God. We have shown that in the Black Christian tradition certain symbols, images, and stories are more central than others. Certain ideas become dominant. As a result, scripture as "Word" conveys a variety of understandings.

For example, if we see the Bible as the Word of salvation, our goal will be to help people to know God and have a personal relationship with Christ. If, however, we understand the Bible as the liberation story of the people of God, our goal will be to help our members hear and understand this story and to make connections with their own story of liberation. Although these two ways of understanding the Bible are not necessarily exclusive, they do result in different teaching goals. African American biblical scholars and religious educators have wrestled with the issue of goals for teaching the Bible. In the table, I have sorted their thoughts into different approaches, grouping together the educational goal and the central vision of the Bible. The differences are differences of interpretation.

Education Goal	Biblical Interpretation	Key Question
Conversion	Scripture as message	In what way do I need to repent and have my life transformed by God?
Cultural Integrity	Scripture as identity formation	How do we keep faith with our tradition?
Common Identity with Bible People	Scripture as story	How do the biblical stories reveal God at work?
Justice in Action	Scripture as liberation	What work do we engage for justice?
Inclusive Biblical Images for God	Scripture as stories for Black women's freedom	How do we think and reform religious life in terms of the full dignity, equality, and liberation of women and men?

Conversion

The central interpretation of the Bible here is salvation. As a result, the goal of teaching the Bible is for the reader to be confronted with "the mind of Christ." It is the goal of conversion of both the individual and the church. The goal of conversion helps the learners explore the key question: In what ways do I need to repent and have my life, and the life of the church, transformed by God? In order to be converted by God, we need to be taught to memorize and probe the biblical text.

We can learn to use the results of biblical scholarship to understand the meaning of the text in the past and to make this text part of our own world. The emphasis in the educational approach is on scripture confronting the community of faith. The goal of teaching the Bible is to confront us with God, known in Jesus Christ, and to convert us out of sin into a holy way.

The educational goal is accomplished by an interpretation of the Bible that stresses the faithfulness of God and salvation in Jesus Christ. This educational approach emphasizes memorization and analysis of texts and doctrines revealed by these texts.

Cultural Integrity

When the goal is to teach scripture with cultural integrity, then the teacher seeks to make accessible the traditions, narratives, and experiences of African Americans. Educators in this approach are thus interested in the ways in which each generation interprets Black tradition. Black people have interpreted the Bible from their own experience, and have sought the Black church as a part of their identity formation. Its key question is: How do we keep faith with our tradition?

The question of identity organizes Black biblical interpretation. Reid states, "Black biblical hermeneutics must reach back to the antiquity of our oppression."[41] The blood of Black Christians in North Africa and Ethiopia, and the blood of Black Christians shed in the United States, is like a flowing stream. The goal of teaching the Bible emphasizes identity and interpretation. Identity and interpretation always inform one another. The task of a Black biblical hermeneutic involves the interpretation of Black culture and the biblical text. Neither identity nor interpretation takes priority; they act as partners.

The goal of teaching the Bible, then, is to help readers recover the Black interpretation of the text and the application of the text to the life experience of the Black community. Teaching scripture with cultural integrity upholds respect for the traditions and experiences of African Americans. The truths from the traditions and experiences of past generations continue to be identified and used in teaching Blacks to practice a religious way of life and to understand their faith tradition. This educational approach leads to an emphasis on the "recontextualization" of scripture: a process of rediscovering in the Bible persons of color and places in Africa before Christ.

Common Identity with Bible People

In the United States throughout the eighteenth and nineteenth centuries, Black religious communities interpreted and reinterpreted the biblical tradition, adding story and song in each generation, answering the questions: "Who am I as a person of God?" and "What am I called to do?" In time, the stories and their interpretations were woven together to become our sacred texts. Sacred texts are those that function as authoritative texts for the Black religious community. The educational goal, then, is to identify us with the biblical communities of the past in order to link ourselves to God's story. The key educational question in this approach is centered on the biblical believing communities and their stories: How do the biblical stories of the past and our stories today reveal God at work? Educators in this approach are interested in the ways each generation reinterpreted the tradition.

By identifying the methods of interpretation used by Black biblical writers, we will be helped in interpreting the Bible in our context today. The story approach to education is primarily concerned with the question of identity and vocation. The goal of teaching the Bible, then, is to help readers identify themselves with the biblical communities of faith and to link our stories with the Bible story. How do the biblical stories of the past and our stories today reveal God at work? Begin with human experience, past and present, and move to God. This approach leads to education that emphasizes stories: stories of biblical peoples and stories of today's peoples.

Justice in Action

The goal of teaching the Bible is not simply to instill knowledge of God, but to teach the right use of knowledge to transform society. The goal of teaching the Bible for educators is to help us see the injustices within contemporary society and to inspire us to critique the current social-political-economic realities in light of God as liberator. The key question is: "What work are we called to do in Jesus' name to 'proclaim good news to the poor' and 'freedom to the captive?'"

Educators in this approach are interested in the prophetic role of religious education. To carry out the task of religious education effectively, the teacher combines the prophetic word and action. The educational emphasis is on living out our Christian faith in faithful action. The key image in the Bible is a God of justice and freedom. Blacks see the exodus story, a story of God's liberation of Hebrew slaves, as the central story of God as liberator of the oppressed.

This approach emphasizes social analysis and action for justice. It often needs a praxis method of teaching and learning. This method, which interacts action and reflection, has a consciousness-raising function. This educational approach focuses on "what to struggle for" and "what form the struggle must take" based on biblical understandings.

Inclusive Biblical Images for God

The goal of teaching the Bible is to help make the experience and insights of Black women available to the church and world. The womanist approach to scripture is about Black women's claim to freedom to relate to God in the church and world. They are acting out these new freedoms. They are coming out of their experiences and interpretations and expressing themselves. What follows is a critique of the historic Black church–traditionally controlled and defined by Black men–which Black women clergy and theologians say has misunderstood and ignored Black women's progress in the church.

Black clergy women and theologians see the scripture as presenting stories and voices for freedom, as they make readers aware of God who has the power of freedom and who gives that power of freedom to us. As the Christian scriptures are read and taught in conjunction with Black women's resources, African American Christians are witnessing the birth of this power of freedom in Black women's humanity bound by male dominance and control of Black religious institutions.

The educational goal of inclusive biblical images of God leads to teaching believers to not only seek specific female images for God in the scriptures, but to name God in liberating, nonhierarchal images and tell their own stories. Black women are discovering the liberating elements of women's experiences as powerful resources to re-image the biblical story. Educationally, this approach provides another way of appropriating the biblical texts, through women's stories, prayers, and songs. It can also connect learners to the rich heritage we have in Black women spirituality, as witnessed by the popularity of Black women's conferences and programs.

Nonetheless, religious thinking and teaching cannot help but be changed by the impact of womanist interpretations of scripture. Even those who resist change will have to struggle with the issue if and when they decide to repudiate Black women and the womanist challenges to church, culture, and congregations. Central to womanist understanding of scripture is commitment to practice/action and equal commitment to remember suffering and oppression. Those who truly follow this goal eventually find themselves moving from prayerful reflection on scripture out into the church and world to engage in action. Most clergywomen and educators realize that transforming action in the world is imperative. Black clergywomen as leaders, who used to be peripheral in the Black church, are revitalizing the church at the center.

In sum, as we engage in Bible study, we will want to use all five approaches. As we discuss the meaning of biblical texts, we may need to name which set of understandings is guiding our thinking.

Conclusion

Historically and practically, the scriptures have provided the content for their curriculum in the church. Curriculum refers to a body of content to be covered in the educational process. The Sunday school serves as the Bible teaching arm of the Black church. Although the Bible is the curriculum for all of the church activities, most view the study of scriptures as being confined to the church school hour and mid-week Bible study. As African Americans recall their own roots, many have pressed toward the mark of creating a curriculum for African Americans.

Producers of curriculum, editors, and writers now take the African presence in the Bible seriously. Black Christians need to see biblical people as real persons who look like them. Materials should convey respected Black scholarly understanding of how the Bible was written. People who choose curriculum need to be sufficiently conversant with biblical study in order to recognize the interpretations used by editors and writers.

Furthermore, the identification of authentic persons of color in biblical study is inspirational to Black believers. The literature ought to provide a sense of belonging. If one is unable to feel involved in lessons, one will not own the lesson. African Americans need to understand the biblical stories that discuss the African heritage. Rev. Walter McCray wrote, "We believe that this present treatment of the Black presence in the Bible offers a fresh perspective for a growing constituency of Christian Black educators and learners who seek to maintain a good respect for reliable biblical and historical information."[42]

This survey of the role of the Bible in African American life and thought demands the attention of theological educators, which is the focus of the next chapter.

PART TWO

CHAPTER FOUR

Hearing and Understanding Contemporary African American Theological Voices

From the middle of the twentieth century to the beginning of the twenty-first, we begin to hear a variety of theological voices in the United States. The voices range from African American evangelicals–a voice that conveys a personal relationship with Jesus Christ–to a liberation voice that speaks to the harsh reality of sin in the structures of the church and society. Appreciating the range of voices that are part of our tradition is important to us as educators. Identifying the theological voices in our tradition provides us access to how we have come to be the people we are. It focuses our attention on the ecclesial, historical, cultural, and spiritual forces that shape us. Understanding the place of Blacks in society and in the church is inextricably linked to the way Black faith develops, when we "drink from our well."[1] Very simply, we cannot move from standing by the well to drinking from it without discovering our own voices.

In the Black Christian tradition, hearing and understanding God's voice and responding to God with one voice, one individual perspective, one cultural interpretation, and one theological perspective cannot really come close to capturing the totality of the African American religious experience. This chapter aims at hearing and understanding the range of theological voices that are part of our Black Christian tradition. We seek a more clear understanding of the theological landscape of African American faith by defining Black theologies, describing the practices of reflection, and identifying and discovering our contemporary voices. In order to gain a greater understanding for our faith, we will look at various voices. The spiritual journey requires that we attend to our voices and to the possibilities that they contain. We cannot walk on the journey of faith if we do not notice our voices and what they reveal to us about ourselves. Let us now turn to hear the voices of African American theologians and educators in our Black Christian tradition. Black theologians and educators variously describe the journey in faith. From their different perspectives and distinctive purposes, all still focus on a process of spiritual growth and liberation.

Defining Black Theologies

Through much of the twentieth century, the voices of people of color and women were excluded. In spite of such resistance by Whites, people of color never ceased thinking theologically. Black theologies differ in that each speaks to the particular realities of a group of people who have been silenced. Black theological understanding is important for all members of the church. We define Black theology as reflection arising out of the Black religious experiences of the church and resulting in faith-informed interpretations that serve to guide the ongoing life of Christians. Theology belongs to the church as a constitutive dimension. Theology as discipline and life within the church is integral to its educational ministry. Many great theologians, educators, and religious leaders have been contributors to theological discourse throughout the history of the Black church from slavery to the present. Today seminaries have Black scholars on their faculties. These thinkers are popularly known as Black theologians.

African American theology is the collective experience of African Americans as reflected in their history and contemporary life. One is speaking of a complex array of individual and collective experiences of members whose stories find a common ground in a paradigmatic event in United States history: slavery from 1619–1865. Although not all Blacks in the United States are descendants of slaves, all Blacks are subjected to racism predicated on the dominant cultures' continued collective unconscious belief that most Blacks are intellectually, culturally, and morally inferior to Whites. This belief is still prevalent in the United States. There has always been theological reflection upon the life and faith of the Black church. African American cultural history has been sustained by informal theological expression. However, there has not always been sustained academic examination of the varied theological expressions of the Black religious experience. Black theology did not commence with the writings of Black religious leaders and educators in the 1960s. The oral tradition of Black theologizing has always sought to interpret and apply the content of Christian faith to the Black religious experience.

We have pointed to the attempts made by Black religious leaders and educators to construct a systematic theology pertinent to Black Christians.

The early writings uttered the quest for freedom. Later literary endeavors by trained Black professional theologians and pastors affirmed liberation. Historically, in part, the Black church was a response to White domination. The Black church generated theologies and established educational models to ensure, among other things, educated leadership within the church. Many of the polemics and critiques written by Black theologians in recent years challenged Black churches and educators to embrace Black liberation theology. A lot of ink has been spilled on this matter. Black theology as a discipline owes its existence to the seminal work of James Cone. Cone used the contemporary struggle of the civil rights movement of the 1960s and the burgeoning growth of Black Power in the latter half of the decade as resources for understanding theological discourse. Cone maintains there is more to theology than faith thinking. Cone calls for a liberation view of theology, with thoughts and actions engaged in the struggle for freedom.

What is Black theology? Black theology begins when one asks, "What does it mean to be Black and Christian?" It is important, first and foremost, to differentiate between Black theology, in the first instance, as all forms of Black systematic religious thought and, in the second instance, Black liberation theology being one particular form of it. This does not mean that the two kinds of Black theology have nothing in common. They are, I believe, trying to answer the same questions about God, human beings, nature, and the world we live in. Both forms are necessary for a full understanding of the faith of African American Christians. In my judgment, a redefined Black theology represents the entire range of Black theological voices.

Here we can learn a great deal from the theological insights of Cone, William Bentley, and Katie Cannon. All voices tend toward their different political, cultural, and spiritual concerns. Yet, what is important and fundamental is their joint work on pursuing salvation and liberation for the Black community. The broadening of the definition is vitally important in order to account for diversity of beliefs and practices in Black history and experience. Thus, to synthesize the best contribution of Cone and Bentley does not force Black Christians to remove or hide their unique identity. Accordingly, a redefined Black theology separates itself from the dominant exodus motif of liberation theology. In sum, a new Black theology has to be accountable to God's diverse expressions in the overall Black community. Given this definition of theology, I now intend to examine the practice of theological reflection expressed in Black theologies.

The Practice of Reflecting on Our Faith

Theological reflection, according to Patricia O'Connell Killen and John DeBeer, is "the discipline of exploring individual and corporate experience in conversation with the wisdom of religious heritage."[2] In this case, theological reflection puts our experience into a genuine conversation with our Black Christian heritage. This conversation opens the gates between our experience and our heritage. It helps us access the Black Christian tradition as a reliable source of guidance of what God is doing now in our lives. Theological reflection is the process of seeking meaning from our Black Christian heritage. Such conversation is the stuff of theological reflection. It invites us to bring our lives to the Black Christian heritage in a way that is liberating and life-giving.

To reflect on our faith involves a process of how to think theologically. It offers a framework in which to do ongoing theological reflection. We focus on the process of thinking theologically, calling it by one of its best-known names: theological reflection. This process is in many respects like a craft. It involves working with various resources or sources, which can be learned and honed over time by practice. Theological reflection involves conversation. The voices of others are heard. Some of these voices, like those of the biblical writers, come from texts of centuries past. Others are those of our contemporaries. Still others are our own. To engage in theological reflection is to join in an ongoing conversation with others that began long before we ever came along and will continue long after we have passed away. The voices of Black Christian thinkers throughout history have had no hearing outside their immediate and very limited space.

African American Christians came to feel that theology is conversation that is closed or stacked against them. African American or womanist theologies of our times are foremost among those that offer alternatives to it. Limiting the circle of conversation partners is always the theologian loss. Opening the circle of conversation of theological voices among the varied members of the body is essential for the church's theological well-being. A model of theological reflection based on conversation allows for an appreciation of diversity. What sources go into theological reflection? What sources are our starting points? There are at least four important sources in Black theological reflection: scripture, tradition, culture, and experience.

The first source is *scripture*. The Bible is an integral element in the life of the Black church, and in theology as well. African American Christians share with all other Christians the conviction that scripture is the primary source and guidance for theological reflection. It is the primary source of the songs, sermons, symbols, images, and hopes by which the African American Christian community came into existence and that still confirm and nourish its faith and understanding. Scripture is an important source for African American Christians.

The second source is *tradition*. Black Christian tradition consists of the corporate and communal experience of early Black Christians. Black Christian tradition as a historical process preserves and transmits the faith traditions of struggle, memories, interpretations, liturgies, rituals, beliefs, and doctrines from generation to generation. It reflects the sum total of the African American Christian past and present. All Black theologians writing from within the Black church draw on Black Christian tradition as a source for their theologies. Not only the content of the Christian message, but the teachings, writings, rituals, and customs of the church are referred to as tradition.

The third source is *culture.* Black culture in the United States is an endless well of cultural resource. It includes both historical and contemporary aspects that influence Black Christian self-understanding. Black culture as the concepts, stories, symbols, songs, arts, and values for conduct serves as an indispensable component in theological reflection. The emphasis, then, is an understanding of theology shaped and formed by the Black cultural experience. Thus, cultural awareness and race pride affirm creation.

The fourth source is *experience.* Experience plays a significant role in theological reflection. African American Christian experience is not only deeply private and inward, it is also corporate and active. African American Christian experience has been oppressive and liberative. The life of faith embraces the totality of our life experiences. In the experience of slavery and segregation, Blacks clearly experienced God. Through prayer, the uplifting presence of the Spirit and the experience of God and oppressive power in the world all enhance our theology of faith.

With respect to sources, now let us turn to how these sources are drawn upon in the following types of Black theological expressions: *evangelical, proclamation, liberation, Pentecostal, womanist,* and *spiritual.* What I seek is to demonstrate that a variety of voices speak from different perspectives. Nonetheless, they also constitute a voice-story about African American hearing and understanding. Each voice is distinctive as it contributes to the overall rhythm of coming into being. Six processes for theological reflection follow. All stem from our basic framework for theological reflection: focusing on some aspect of experience, describing that experience in cultural context,

THEOLOGY	SOURCES
Evangelical	Experience, culture, scripture, tradition
Proclamation	Experience of oppression, scripture, culture, tradition
Liberation	Experience of oppression, culture, scripture, and tradition of struggle
Pentecostal	Experience of Holy Spirit, scripture, culture, and tradition
Womanist	Women's experience, culture, scripture, and tradition
Spiritual	Inward experience, culture, scripture, and tradition

placing our experience into genuine conversation with our Black Christian heritage, and identifying from this conversation new interpretations from scripture for living and action. The following chart shows the framework for theological reflection used by each theology in this section. The chart illustrates that each draws on the sources in a variety of ways.

Identifying and Discovering Our Theological Voices

To understand a theology it helps to know about the individuals who fashioned it and the context in which it was fashioned. In this section I will draw on the work of contemporary theologians and educators in explaining how these theological constructions understand the theological task, including perhaps most especially what they mean by *theology*.

Evangelical Theology

Evangelical theology emerged in the eighteenth century during the First and Second Great Awakenings in America.[3] Black evangelical heritage, to which the present Black church is heir, began with evangelical zeal directed toward the poor and disinherited. Methodist and Baptist preachers proclaimed a simple gospel of salvation to all who would listen. Among the poor and disinherited who listened and responded to the gospel message of the Methodist and Baptist preachers were enslaved Blacks who had been brought to America in chains. The Great Awakenings brought about a change in religious thought. Conversion became the culmination of the Christian experience for each person, available to all.

When enslaved Blacks accepted the evangelical faith, it was more for existential than for doctrinal reasons. They found this new movement ethically and spiritually attractive. Evangelical preachers, by preaching Jesus frees, offered enslaved Blacks a vision of God's justice, either now or in the future. By the late nineteenth century, the foundations of Evangelical Protestantism were well in place. It was a religion, especially as exemplified by the Methodist and Baptist denominations, that upheld the verbal inspiration, inerrancy, and sole authority of the scriptures. It also emphasized the supreme importance of proclaiming the word of God in preaching.

The Black evangelical tradition also regarded primacy of religious experience, the conviction of sin, the need for repentance, and religious personalism as central tenets of the Christian faith. Black evangelical theology comes out of the heritage of Black culture and religious experience. The extent of the impact has varied over the centuries. The sources of Black evangelical theology are Black experience, culture, scripture and tradition, and the norm as Jesus Christ himself.

William H. Bentley observed that Blacks within the major Black denominations have suffered historical amnesia about its evangelical heritage.[4] Theological voices in Black evangelicalism are comprised by traditional evangelical orthodoxy, nontraditional orthodoxy, evangelical social gospel, and nondenominational evangelical orthodoxy. In the cultural context of Black evangelicalism, there are those who hold to the fundamentals of evangelical theology, yet see no conflict at all with a strong socio-political emphasis. Yet, at the same time, there are Black evangelicals who desire to divorce Black culture altogether from the Black church and see it as a hindrance to truly biblical Christianity within the Black church. Within Black evangelicalism the differences are not theological but socio-cultural: the role of social involvement and Black culture.

Ronald E. Roberts's (1985) unpublished doctoral dissertation "Leadership Studies in Black Evangelicalism," provides understanding of the Black evangelical heritage. For Roberts, to be a Black evangelical one must uphold the fundamental beliefs of orthodox and historic Christianity. Such fundamental beliefs include: the Bible as the inspired word of God; the deity of Christ; the virgin birth of Christ; the substitutionary atonement of Christ; and physical resurrection and future bodily return of Christ.[5]

Black evangelicalism is influenced by its Black heritage and at the same time by its White evangelical training and teaching. The educational experience of many Black evangelicals from college to seminary has been influenced by White evangelicalism. White evangelicals have written most of the literature that Black evangelicals read. Many of the Black evangelicals who are ministering today have come out of the traditional Black church. White evangelicalism reached others outside of the church scene altogether.

The nineteenth century witnessed the rise of historic Black denominations. In the historic Black denominations there are leaders who are orthodox in their theology. Their belief is rooted firmly in biblical orthodoxy and historic church doctrine. The authority of the Bible, experience, and church tradition are sources of reflection. In his study, Anthony Evans points out the Black church is basically orthodox in its theology. He states, "Historically, the Black church in America has held to the mainline assertions of conservative Protestant theology. Doctrines such as the virgin birth, bodily resurrection of Christ, and the physical second coming marked the essence of Black belief."[6]

Traditional evangelical orthodoxy displays a highly transmissive view of Christian education in which the teachers of the Christian tradition hand on the content of Christian tradition from one generation to the next. This tradition is treated as constituting God's saving Word to humanity. For some, the transmission of the content of the faith has an instrumental function, serving as a means of precipitating a contemporary personal encounter with God. Traditional orthodox Black churches reject emotional display in the worship service and the doctrine of miracles, prosperity, and healing taught by the Charismatic movement. Nontraditional orthodox church–oriented Black evangelicals are those who made a break with the traditional Black church; their worship is nontraditional and sees the task of the church as the proclamation of the good news of salvation in Jesus Christ.

Black evangelicalism took on another shade of meaning in the early twentieth century. This period saw the emergence of Social Christianity, or, as it was later called, the "Social Gospel." Although the Black religious tradition beginning with the spirituals contains elements that predate and anticipate the social gospel's concern with the total person, it was not until the end of the nineteenth century that Black church leaders began to explore the social gospel. Black social gospel advocates believed that the teachings of Christianity and the gospel of Christ were concerned with more than just the spiritual welfare of humanity. Christ's gospel addressed the total life experience: political, social, economic, and spiritual. As a result, social gospel ministers committed themselves to the "social salvation" of humanity—the meeting of all pressing needs.[7]

The social gospel movement tended to have a weak record on issues of race relations until African American church leaders such as Reverdy Ransom began to rethink the social gospel in light of race consciousness. One observer of Black social gospel advocates in the historic Black church argues:

> Most ministers rejected the social gospel, fearing that it placed too much emphasis upon social concerns. A minority of church leaders recognized the gospel's mandate to heal the whole person. It was understood by this segment of the church that a commitment to the gospel meant addressing the full range of human needs, in part revolving around the removal of racism's harmful effects.[8]

Charles S. Smith and Ransom, the premier social gospel advocate, represent this perspective. For these clergymen, social salvation was the message of the gospel.

In the late twentieth century, a host of new nondenominational Black evangelicals surfaced who placed great emphasis on the teaching of the word of God in the Black church and on practical Christian living. New nondenominational evangelicals place emphasis on "what God is revealing in my life now." It encourages reflection on personal experience and its significance. Some Blacks are leaving historic Black denominations, saying that the churches place little emphasis on clearly preaching the Bible.

During the course of the late twentieth century a number of Black evangelical pastors and thinkers emerged, such as William E. Purnell, Tom Skinner, Carl F. Ellis, William Bentley, Anthony Evans, E.V. Hill, Frederick Price, and Melvin Brooks. They were determined to develop a rationale and apologetic for Black Evangelical Christianity and were at the same time willing to engage in constructive theological debate with proponents of contrary views. Granted, there are a variety of meanings appropriate to the word *evangelical* in different historical and cultural contexts. However, it has most often been associated with the doctrine of salvation by faith in Christ alone. Black Evangelical Christianity transcends denominations and their respective polities.

While evangelical thinking moved from traditional evangelical orthodoxy to social gospel and nondenominational evangelicalism, Black Evangelical thinking has undergone significant modification in its expression. But, with its firm commitment to biblical authority and personal evangelism, nondenominational evangelicalism, unlike its orthodox counterpart, has enjoyed dramatic growth. Aided by the contemporary emphasis on experience and electronic media, and by defectors from the institutional Black church, it gives every indication of becoming stronger in the future. Nonetheless, certain questions are being raised today that no longer allow us to assume these doctrines are held by the entire Black church. Without question, evangelical theology is the predominant form of religious expression in the African American community, but other theological traditions of historical quality and social significance exist in African American religion.

Proclamation Theology

What is proclamation theology? How does proclamation theology influence the education of Black Christians? Does it play a significant role in religious education? What are its theological and educational contributions? In pursuing these queries, it is necessary to proceed by examining first the development of proclamation theology and later the principal educational methods to which it gave rise.

Theology as proclamation is crucial for the African American church. James H. Evans correctly observes that African American beliefs and practices are not learned primarily through detailed, systematic theologies, but through the spoken word of Black preachers as they reflect on scripture, tradition, and experience.[9]

Preaching in the Christian tradition has always proceeded from the presupposition that God has presented Godself in the person of Jesus Christ. However, the preaching posture in terms of content and style assumes many forms. The form is determined by myriad factors such as the preacher's particular personality, religious experience, intellectual pilgrimage, worldview, hermeneutical posture, and theology. Hence, there exists among Christians in America that brand of proclamation that can be described as "Black preaching."

Preaching has been a main factor in the ministry of African American churches since their inception. The genius of Black pastors to make the Bible relevant may account for the level of acceptance their messages enjoy. Although the pulpit has been a platform for addressing many of society's ills, both social and spiritual, a strong emphasis has been placed on sound doctrine. If preaching is to have contextual relevancy, it must address the audience under consideration.

Henry Mitchell explained, "Black preaching is conditioned by the sociology, economics, government, culture, the total Black ethos of the ghetto. It is also affected by both Black summa theological and, in particular, a theology about itself."[10]

The Black church has enjoyed a distinguished degree of prominence in terms of the preaching ministry. From the 1700s to the present, numerous luminaries have had great pulpits in the Black community. One only has to be reminded of Richard Allen, Andrew Bryan, J.W.C. Pennington, Samuel Ward, Gardner Taylor, Samuel Proctor, and T.D. Jakes. A great deal of emphasis has been placed on preaching and worship. However, the gift of preaching in the Black church has led to little systematic theological reflection on the proclamation of the gospel. The works that have been written tend to focus on sermon-building, biblical interpretation, and methods of delivery; few concentrate on the need to develop a theology of Black preaching. There is a real need to begin to develop a body of literature highlighting the importance of the interrelationship between theological reflection and Black preaching. What are the origins of proclamation theology? Proclamation theology derived its name from Bishop Joseph A. Johnson, who served as professor and bishop of the Christian Methodist Episcopal Church. Bishop Johnson's work, *Proclamation Theology*[11], must be considered the first major systematic theological treatment of preaching in the Black church. Johnson must be considered the major contributor to the proclamation perspective. Johnson believes that proclaiming the word of God has been and continues to be the primary concern of the Black preacher. Proclamation theology, a preaching theology addressed to the oppressed and oppressors, is evangelistic and offers salvation to all. The sources of proclamation theology are the experience of oppression, Black culture, and Christian tradition.

Proclamation Theology grew out of a need for students to master the art of translating theology so that it could be used homiletically in the proclamation of the word of God. Johnson argues that the central function of the Black church involves the preaching ministry of the Black church. Teaching is derived from and based upon the proclamation of the gospel. Johnson states, "The proclamation of the word of God has been and continues to be the basic concern of the Black preacher."[12] He further states, "The systematic theology which is of primary interest to me is a theology which can be preached, a theology which is faithful to the Hebraic-Christian tradition and more particularly to the Black classical preaching tradition. My primary concern is the elucidation of a theology that can be used and preached by preachers, regardless of race."[13]

For Johnson, proclamation theology is the authoritative word of God proclaimed from the pulpit and taught as an integral part of Christian education. It is the proclamation of the faith in which the gospel of salvation is the central theme. We all encounter the word of God in the person of Jesus Christ. Proclamation theology is Christian theology precisely because it utilizes God's revelation in Jesus Christ as its point of departure and also as a norm for interpretation of the meaning and significance of human existence. Johnson states proclamation theology "begins with the existential situation in which oppressed Blacks exist and seek to determine the message of Christian gospel in this situation of oppression."[14]

Proclamation theology emphasizes the dynamic aspect of the gospel as well as the rational aspect on which theological reflection concentrates. Proclamation theology is concerned both with the manner of God's speech to Blacks in the context of Black presence and experience and also with the message and action of God in situations of racism. Proclamation sets forth the message of the church. The message of the church sets forth God's offer of salvation to all who will accept Jesus Christ as Lord and Savior.

In recent years contemporary scholars have sought to describe at a more systematic level of reflection a theology of Black preaching. Henry Mitchell, in *Black Preaching,* argued for theological reflection on the emotive/celebrative encounter between preacher and pew that has historically characterized the Black religious experience.[15] Edward P. Wimberly, in *Pastoral Care in the Black Church,* viewed the African American sermon as therapeutic. He explained, when preaching has as its primary aim the care and concern for the person in crisis, this is pastoral care.[16]

James Forbes, in *The Holy Spirit and Preaching,* added an essential dimension to proclamation theology. He viewed preaching as an event in which the preacher proclaims the living word of God in the power of the Holy Spirit. The preacher and the spirit are thought to be partners in the proclamation of the gospel.[17] Carlyle F. Stewart, III, in *African American Church Growth,* explained that Black preaching raises the critical consciousness of the congregation. From the perspective of the theological convictions articulated, the preacher helps the congregation think critically about God, Christ, and the world.[18]

James H. Harris, in *Preaching Liberation,* considers the centrality of theology in preaching. He believes that in order to preach the gospel the preacher needs to have a clear understanding of God, Christ, and the Holy Spirit.[19] Cleophus J. LaRue, in *The Heart of Black Preaching,* provides a theological-historical analysis of the distinctiveness and dynamics in Black preaching. He views the African American sermon as a conversation of belief, context, and life experiences of the preacher. His analysis of the way in which African Americans conceive of God is best viewed through a cursory examination of Black theologians thoughts about God. He states, "four themes have been central to the ways in which African Americans understand God to be at work: freedom and particularly; love and partisanship; personhood and creativity; and survival and liberation."[20]

Proclamation theology denotes the theological and educational content of preaching. Proclamation theology also intends to provide the core and basis of all guidance and instruction for Christians. However, those who theologized from the proclamation point of view do not dominate the academy. Those who offer leadership tend to be preacher-theologians and may well be the principal reason that proclamation theology retains a measure of influence today.

Liberation Theology

Black liberation theology arose in the Black church in the 1960s in the midst of the struggle of the Black community for liberation from White oppression and domination. Black liberation theology is Christian theological reflection upon the Black struggle for justice and liberation. It was an innovative departure in the history of theological thought in America.[21]

Several factors contributed to its emergence: the civil rights movement, the Black Power movement, the influence of Malcolm X on the Black Nationalist Movement, and the reaction to the negative depiction of Black religion set forth in Joseph Washington's *Black Religion*.[22] James Cone was the first to articulate a Black theology. Cone's "Theology of Black Power" for Black liberation became the major voice in the Black theology movement. James Cone cites the resources of Black theology in his groundbreaking work *A Black Theology of Liberation* as the Black experience, Black history, Black culture, revelation, scripture, and tradition, and the norm as Jesus Christ. These sources and norm remain valid to the present day.[23]

> There is no truth for and about Black people that does not emerge out of the context of their experience. Truth in this sense is Black truth, a truth disclosed in the history and culture of Black people. This means that there can be no Black theology, which does not take the Black experience as a source for its starting point. Black theology is a theology of and for Black people, an examination of their stories, tales, and sayings. It is an investigation of the mind into the raw materials of our pilgrimage, telling the story of how we got over. For theology to be Black, it must reflect upon what it means to be Black. Black theology must uncover the structures and forms of the Black experience, because the categories of interpretation must arise out of the thought forms of the Black experience itself.[24]

There were other voices. Albert Cleage in *Black Messiah* provided a Black nationalist interpretation of the Black church.[25] J. Deotis Roberts in *Liberation and Reconciliation: A Black Theology* insists that liberation must be preceded by reconciliation.[26] Major Jones, in *Black Awareness: A Black Theology of Hope*, believed that Black theology is valid as it moves the Black church toward the new community.[27] Gayraud Wilmore, in *Black Religion and Black Radicalism*, contends that Black radicalism can be best validated in the Black religious experience.[28] Grant Shockley and Olivia Stokes in key articles add a significant dimension to the Black theology discussion with their position on the impact and implications of Black theology for the theory and practice of religious education in African American churches.[29]

Yet other voices heard on Black liberation theology in the 1980s and 1990s represent the emerging second generation of Black scholars in theology, both male and female. Symbol, metaphor, narrative, and testimony exemplify their theological voices. Second-generation Black religious thinkers draw upon Black religious past for expressions of faith that may be translated into contemporary theological expressions. For example, they analyze African American folklore, songs, sermons, and slave narratives for their potential contribution to a contemporary Black theology of liberation.[30]

Scholars who belong to this second generation are both heirs to the Black theological founders and groundbreakers in their own right. One representative work is R. Earl Riggins Jr.'s *Dark Symbols, Obscure Signs: God, Self, and Community in the Slave Mind.*[31] Riggins draws on ex-slave interviews, folk culture, and the spirituals to assess how illiterate poor African Americans have built the founding structures for a contemporary Black theology and ethics. This approach also appears in the book *Cut Loose Your Stammering Tongue: Black Theology in the Slave Narratives,* edited by George C.L. Cummings and Dwight N. Hopkins.[32]

Cain Hope Felder's *Troubling Biblical Waters: Race, Class, and Family* focuses on Black people's relation to the Bible and Black presence in the Bible.[33] James E. Evans Jr.'s *We Have Been Believers: An African American Systematic Theology* moves carefully through the standard doctrines of Black theology and provides an exact definition of Black theology and how it relates to the general understanding of systematic theology.[34] Will Coleman's *Tribal Talk: Black Theology, Hermeneutics, and African/American Ways of "Telling the Story"* puts Black theology into conversation with bodies of knowledge different from theology.[35] He uses philosophical and literary-critical approaches to determine the ways in which slave narratives are indeed a basis for Black theology.

Kelly Brown Douglas's *The Black Christ* explores the historical and contemporary issues surrounding the African American community's gravitation to a Black Christ and offers a theological response to the question of the color of Christ.[36] Liberation theology has developed in different ways. Anne S. Wimberly's *Soul Stories: African American Christian Education* recovers the story method in teaching, relating it to African American heritage.[37] Story-linking is central to Wimberly's theology. It entails a teaching/learning process focused on liberation and vocation. The process seeks to link your story with the Christian story found in scripture and with the African American Christian faith heritage stories.

These works, as Dwight Hopkins outlines in *Introducing Black Theology of Liberation,* represent two different approaches to liberation theology–the political and the cultural.[38] The political theologians are depicted as seeing theology as a mandate for political activism on the part of the Black church and community and for the full empowerment of Blacks. The political theologians also believe that God is a liberator for Blacks just as for the Hebrews. Hopkins sees James Cone, Albert Cleage, and J. Deotis Roberts as representatives of the political group, while Gayraud Wilmore, Charles Long, and Vincent Harding are members of the cultural.

The cultural theologians assert that prior to political action one must first be in touch with the cultural context from which that call to action arises. The theologians of culture note that in order to fully understand and express that theology there must be a return to and retrieval of the roots of the Black experience, especially African American cultural ties with Africa. A new generation of theologians advocates giving more attention to the memory of African values and worldviews.[39] Afrocentricity places the African being at the center of existence and replaces Euro-American cultural beliefs and values. Afrocentricity instructs the Black church and community to base their entire religious life on African values, beliefs, and practices.[40]

These theological voices represent today an amalgam of human understandings of who God is and who we are. What is quite surprising in reviewing these works is the neglect and exclusion of Grant Shockley's and Olivia Stokes's writings as early interpreters of Black theology. Their contributions are absent, even in James Cone and Gayraud Wilmore's *Black Theology: A Documentary History Volume II 1980–1992,* writings of second generation Black theologians.[41] Black liberation theologians have not yet shown a deep concern or respect for educational issues and thus are alienated from Black life in the congregation. If Black theology is first and foremost a pastoral theology, then it has failed to deal with the issues of Christian education.

Contemporary theologians and educators' voices continue to examine and critique the theology of liberation, so that we might think pedagogically how the content might be used, presented, or taught. They include: Fred Smith, bell hooks, Lynne Westfield, Frederick Ware, Anne Wimberly, Evelyn Parker, and Yolanda Smith. For these thinkers the particular object of theological action or reflection is how African American theology relates to the Christian education challenges of African Americans. Once this is recognized, questions about how our religious tradition helps or hampers spiritual growth and freedom become vital. Whether we move from theology to education or from education to theology, the conversation is needed.

Pentecostal Theology

Pentecostalism emerged during the twentieth century as a major presence within the African American community, which created a host of new congregations and denominations, transforming the religious life of historic Black denominations. Throughout the twentieth century, Black Pentecostalism has been a vital movement within American Pentecostalism and Christianity.

African American Pentecostalism came out of the historic Black Baptist and Methodist denominations because of a commitment to holiness. The beginnings of the modern Pentecostal movement can be traced back to 1906. The essence of Afro-Pentecostalism is located squarely in the Black roots of the Azusa Street Revival, of which William J. Seymour was the founder. An observer at one of the services wrote these words:

> Sister Farrar rose from her seat, walked over to Brother Lee, and said, the Lord tells me to lay hands on you for the Holy Ghost. And when she laid her hands on him, he fell out of his chair as though dead, and began to speak in other tongues. Then they went over to the prayer meeting at Sister Asbury's house. When Brother Lee walked into the house six people were already on their knees praying. As he walked through the door, he lifted his hands and began to speak in tongues. The power fell on the others, and all six began to speak in tongues.[42]

Noted Afro-Pentecostal scholar, Cheryl J. Sanders, described African American Pentecostalism as the "Sanctified church tradition."[43] Black Christians who came out of the mainline Black denominational churches and sought the deeper life of entire sanctification and Spirit baptism led the emergence of the "Sanctified church tradition" as a twentieth-century African American Christian reform movement. The five original bodies that constitute the Afro-Pentecostal tradition include: the United Church of America; Fire Baptized Holiness Church of God in the Americas; Church of Christ Holiness, U.S.A.; Church of God in Christ; and Pentecostal Assemblies of the World. They all share a common heritage with regard to the experience of Spirit baptism.

Historically, a denial of access to academic institutions hindered the formal training in theology and restricted the emergence of Black theologians equipped to present the Black experience in the development of Pentecostal theology. Today, things are beginning to change. The 1970s signaled the coming into existence of Black theological writing on Black Pentecostalism. Contemporary Afro-Pentecostal thinkers include Leonard Lovett, James S. Tinney, Robert Beckford, Robert Franklin, James Forbes, and Cheryl J. Sanders. Leonard Lovett, a pastor-scholar in the Church of God in Christ, explores in his doctoral dissertation the relationship between

Black Holiness-Pentecostalism and Black liberation theology. James S. Tinney, who was a pastor professor and community organizer, argued that Pentecostalism is inherently Black in his most notable article "The Blackness of Pentecostalism."[44]

Robert Beckford is even more forceful and to the point. Beckford belongs to a new generation of radical Black Pentecostals. He raises the question that cries out of his context, as a Black urban Pentecostal in Britain, "Is it possible to be a black Pentecostal and black conscious?"[45] Robert Franklin, a Church of God in Christ ecumenist, scholar, and clergymen, recently develop a more explicit understanding of the gift of Afro-Pentecostalism. In his speech at Harvard Divinity School (2005) he set forth six gifts: non-racialism, confrontation of personal/institutional sin, prophetic witness, recovery of African spirituality, ecumenical involvement, and globalization.[46] James Forbes sees the need for Black Pentecostals to engage in the struggle for social justice. Forbes writes concerning "progressive Pentecostalism" that anything that affects our attainment of an abundant life and social freedom is on the Spirit's agenda.[47] Cheryl J. Sanders's groundbreaking book *Saints in Exile* describes how Holiness, Pentecostal, and Apostle churches represent the exilic existence of African American Christians. To live in exile according to Sanders is for the saints of God as being "in the world, but not of it."[48]

Each of these individuals served as teachers while at the same time fulfilling a leadership role as pastors or leaders in one of the Pentecostal denominations. Afro-Pentecostal thinkers represent a significant, if largely unrecognized, scholarly group of intellectuals who have made a significant contribution to our understanding of Black religion. Critiques of Pentecostals by Black theologians may be a service to the entire church. Vinson Synan has called the Pentecostal surge the most significant religious movement since the birth of Black theology. Pentecostals still represent a quiet revolution. They are not headline grabbers. Still, they are continuing to grow. C. Eric Lincoln and Lawrence H. Mamiya tried to fathom the meaning of this revival in the historic Black denominations in *The Black Church in the African American Experience*. Lincoln states that, just as some of the White mainstream church denominations have experienced a charismatic or neo-Pentecostal movement among some of their churches, a similar phenomenon has occurred among some Black church denominations, such as the African Methodist Episcopal church.[49]

The sources of Pentecostal theological reflection are the experience of the working of the Holy Spirit, practice of spiritual gifts, the authority of the living word of God, and Black culture. At the heart of the Pentecostal experience is baptism in the Holy Spirit. Tongue speaking as experienced and promoted by William J. Seymour and his modern heirs was the beginning of an unprecedented religious development. For the first time, a Christian movement developed a whole doctrinal framework called the baptism or filling of the Holy Spirit and attached it inseparably to the experience of speaking in tongues. A fundamental presupposition of Black Pentecostal theology and praxis is the central emphasis on the experience of the working of the Holy Spirit. This experience includes "gifts of the spirit," especially healing, speaking in tongues, and prophesying. Central to Pentecostal theology is the doctrine of the baptism in the Holy Spirit as a second encounter with God (after conversion) in which the Christian begins to receive the supernatural power of the Holy Spirit into the life.

Clearly the Pentecostals place emphasis on the Holy Spirit as teacher, the inspired word of God, teaching from the Bible, tongue speaking, healings, and miracles. The Holy Spirit as teacher opened up a new approach to instruction for Pentecostals. Black Pentecostals perceive the Spirit as working through them in the gifts of story and song, testimony and prayer, vision and dream, dance and shouting, and the drama of the sermon.

Pentecostal belief means that Jesus Christ not only saves people from sin, but also heals sickness and delivers them from the power of Satan in all its various manifestations. Again, the beginnings of the modern Pentecostal movement can be traced back to 1906. More recent neo-Pentecostalism or charismatic renewal arose around 1963 within the mainline Protestant churches; they also spoke in tongues but did not see tongues as the necessary evidence of the Pentecostal experience.

Neo-Pentecostalism also has tended to be aggressively concerned with the proclamation of the gospel to bring nonbelievers into the Christian faith and Spirit baptism. Speaking of neo-Pentecostals, Walter Hollenweger describes these people as follows: "Most of them, but not all, are rather evangelical. But all of them want to stay within their churches and try very hard to remain faithful to their liturgy and theology."[50] In Neo-Pentecostalism, spiritual authority rests ultimately in the present activity and teaching of the Holy Spirit at least as much as in the Bible itself, whose essential truth is made known to individuals only by the power of the Spirit. During the last quarter of the twentieth century, Black Pentecostalism found prominence as a religious preference of the members within the new Black middle class. Black neo-Pentecostalism has entered its second century as a major tradition within the Black church and American Christianity.

Black Pentecostal theologians recognize that they can speak in tongues *and* be critical thinkers. They are beginning to ask very searching educational and pedagogical questions. Pentecostal theological reflection in Christian religious education is a must for the future. In my view that is the single most important topic for the church for the twenty-first century.

Womanist Theology

The close of the twentieth century witnessed the rise of Black women in roles of responsibility and leadership, especially as ordained ministers and theologians. Historically, those who did have such roles, few as they were, were constantly challenged by both men and women as to the propriety of their roles, their ability to fulfill them, and the validity of their calling.[51] Today this situation is slowly changing in the Black church. Womanist theology grew out of the failure of the historic Black church to address the issues of women of color.

As Black women began to critique the Black church, they also began to critique Black theology. Jacquelyn Grant provided an early critique of Black theology in her 1979 article, "Black Theology and the Black Woman."[52] In this article she recognized that by ignoring the experiences of Black women, Black theology rendered Black women invisible in their theologies. Grant ended her assessment by charging that with Black women representing more than 70 percent of the Black church, no authentic theology of liberation can arise out of those communities without specifically addressing the liberation of women.

Feminists propose a theology that emerges out of the particular experience of women. Liberationists propose a theological approach out of the experience of oppressed people. Womanist theologians suggest a theology that emerges out of the experience of African American women. Womanist is a term developed by Alice Walker to embody the African American woman's experience. It speaks of surviving in the struggle, of being in charge, courageous, assertive, and bodacious. It speaks of being fully-grown and responsible enough to contemplate and dialogue theologically independent of other races and gender.[53]

The womanist theological viewpoint recognizes the Bible, Black women's culture-history-experience, church tradition, and Jesus Christ. Womanists argue that theology developed in Europe and America has excluded the majority of humanity. Only when Christianity and theology are contextualized do women and other oppressed groups become participants rather than recipients of dogma. As participants, the oppressed are able to dialogue on the gospel for the oppressed. The womanist theological perspective reflects inclusiveness. It does not deny the value and worth of African American men. The perspective considers both race and gender as valid experiential ground for "doing" theology. Both Protestant and Catholic women theologians have taken up this understanding.[54]

Womanist theology insists that full liberation can only be achieved by the elimination of not only one form of oppression, but of all. Grant believes that womanist theology must engage the issues of racism, sexism, and classism to avoid becoming another bourgeois theology. She asserts, "To speak of Black women's tri-dimensional reality, therefore, is not to speak of Black women exclusively, for there is an implied universality which connects them with others."[55] "Womanist" symbolizes Black women's resistance to their multidimensional oppression as well as their self-affirmation and will to survive with dignity under dehumanizing social-historical conditions.

Womanist theology, like Black liberation theology, has influenced theological education more than it has shaped Christian education in the local church. Womanist theology is not taught in Black churches, state and national conventions, annual conferences, or Christian education congresses. While the rise of women as ordained clergy, pastors, church executives, and scholars in recent years has established the bases for women's liberation, a significant majority of Black Christians are unaware of its meaning.

Contemporary womanist theological educators are serious about ensuring that practice and theory are connected. Several, such as Anne Wimberly, Lynne Westfield, and Yolanda Smith are particularly significant in their explorations of educational questions. Anne Wimberly envisions a theology that regularly utilizes cultural sources from within the Black community for ministry. These sources include African American stories of faith. Anne Wimberly's model of story linking explores themes of liberation, vocation, and decision-making through the sharing of personal, biblical, and African American faith heritage stories. The theological implication of this approach is that stories serve as a source for theological reflection.

Lynne Westfield explores the relationship between Black theology, womanist theology, and Christian education. Womanist religious education is committed to a "life of the mind" along with full regard for expressions of the body and soul.[56] For Westfield the location of womanist dialogue has been the classroom. The classes became opportunities to explore the current realities of Black women. She experimented and found several components for effective womanist pedagogy. Westfield envisions womanist pedagogy as a form of resistance to narrow perspectives of classroom education. The most important and enduring essential for womanist theology is "hospitality." Yolanda Smith has developed a more extensive analysis of womanist theology/pedagogy in her search for a new paradigm that is more effective for African Americans. She developed a tri-collaborative model for teaching the triple-heritage. The three-level heritage includes Christian, African, and African American traditions. Each brings sources for theological reflection. Smith uses the spirituals as a location where each of these heritages overlaps.[57]

Nonetheless, there is a growing understanding and acceptance of women in leadership roles in the Black church, as exemplified by the election of Rev. Vashti McKenzie, the first Black female bishop of a historic Black denomination, the African Methodist Episcopal Church. Perhaps Bishop McKenzie's journey from Black theology to womanist theology suggests there will be a conscious and systematic approach developed to gradually infuse the church with concepts of womanist theology. McKenzie, in *Not Without a Struggle*, writes that the womanist theology challenge is to make relevant application of theological perspectives for African American women and the African American community at large. The academy and the congregation must come together to formulate, prepare, and express our common struggles, which broaden our expression of our knowledge of God.[58] This is important in the Black church, especially since the majority of Christian educators are Black women and the vocation itself has been seen as a woman's vocation through much of its history. Most Black churches face problems finding people to fill the educational ministry positions in local churches.

The responsibility for educating the congregation is often perceived as a sacred task, but its place in the church is almost always along the sidelines. Every woman and man called to teach and practice Christian education with excellence will not reverse the problem alone. We need a fundamental rethinking of Christian religious education that includes Black women's story of struggle.

Spiritual Theology

What is African American spirituality? What are the ways in which African American Christians have conceived and expressed their relationship to God? At the close of the twentieth century, Black Christian theologizing has focused in the area of spirituality, articulating the divine-human relationship and working out the concrete ways in which it is expressed in Black religion and culture. Spirituality has to do with one's relationship with God, with the way in which that relationship is conceived and expressed. The way in which one conceives of God is theology. There is an obvious relationship between theology and spirituality. Theology needs spirituality. Spirituality needs theology. Spirituality needs understanding, and it is such understanding that theology supplies.[59]

It is important to note, too, that the now very popular term "spirituality" has only recently come into common usage. Today we describe the spiritual life within the context of a particular historical period (Ancient African Christianity), a commanding figure in religious history (Daniel A. Payne or Howard Thurman), or a specific theological tradition (Methodist or Pentecostal); it is also possible to speak of culturally or racially determined spiritualities (African, African American).

While today we tend to use the terms "spiritual theology" and "spirituality" interchangeably, we must be careful of the nuances involved. While spirituality tends to be a more universal term dealing with lived experience, spiritual theology is more often theological reflection that informs the lived experience. Here we will be dealing with both spirituality and spiritual theology, in light of the African American religious experience. The sources for this theological approach suggest that our experience must be tested in the light of reasoned reflection on scripture, Black history-culture, the teachings of the church, and the communal struggle for freedom lived out by each of us in a personal relationship with God.

Jamie Phelps, in "Black Spirituality," writes that Black spirituality is a vital and distinctive spirituality forged in the crucible of the lives of various African peoples. The common spirit found in people of African descent is an attitude that sees all of life in the context of the encounter with the Divine, which is rooted in a distinctive and ancient worldview.[60] Also, there is a very new and self-conscious effort to construct a Black spirituality that simply rejects traditional Christian norms for assessing the value and authenticity of Christian spiritual practice. Some Black scholars today speak of Black cultural spirituality, a spirituality that exists alongside Black Christian spirituality.[61]

Contemporary Black theologians have been criticized for ignoring spirituality in their analysis of Black religion and the Black church. Critic Calvin E. Bruce writes that any workable theological system addressing African Americans should posit the importance of the African American spiritual temperament as an indispensable starting point.[62] Bruce also emphasizes that African American spirituality and African American religion are quite often used interchangeably when discussion focuses on the faith of the African American community.[63] They may be related, but they are not identical.

Flora Wilson Bridges, in *Resurrection Song: African American Spirituality,* also writes that Black theology has neglected or ignored the African-based spirituality that is the foundation of the culture of African Americans, their religion, and their struggle for freedom in the United States. Bridges argues that African American spirituality is the underlying spiritual matrix that helped African Americans forge their own worldview, which in turn helped them to be more resilient; less malleable to racial, social, and economic exploitation; and able to live with some sense of dignity and cultural cohesion as a community.[64]

How shall we articulate the characteristics of an "African American spirituality?" The chief characteristics of Black spirituality are historical, cultural, spiritual, and theological. The first characteristic is historical. Ancient Christianity is not, as many think, a European religion. Christian communities were well established in Africa by the third and fourth centuries. In Egypt and Ethiopia, traditions of worship, monasticism, and spirituality have remained authentically African and Christian down to the present day.[65] Black history is replete with examples of how spirituality has enabled Blacks to survive amid subtle and flagrant forms of racism. There are many accounts of a remarkable flowering of Black spirituality in the eighteenth, nineteenth, and twentieth centuries in America, and these accounts relate this occurrence to the social and political conditions of the period.

The second is cultural. The studies of slave religion have demonstrated the complexity of the interrelationships between belief, culture, and social constraints. Carlyle Stewart writes that African American spirituality is the practice of freedom. This freedom to create a culture, to fashion a uniquely Black worldview while surviving the perils of oppression, is one of the most important characteristics of the African American experience.[66] According to Flora Bridges, "African American spirituality inherits its distinctive hue not only from the experience of the enslaved in America. An intricate symbiosis of African and American cultures also threads its way through various dimensions of Black American culture."[67] There is thus a culture, a reality and ethos that is authentically African American, made possible and sustained by firm belief in God.

The third characteristic is spiritual. No matter where they live, Black people are fundamentally African people whose perspective and way of life have been conditioned by their roots in Mother Africa. African and African American theologians identify experiences in which African spirituality foreshadowed ancient Christianity. They note a distinctive worldview in traditional religious proverbs, oral traditions, social ethics, and moral codes.[68]

The suffering witness of slave Christians also constitutes a major spiritual legacy. Howard Thurman says, "By some amazing but vastly creative spiritual insight the slave undertook the redemption of religion that the master had profaned in his midst."[69] Out of this legacy of suffering the music arose that constituted one of this nation's most significant contributions to world culture. The Negro spirituals captured the suffering of enslaved Blacks. They reveal the capacity of the human spirit to transcend bitter sorrow and to resist the persistent attempts of evil to strike it down.

Calvin E. Bruce writes that the legacy of Black spirituality is made possible by strong faith in God. Faith has taught us that we can, indeed, steal away in the morning hours and "have a little talk with Jesus, tell him all about our troubles." Blacks have always had a lived theology that served to liberate the spirit from all forms of bondage. The fact is Black Christians have been able to live a theology that awakened the human spirit to the occasion, to live engagingly in the profane world, and, in special moments, to step into another sacred realm of spiritual being.[70]

The fourth characteristic is theological. Howard Thurman has been viewed more as a religious philosopher and mystic than theologian. Only since theology has begun to expand its ideological and methodological parameters into the spiritual and philosophical disciplines has Thurman come to be understood as a theologian in his own right. Howard Thurman engaged in theological reflection on the spiritual life. He was the mystic and spiritual thinker *par excellence* of the Black religious experience.

Howard Thurman was one of the great mystics of all time. His mysticism was practical, urging us toward involvement and engagement in the real world of social and ethical issues. The heart of religion for him was its moral and personal core. His mysticism was not introverted. Luther E. Smith called Howard Thurman the theologian of mysticism.[71]

In Thurman we encounter a genuine Black spirituality. In his work *The Luminous Darkness,* Thurman is intensely concerned about what segregation does to the human spirit.[72] For Howard Thurman, the main task of the writer about spirituality was to demonstrate that Christian commitment provided a unifying factor in life. His own experience of religious conversion, combined with his subsequent studies of the mystical tradition, convinced him of this. Thurman's investigations into the spiritual life were catalytic in moving African American spirituality in new directions.

Howard Thurman contributes the missing link in Black theology. For him the engagement in raw, spiritless, social action not only is emotionally unhealthy, but it is nonproductive. Only meditation and the disciplined spiritual life can be faithful to the cross of Jesus Christ. As he puts it:

> It is good to make an end of movement, to come to a point of rest, a place of pause. There is some strange magic in activity, in keeping at it, in continuing to be involved in many things that excite the mind and keep the hours swiftly passing. But it is a deadly magic; one is not wise to trust it with much confidence…Bring in your scattered parts, be present at all levels of your consciousness.[73]

Thus the spiritual life and Christian praxis need each other.

In sum, the challenge for Christian educators is to offer education in spirituality to clergy and laity within the Black church who now hunger for understanding and deepening of their relationship to God. The roots of spirituality are in the convictions of the Black foremothers and forefathers of the faith. Their faith is a consequence of their struggles with God, not of purely academic research. Black Christians in search of spiritual renewal need to return to their origins. The theological foundations explored in this chapter provide an essential ground for exploring the relationship between theology and Christian religious education in the Black church.

Conclusion

Theological reflection of African American Christians contributes to theological reflection in ministry. The theologies discussed in this chapter reflect that various historical streams converged to shape contemporary perspectives of African American Christians. These streams were both internal and external to Black communities, tied with the histories and philosophies of the times, reflected in churches. The resulting ideas became embedded in the traditions of the religious communities. These theologies are part of twentieth-century scholarship and inform the work of contemporary thinkers. Some theologians support the status quo; some stand in challenge to the times.

Our challenge today is to recognize the multiple theological voices of African American Christians. In order to create an environment where everybody's voice is heard, we must develop the art of listening. As we dialogue with different theological perspectives, our hearts and minds open to new spiritual understandings. Theological reflection articulates reasons for our judgments and subsequent actions. Explaining the rationale behind why we believe and why we educate is central to the theological task.

Theological reflection is insufficient if it is done in isolation. True theological reflection occurs in the context of community. It is communal and dialogical. Its formation occurs in sharing, talking and listening to other voices than our own. We cannot walk on the journey of faith if we do not listen to voices and what they reveal to us about ourselves. Whether it happens at the ministers' meeting, while reading a book, during Bible study and feedback with other friends and family members, or from the writings of professional theologians, the convictions of the community of faith form our theology.

Knowing why we believe what we believe allows us to enter conversation with other Christians. The community of faith is not only a community of worship; it is also one of theological inquiry. We offer our thinking about the faith. We listen to others. Theological conversation occurs. Each voice supplies a piece of the theological puzzle necessary for assembling the overall picture of the gospel and ministry. Our prior reflection on theology and ministry will inform our practice. If we are attentive to the Word, our faith will have its impact on what we do. As African American Christians, we are called to listen and to forge an ever-growing understanding of the meaning of the Christian message in our lives, in the church, and in the world.

CHAPTER FIVE

Understanding the Relationship between Theology and the Dynamics of Educating African American Christians

For the past four decades a major discussion has taken place in the emerging field of African American Christian education concerning the relationship between religious education and theology, particularly liberation and womanist theologies. In the earlier years of this conversation the participants were mainly theologians. In the past three decades professional religious educators have joined the debate. At the heart of this debate is an unresolved problem about the relationship of theology and religious education. The debate first took place among African American theologians who chose Black liberation theology as the theoretical foundation for religious education. Theologians such as James Cone, Jacquelyn Grant, J. Deotis Roberts, and Grant Shockley share this perspective. African American religious educators entered this debate in the 1970s, 1980s, and 1990s over the roles of proclamation, evangelical theology, womanist theology, and African American spirituality. William Bentley, Tom Skinner, Joseph Johnson, Lynne Westfield, and Flora Bridges share this perspective.

African American theologians and educators have divided into two groups: those who view religious education as a branch of pastoral theology (James H. Harris, Forrest Harris, Lora-Ellen McKinney, and Anne

Wimberly) and those who attempt to situate religious education as a separate interdisciplinary field (Lynne Westfield, Fred Smith, Yolanda Smith, and Evelyn Parker). These thinkers have shaped the horizons of thought on which theology and education are related. In the previous chapter I identified the major schools of theology that govern African American religious thought. In this chapter I develop an understanding of the relationship between theology and the dynamics of educating African American Christians. I also explore the relationship between a wide variety of contemporary Black theologies and the teaching of African American faith.

In the first section I present a brief summary of the relationship between theology and teaching in the African American church. I conclude this first section by arguing for the maintenance and development of the connection between theology and religious education, especially church education. In the second section I explore how various expressions of theology shape the dynamics of educating African American Christians. I conclude this section by evaluating how these theologies promote theological understanding. My contention is that in the history of African American Christian education a number of theologies have occupied a dominant place in African American churches.

The Relationship between Theology and Education in the African American Church

The history of the relationship between theology and education in the African American church shows that evangelical theology, proclamation, and Pentecostal theology occupy a dominant place in Black churches. Evangelical faith has continued to play a central role in African American Christianity up to the present time. Evangelical theology shapes thought and teaching in the Black church. The historic Black denominations have created curricula influenced by evangelical theology. However, James Harris and others have made sharp criticisms of prevailing Black evangelical theology. Harris rejected particularly such concepts as personal salvation and evangelism. His discussion did not deal so much with the place of theology, but rather with the type of theology that should undergird religious education. He argues for "teaching and preaching liberation" with more emphasis placed on what the church is teaching and less upon how it teaches.[1]

With the emergence of the Pentecostal movement in the early part of the twentieth century, and neo-Pentecostalism in the late twentieth century, the thought and teaching of the Holy Spirit and gifts of the Spirit arose. Like liberation theology, Afro-Pentecostal theology seeks to illumine an overlooked dimension of African American religious life: Word and Spirit. The history and identity of Afro-Pentecostal theology has been characterized by Cheryl Sanders as the "Sanctified church tradition."[2] In both evangelical and Pentecostal traditions we see the role of "proclamation" in the religious education process. Liberation theology and womanist theology retain a position of importance in the academy, but they have been less relevant to the life of the church. At the same time, spirituality has surfaced and appears more and more relevant to the meaning of life for Black Christians.

Until recently there has been little African American participation in the discussion of the relationship between theology and religious education. A particular theology stands in the background for every educator. It may not be clearly articulated or at the forefront of one's consciousness, but it becomes evident as various educational concerns are faced. In this section and pointing toward the approaches presented by the several theologians, we focus on the basic question of the role of theology in the religious education process. As stated by Padraic O'Hare, "there may be several points at which theology and education are related...theological reflection provides the religious educator with systematic investigation of the meanings and shared symbols of the religious community...it is indispensable throughout the education act, and most especially at the pre-educational moment in which the teachers seek to know his/her own mind, what to value, what to transmit."[3]

What should be the relation between theology and education? Sara Little lists five possibilities: "theology as content, theology as norm, theology as irrelevant, doing theology as educating, and dialogue between theology and education."[4] Norma Thompson, writing on a similar question, adds another possibility: "theology behind the curriculum."[5] My own position privileges three possibilities: that theology stands behind the curriculum, theology as content, and dialogue between theology and education. I discuss these possibilities in relation to the theologies presented. The Black church seems to be in search of a language, grounded in scripture, experience, church tradition, and action, by which it can guide its life. According to Richard Osmer, this suggests a broader shift in our thinking about the role of theology in religious education. He states that there is "a shift in fundamental assumptions about the nature and purpose of theological reflection, and the manner by which theology makes its contribution to function in the church."[6] What is the relationship between theology and religious education in the African American church?

James Cone published the first work in Black liberation theology, which was the essential theme. For Cone, liberation theology should serve as content for church education. The sources for this theology are found in the spirituals, songs, and sermons of our people. He further stressed that Black churches ought to be thinking churches; that is, churches that engaged in critical theological reflection.[7] J. Deotis Roberts and James H. Harris contend that Christian education in the Black church is the process and content of teaching about the Christian faith and the formation of Black Christian identity. For Roberts, Christian education is what Black theology comes in. Its point of entry is through the educative process. He says, "The involvement of Black theology in the educative process should begin with Christian education in local churches."[8] James H. Harris believes that the task of Christian education in the Black church is the development of faith and self-esteem among African American Christians. He says, "Christian education and Black theology, working in concert, can dramatically change our churches and communities."[9]

Grant Shockley expanded the project of Black theology to include the practice of education. He has correctly indicated the need for religious education for liberation, guided by Black theology. Shockley believes that Black theology's relevance to religious education has caused the Black church to see religious education from an entirely new perspective and has been instructive at the point of letting us know that any religious education must grow out of and center around the experiences, relationships, and situational dilemmas that Black people face.[10] Olivia Pearl Stokes critiqued religious education in the Black church through the lens of Black theology. She wrote that the central task for all Christian educators is "translation of Black theology, and its underlying concepts and implied theoretical assumptions, into goals, objectives, curricular designs, educational materials, and teaching methodologies."[11] Lynne Westfield and Yolanda Smith see the relationship between theology and education as dialogue. Westfield explains the relationship between Black theology, womanist theology, and Christian education, and Smith examines how the triple-heritage of African American Christians (African, African American, and Christian), through the African American spirituals, shapes and informs Black Christian faith and identity. Both contain a number of sources to assist educators gleaning insight for what we teach (content).[12]

For Anne Wimberly, theology is in the liturgy of Black church worship. Practicing God's presence through worship and liturgy is the focus of her work. Wimberly says, "Songs, along with prayer and sermons, are actually a narrative means of forming a participatory habitation for evoking our awareness of the qualities of God."[13] Worship carries us to a place where there can emerge a source of knowing that we know God. Worship deals with an instructional awareness. The emphasis here centers on recognizing the instructional aspects of a corporate worship experience and making use of learning opportunities for spiritual growth.

Reflections on How Theology and Education Connect

As a church leader I am called upon to defend, define, and interpret the faith to the faithful. I am often asked to lead workshops in congregations of continuing education events for ministers and laity. In these ways I contribute directly to the teaching ministry of the church. Therefore, here I share some of my reflections on how theology and teaching connect.

There are eight points at which theology is related to the teaching ministry of the Black church.

First, the church is the context within which we derive our distinctive Christian interpretation of God and the world.

Second, the church transmits the faith of the community. The Black church is called a community with its roots in Black history; it is a community in which Christ is presently at work. The Black church's historic and contemporary aspects are both important for the church's teaching ministry, for teaching must never be exclusively concerned with passing on the tradition or with present experience, but with both in relation to one another.

Third, the church teaches through its organized life. In order to carry out the great commission to teach throughout the world, it must equip its members. Therefore, the ministry of the laity is significant for understanding the Black church's teaching ministry.

Fourth, we teach and learn the history of a congregation in story form. Black congregations convey the experience of corporate life through story. Theological reflection upon Black church life can unearth the stories. African American folklore, songs, sermons, slave narratives, and biographies are sources for Black theological religious education reflection.

Fifth, most teachers in the Black church use the Bible for knowledge of the scriptures. However, they use other resources in the teaching of creeds, confessions of faith, and doctrines. These forms of theological expression have been used for understanding the faith. Therefore, we need to know and examine new ways of thinking about Black church tradition.

Sixth, the church has a faith to communicate. The church introduces people to the faith, presenting faith as knowledge about the heritage of Christianity and the Black church tradition (creeds, doctrines, customs, and confessions of faith). Theology as faith can be presented in the form of knowledge about the Christian faith and witness to one's own relation to God. Both are parts of theological content of teaching.

Seventh, we teach in order to develop an awareness of certain theological questions. Both professional religious educators and church educators interpret faith as they share it. They are theologians.

Eighth, theology promotes the formulation and the application of doctrine as well as the organization of rituals and ceremonies. Black educators need an adequate theology to explain faith in God to others. Having such a theology means they have enough confidence to offer their faith to others.

Christian education is the structure for teaching and applying such teaching to every phase of the church's ministry. Theology influences both the content and process of religious instruction. Sometimes this influence is direct and articulated, as when one explains the relationship of baptism and holy communion. In these instances, the theological understandings must be explained to the learner in keeping with his or her developmental level. In every instance the teacher has thought out the explicit theological teachings and everyday living experiences, making them mutually enlightened to each other. At other times the theological influences are indirect and operating as underlying, though unexpressed, assumption. Theology can also be in the background. It can be discovered, for example, while studying the internal ordering of the components of a teaching-learning session. For example, is the relation of Christ-church-sacraments clear, or do medals for perfect attendance seem as important as the resurrection?

Whether direct or indirect, this influence of theology is important because it is one of the chief shapers of the components of the teaching-learning experiences. Religious instruction necessarily includes the articulation of religious faith in theological language and theologically shaped rituals. Examining briefly the components of religious education, one easily discovers the influence of theology. Both the teacher and the learner bring with them all their previously acquired theological convictions–their own perceptions of Christianity. Certainly there can be and often is a wide range of theological orientations even within a given denomination, even within a single congregation. One can find theological orientations ranging from conservative evangelical through all shades of progressive Pentecostal or liberationist.

Black Theologies and Christian Religious Education

When I began my vocation as a Christian educator, I was concerned about Black theology and its relation to the field of religious education. Until the late twentieth century there had been little theoretical interest in religious education in the Black church. Through the nineteenth and twentieth centuries, religious education was conducted by means of straightforward didactic methods, such as storytelling, sermon, and song, with a heavy emphasis upon memorization of texts, especially the Bible. It was assumed that the purpose of these activities was to convert Blacks to Christianity and enable the learners to "get right with God," or to be saved, by knowing the word of God and right doctrine.

With the emergence of such leaders as Grant Shockley, Olivia Pearl Stokes, and the like, religious education in the Black church came to have a sense of integrity as a discipline of its own. What these leaders tried to do was to take seriously the educational nature of religious education. Since 1970 there have been new directions in both educational theory and in theology. The emphases on Afrocentricity, Black spirituality, multicultural pluralism, and praxis are some current phases. In theology, changes in Black theology, womanist theology, and other forms of thinking have contributed to the disciplines of both theology and religious education.

There is disagreement among Black theologians and educators as to whether the basic and guiding purpose of religious education ought to be liberation. As Black theologians evaluate one another, a spectrum develops that includes several views: evangelical, proclamation, Pentecostal, liberation, womanist, and spiritual. This section illumes whether or not theology is decisive in religious education. Education must be theologically responsible. According to Little, "that concern for theology is imperative for the educator, influencing how one selects content and chooses an appropriate consistent process for education."[14]

These theologies, all derived from the Black Christian tradition, provide a wide variety of starting points and conclusions, and each theology leads to its own distinctive theory and practice of religious education. There is overlapping, but the emphasis is different in each case. What are the implications for theory and practice? What specific pedagogical/ instructional procedure or set of procedures does that particular form of theology directly generate?

Evangelical Religious Education

Various leaders and theologians in the Black church expressed evangelical theology with its roots in history, beliefs, and practices of Christian orthodoxy. The twentieth century began with the dominance of evangelical approaches to Protestant religious education. At the end of the twentieth century, this approach had resurgence with the growth of African American nondenominational evangelical churches. The strength of the nondenominational evangelical wing is seen not only in membership numbers but in its creative ability to communicate biblical truths in the pulpit and classroom. If faith comes by hearing, then people hearing these truths taught and preached will likely live by these truths.

A number of prominent Black theologians, pastors, and educators have offered rationales for Christian education based on evangelical theology. Calvin Bruce, a prominent evangelical theologian, made in strong terms the evangelical case for the relevance of the Bible in Christian education. He states, one cannot "ignore the profound significance of the Bible for the edification and enlightenment of the Black Christian community of faith. Abundant informal evidence indicates that most Afro-Americans have been reared on a diet of bibliocentric faith and are not easily convinced that theology minus God or his Word can meet their spiritual needs of existence."[15] Another evangelical educator, Ronald E. Roberts, has outlined the principles of Black evangelical Christian religious education. He states that Black evangelicals "hold to the central tenets of the Christian faith and while recognizing the validity of and significance of the Black experience in America, views the scriptures as the central criteria and the final arbiter in matters of faith, conduct, and practice."[16]

Most Black evangelical educators stress the transmission of a biblical content as primary in Christian education. However, James Harris sharply criticized the traditional evangelical approach to Christian education. Harris argues that evangelical theology has actually been unbiblical because it has essentially ignored the biblical teachings that God is on the side of the oppressed while purportedly insisting on belief in the sole authority of scripture.[17] Harris seeks a Black liberation education for Christian educators.

What does evangelical theology contribute to our understanding of Christian religious education theory-practice? Evangelical theological understanding and practice of religious education focus on personal salvation and living religiously. Living religiously means living/doing right, love of neighbor/God, and modeling/teaching family values. Here the approach is on understanding the faith and the experience of Jesus. Evangelical theology in relation to education is content to be taught and lived. The evangelical element in Christian education is when people make a decision for Christ and are saved. Education at this point is evangelical.

Black evangelical Christian educators focus a sharp eye on understanding Jesus and applying the meaning of conversion to everyday life. Once a person accepts Christ, the new believer embarks on a process commonly know as sanctification, with the eventual goal of living a Christlike life. They live out that goal within the context of the Black church and community. What are the theoretical and practical implications?

On the basis of the theological framework presented, several factors emerge. First, the fundamental truths of evangelical faith and life are founded on the primacy of scripture over religious experience. Evangelicals agree that God inspired the Bible; the Bible is the preeminent source of the knowledge of God. The Bible and the tradition are a fixed deposit of beliefs on which the community can draw. Evangelicals believe that, when the community understands the Bible, the community can then apply biblical truths. Second, the church, as an ecclesial body, is the context for educating Christians in the understanding and living of Christian life, through its teaching, preaching, and worship experience. And third, the church's theology and faith, as expressed first in scripture and also in Black history, culture, and experience, provides the basic content for articulating educational goals.

What is the primary pedagogy of evangelical theology? Whether it is E.K. Bailey, William Bentley, William Perkins, Dwight Perry, Melvin Wade, Stephen J. Thurston, or Anthony Evans interpreting the gospel through preaching, one benefits by the varying views. In other words, the religious reality becomes available or comes into existence only when it is spoken. Theology is offered through preaching from the pulpit and teaching in the Sunday school classroom. Both preacher and educator become theologians interpreting and making available knowledge about the tradition and the community out of which the tradition emerged. The theory of learning here is, "What I teach, you learn and live."

Traditional evangelical theology of the Black church has historically served as the criterion for the interpretation of experience among African

American educators. Evangelical theology sees religious education as teaching for living. Didactic pedagogy has been the method to teach religion. A favorite teaching form is the verse-by-verse sermon in which the preacher states the lessons from the text as they unfold. Evangelicals ask what they can learn from the text. The strength of the contemporary evangelical approach is the teaching sermon. The teaching sermon offers much in today's Black church.

Kergymatic Religious Education

Preaching is the center of the Black church experience. However, "proclamation theology" was never a household word in thinking and writing on the Black religious experience. One is hard pressed today to think of influential books of how proclamation theology influences the education of Black Christians. Nonetheless, today proclamation theology seems to play a significant role in religious education, albeit without the recognition it deserves. Joseph A. Johnson, the main contributor to proclamation theology, emphasizes that the core content of the Christian faith is "proclamation." Proclamation theology sets forth the message of the church. The message of the church is about God, Jesus Christ, and humanity.

Proclamation theology is evangelistic in nature; it sets forth God's offer of salvation to all who will accept Jesus Christ as Lord and Savior. Proclamation theology, unlike its Euro-American counterpart kergymatic theology, is shaped by the Black religious experience. It is concerned with the development of a statement about God and humanity in the light of Black awareness, Black dignity, and the oppression of Black people.[18] It also sees religious education as teaching for salvation and transformation. Proclamation yields teaching, expressed in the words of the sermon, song, and sacraments of the Black church. The proclamation further yields teaching through guiding, reconciling, and nurturing in worship. The sermon is part of a teaching and learning environment when it helps the congregation learn how to grow in Christ. The preacher can help the congregation enhance the educational qualities of the congregation. Christian educators along with theologians can help preachers develop a theological curriculum that can be taught from the pulpit. What are the key ideas about God, Jesus, the Holy Spirit, the church, and the world?

What are the educational practices to which proclamation theology gave rise? Methods for Christian teaching are didactic. The proclamation event becomes the greatest moment for the Black preacher to educate the people he or she serves. Anne Wimberly's new work, *Nurturing Faith and Hope: Black Worship as a Model for Christian Education,* views the sermon as the central and perhaps singular pathway through which nurture of faith and hope are carried out in the Black worshiping congregation.[19] The task of preaching centers in what Harris calls "uplift education."[20]

The Black preacher's pulpit is more than just a preaching station. It is the place where the preacher leads the congregation in thinking critically about God, Christ, the Holy Spirit, the church, and the world. The preacher helps the congregation interpret God's will for justice and love. This makes for the didactic (teachable) moment in Black preaching.

In the didactic process, teaching is explaining and preaching is the proclaiming of that which has been explained. Didactic means teaching or imparting information and inspiration into the hearts and minds of the members. Preaching as theological interpretation is didactic. From the perspective of the theological convictions articulated, the preacher helps the congregation remember God's purposes of love and justice, and helps the congregation name sin and its effects and agents. The preacher encourages the congregation to recognize its own brokenness. Ronald Allen states that the pastor is not the only theologian in a congregation. Indeed, all Christians should be theologians. Most preachers can recall occasions when grandmothers, day laborers, and children clarified their theological perception. However, the church sets the preacher aside so that someone in the community is specifically responsible for helping the church reflect theologically on its life and witness.[21]

On the contemporary scene, Black preaching has a variety of styles. Black preaching is still rooted in the gospels and a storytelling tradition. In the telling of Jesus' story, Henry Mitchell affirms the most certain statement one can make about Black preaching style is that nothing is certain or fixed: "Styles of Black preachers range all the way from those known to proclaim the gospel from ladders and coffins and in other spectacular ways, to others noted for standing flatfooted or in one place and hardly raising their voices."[22] Who has embodied the sermon as a teaching event? What are some models of didactic teaching? Some Black preachers view every sermon as a teaching event whose purpose is to build up the congregation in faith. Because teaching is a creative act, there is no single form. The following "ministers-as-teacher" embody the best of the didactic preaching.

John R. Bryant, bishop in the African Methodist Episcopal Church, brings to the preaching moment an expositional style. His sermon always comes straight from the text. The didactic aspect of expository preaching offers clarity of thought for the hearer. Gardner C. Taylor represents a poetic preacher-teacher. As the retired pastor of Concord Baptist Church in Brooklyn, New York, he is considered the "dean of Black preachers." This form allows the people to experience the music in the language of preaching, as well as to make clear and colorful the story of salvation. The late Frederick G. Sampson embodied the philosopher-preacher-teacher. His sermon discourse moves in and out of biblical narratives, Shakespeare, Hume, Dubois, and others with ease. He wrestles with ideas and drives home his ideas with scripture and illustrations. The didactic quality allows the hearer to be exposed to new and fresh ideas of life. The didactic aspect of preaching uses the preaching moment, whatever the style, to enlighten and strengthen the congregation in faith. Style and presentation in the Black preaching tradition is rich and varied. These have been just a few of many who embody the best of didactic preaching.

Historically Black preachers have been the leading educators in the Black community. Today more than ever proclamation needs to be didactic. In the Black community there is a generation of people who have no church background. There are people who do not carry the Christian fervor of generations past. They have never stepped into a church for any reason. These individuals are unaware of the foundations of faith. They do not know how to use a Bible. Even people who have sat in our pews for years are biblically illiterate. Therefore, didactic preaching becomes an important element in the development of Christian character. There must be preaching in our teaching and teaching in our preaching. In the Black church, the sermon allows the Word to live for the people, and that is what becomes the didactic nature of Black preaching.

Liberation Religious Education

The dominance of evangelical orthodoxy came to an end in the Black church during the 1960s. What has emerged among Black churches is pluralism of theologies. The same can be said of approaches to Christian religious education in the Black church. The emergence of Black liberation theology as well as the role that religious education might play in socio-political liberation and the struggle for social justice marked the changing of the guard. The theme of liberation has permeated Black Christianity since slaves were converted. However, Black liberation theology is a different approach. Black liberation theology is a Christian theology developed systematically from a Black perspective. There are many different Black liberation theologians (e.g., James Cone, Albert Cleage, and others) and even they do not agree on everything.

Albert Cleage offers a religion of Black power based on the normative authority of the Black experience, the image of a Black Christ under whose leadership the Black church will lead Black people from slavery to freedom within a separate, Christian Black nationalist state. Black liberation theology and education's most radical approach found expression in Albert Cleage's *The Black Messiah* and *Black Christian Nationalism.* He favored a stronger emphasis on the liberation of Black people. Cleage asked for a thorough rethinking of the place of Black history, culture, and theology in the education of Blacks. He described this model of education as teaching for liberation, or prophetic education.

James Cone's theology of liberation focuses on radical change. In the Old Testament the Exodus God is the God of the oppressed, and in the New Testament Jesus takes upon himself the oppressed condition so that all people may be what God created them to be. J. Deotis Roberts interprets the task of Black theology as a doctrine of reconciliation and argues that Black theology is incomplete without it.[23] Major Jones states that liberation theology must be accountable to the Christian ethic of love.[24] In addition to their differing views, however, most Black liberation theologians agree on several themes. The controlling theme of Black liberation theology is the idea that Jesus is the liberator of the poor and oppressed. The crucial focus is liberation now, liberation in this world, and liberation as socio-political and economic justice. In Black liberation theology, God is on the side of the oppressed and opposes oppressors. God wants justice and equality in the world.

How much influence has Black liberation theology had among Black clergy? Lincoln and Mamiya indicate that Black liberation theology has only limited influence on the ministers, based on the results in their national survey of Black ministers. They asked ministers: "Have you been influenced by any of the authors and thinkers of Black liberation theology?"[25] Only about one third of the Black ministers indicated any influence from this theology. One critical question must be asked of Black religious scholars and church educators who are attempting to develop an educational program to complement Black theology: Why has Black liberation theology engaged globally, but failed locally? Is Black theology adequate? The strength of Black theology is that it embraces Black people in their Blackness. It fosters a sense of self-esteem and pride as they come to understand that who they are is not abhorred, but valued by God. Though Black liberation theology was born out of Black faith, it ironically has not made significant inroads in Black churches.

Is it because most Black clergy still aren't seminary trained? As a result, awareness and relevance of Black liberation theology to local church pastors and educators is nonexistent. In addition, seminarians are not trained to methodologically infuse Black theology into Christian education into the local church. Gayraud Wilmore has argued that the reason Black liberation theology is failing to reach pastors and congregations is because it must concentrate not just on the fight against social political-social injustice, but also on the pastoral concerns of Black Christians.[26] As Wilmore explains, it must be both political and pastoral.

In the 1960s the questions of the relevance of the church and religion to the problems of the world, the rise of liberation theology, resulted in equating of religious education and social action. Grant Shockley and Forrest Harris discuss the relation between social action and church action and conclude that social action is an appropriate work of the church, that it may be education if reflected upon, but the educational task of the church with respect to the problems of society is to help church members develop a mentality for social justice.[27]

Black liberation theology draws its educative nurture from the integration of faith reflection and practice. It emphasizes praxis, the dialectical connection of action and reflection, a praxis-oriented education.

A liberation approach to teaching seeks to help the community name oppression in particular situations. The teaching conversation in this approach aims to identify the historical persons and processes through which God is working for liberation. The educator teaches liberation. The educator needs further to help the community respond to the movement of liberation, so the liberation approach includes teaching for action.

The new direction of liberation theology affected education theory and practice, especially its engagement character. African American educators such as Grant Shockley and Olivia Pearl Stokes have identified with and utilize theology of liberation and the pedagogy of the oppressed of Paulo Freire. They have argued for a more explicit social and cultural role for religious education. Grant Shockley proposed a liberating education appropriate for Black churches. For him this education entails a critical reflection on praxis that is sensitive to forms of human injustice, discrimination, and racism. Shockley consistently used the language and themes of liberation in his corpus of work. Shockley has made the most sustained attempt to relate liberation theology and Black theology to religious education. He has made a persuasive argument that religious education in the Black church should be grounded in a biblical-theological foundation concerned with liberation.[28]

Liberation theology has offered a radically different approach to education for Black congregations. Olivia Pearl Stokes has made an analysis of Black culture the focus of her approach to a liberating education. She begins with an understanding of Black culture in order to make us sensitive to the content and context of Black culture. She then moves to an analysis of models and methodologies of teaching to see how Black theology and culture is in the content of teaching. She calls for a Saturday ethnic school that would offer a curriculum centered on Black history, Black church history, and contemporary issues viewed from the Black perspective.[29] The school's major thrust would be to celebrate the genius of the Black experience, as expressed in the life of the individual, the Black family, and the Black Christian community. It would aim to develop creativity within its members, to express their religious insights through drama, music, dance, painting, poetry, and creative writing.[30] Lastly, Olivia Stokes recommends that teachers of religious education be involved in cultural activities themselves.

In the 1980s and 1990s the voices of several African American Christian religious educators began to be heard. Contemporary Black theologians and educators' contributions call for a serious engagement of aspects of Black popular culture and Afrocentricity in Black theological reflection. Anne S. Wimberly's storytelling approach, Evelyn Parker's wisdom formation approach, and Yolanda Smith's triple-heritage approach all encourage critical reflection on education practice. Michael Dyson in *Between God and Gangsta Rap* makes insightful use of hip-hop and rap music to draw attention to the importance of understanding the current realities of Black youth culture.[31] His appeal is to the churches to take more serious account of the musical traditions of Black youth. Learning from second-generation Black theologians, J. Deotis Roberts shows how Afrocentricity relates to Christian faith, theology, and ministry. Afrocentricity is Roberts's concern in *Africentric Christianity: A Theological Appraisal for Ministry*. Roberts is one of the first Black theologians to enter into meaningful dialogue with Afrocentricity and Black Christianity.[32]

For hip-hop, rap music, and Afrocentricity to find a way forward into full promotion of liberation among Black people, each approach needs to enter into meaningful dialogue with the Black church. This process has, in some small way, been set in motion by a new generation of young minds, unlike their parent and grandparent generations who do not feel a need to isolate or protect themselves from the radical elements in the community. Neither do they feel a need to surrender their spiritual foundations in order to facilitate the demands of these cultural developments. Some Black congregations are utilizing Afrocentric-based curricula developed by independent Black publishers. To date, the translation of liberation theology into curricula content and method has been moderately influential among the historic Black denominations. Some theologically oriented writers have been influential in working with the historic Black denominations in developing curricula for Christian education. In my own spiritual quest I continue to utilize both Afrocentric and Black theology. In my frequent wanderings between both Black and Christian, I find that my own liberation is most fully realized by a meaningful conscious intersection between the two.

Black liberation theology as explicit curriculum now is beginning to appear in Black congregations. For example, the following congregations have developed programs and ministries which speak to issues of cultural liberation and social justice: Trinity United Church of Christ in Chicago, Pastor Jeremiah Wright; Hartford Memorial Baptist Church in Detroit, Pastor Charles Adams; Bethel AME Church in Baltimore, Pastor Frank Reid; Hope United Methodist Church in Southfield, Mich., Pastor Carlyle Stewart III; and First Afrikan Church in Atlanta, Pastor Mark Lomax.

Black liberation theology raises new questions for religious education about racism and sexism in communities and churches in the United States and the world. The implications for religious education at the local church level are several: one, through praxis-oriented learning all persons should have a clear view of their responsibility as Christians; two, through direct political action persons can bridge the gap between proclamation and practice; three, liberation-oriented education will require an enabling style of leadership, committed to the Black church as an agency for social change; four, education and theory in the Black church has been affected by the new direction of liberation theology, especially its direct action character; and five, an Afrocentric pedagogy moves the African American

Christian from margin to center. Afrocentricity is the concept of Africa as the focal point for centeredness. It is, as Cheryl Gilkes has observed, "a commitment to standing in the middle of the Black experience…and starting one's thinking there."[33] Black liberation theology has caused the Black church to see Christian religious education from a new perspective—a worldview that illuminates a new future: a future in which Christians know that they can be free if they want that freedom enough to suffer, sacrifice, and perhaps die for it.

Pentecostal Religious Education

Black Pentecostals, like other Black Christians, have been perceived as not interested in formal theology. In the past, due to a denial of access to academic institutions, Black Pentecostals remained outside the centers of learning. This hindered formal training in theology and restricted the emergence of Black theologians equipped to present the Black perspective in the development of Pentecostal theology. Early Black Pentecostalism was born in the Bible school tradition among people with very little formal education. In the early years of the movement, religious education was primarily training in piety-education geared to the study of the Bible and literal interpretation of the text. But with the increasing middle-class nature of the major Black Pentecostal denomination Church of God in Christ (COGIC), more young clergy were educated in their church-related college, C.H. Mason Seminary.

New Black Pentecostal leadership and theologians emerged in the 1970s. They advanced new images of Black Pentecostalism. Different writers began to propose a redefinition of Black Pentecostal denominations as "Sanctified." The label "Sanctified church" distinguishes Apostolic, Holiness, and Pentecostal congregations from those of other Black Christians, especially Black Baptists and Methodists. Most Pentecostal theologians view their movement primarily as an experience movement rather than a theological one. They all agree the early Pentecostals were seeking experiences of pneumatic power. Theological understanding developed out of the experience. We now have a contemporary generation of Black theologians producing a pneumatology of their own. Pentecostalism has come to a crossroads. From its own ranks there comes a challenge by Pentecostal scholars and educators who are asking very searching educational questions. There is a challenge for a spirituality that does not blank out critical thinking and reflection. It is now possible to speak in tongues and to be a critical thinker in the church and university at the same time. This was not possible in the past.

As we listen to Leonard Lovett, James Forbes, James Tinney, David Daniels, Robert Beckford, Robert Franklin, and Cheryl Sanders, we hear the role of the Holy Spirit as teacher, whereas most historic Black denominations place emphases on the need for institutional roles and agencies by which the church can teach with authority. Here the emphasis is placed on the individual's personal relationship with Jesus and the role of the Holy Spirit as a continuation of the presence of Jesus. All who abide in Jesus have within them his Spirit, which serves as an inner witness to bring to mind the things he has taught. Teaching is tied to Spirit, not structure.[34] However, Pentecostals such as the Church of God in Christ, the largest Black Pentecostal religious community, function under authority structures (bishops, elders). Clearly, both models of teaching through structure and Spirit are important for the religious education process.

Black Pentecostalism attempts to integrate Spirit baptism, gifts of the Spirit, and new forms of ministry. Even though early Pentecostalism placed emphasis on the role of the Holy Spirit as teacher, neo-Pentecostalism places emphases on new institutional roles such as publishers, traveling evangelists, teachers, and lecturer-preachers in religious education. Early classical Pentecostalism had much less dependence on the printed word than neo-Pentecostalism. Yet one has to be impressed with the importance of the electronic word in the neo-Pentecostal movement, which reflects a dependence on literacy. From its beginnings it has employed the mass media very effectively. Especially important has been its distribution of books, pamphlets, audiotapes, and videotapes. For example, Frederick Price, the Word of Faith pioneer, gained fame as a television religious teacher after founding Crenshaw Christian Center in Los Angeles. This movement stresses knowledge and study of God's Word. Its principal disciplines are proclamation and teaching.

Emerging Black Pentecostal leadership and churches include Gilbert E. Patterson of Memphis, Bountiful Blessings Ministries and Chief Bishop of the Church of God in Christ; John A. Cherry of Temple Hills, Maryland, Macedonia Ministries; Paul Morton of New Orleans, St. Stephen Full Gospel Baptist Church, who organized a new-Pentecostal Baptist fellowship: the Full Gospel Baptist Fellowship; and T.D. Jakes of Dallas, pastor of Potter's House Church. Also, African American women clergy such as Juanita Bynum, Claudette Copland, Barbara Amos, and Jackie McCullough have become major preachers with national reputations. African Methodist Episcopal Bishop John Bryant, in partnership with his wife, the Rev. Cecelia Bryant, and several protégés, has initiated a "Neo-Pentecostal" movement in his denomination that exemplifies this tradition today.

What are the educational implications of Black Pentecostal theology? There are a couple of important educational implications. First, any adequate educational approach relevant to ministry must take into account the reality of the Holy Spirit.

Pentecostal worship is a component of the curriculum of education. Black Pentecostal worship services concentrate on proclamation, praise, and the power of the Holy Spirit. The worship service educates. Worship may occur at any point in the educational process, and most naturally during

Sunday morning. Christian education takes place whenever the Bible is used; it helps the congregation to engage in living dialogue with God through word, gesture, rite, and song. For instance, when the congregation prays for healing, those who are praying learn how to offer such a prayer. When the prayer of healing is followed by an assurance of healing, the congregation learns that God heals. The service of worship teaches in everything it does. Christian educators can help pastors realize that worship teaches. Christian educators and theologians can develop a worship curriculum that focuses on the Holy Spirit. Many Black congregations are beginning to do the serious educational work of reshaping this particular ecclesial form.

The other approach is more personal and refers to teaching for living, faith in life. Pentecostals love the Bible. They take a Pentecostal perspective to an understanding of the Bible. This has often led to the perception by non-Pentecostals that Pentecostals have an inferior understanding of the Bible. This misunderstanding persists because non-Pentecostals have failed to understand the approach of Pentecostals to hermeneutics. Pentecostals are more appreciative of Christians living by the Bible than Christians having only an intellectual understanding of the Bible. A Christian education geared to such a theology as we have described, with the resulting educational theory and practice, will yield signs of renewal and reform that may let the church be the church.

Finally, Black Pentecostal theologians and educators have an opportunity to revive Christian religious education theory and practice. The consequences of this development will broaden our understanding of spiritual renewal. Other Black congregations would do well to examine how these forms of ministry help to formulate a new understanding of Christian religious education.

Womanist Religious Education

Another voice not heard in contemporary AACRE comes from womanist theologians and religious educators who have pioneered approaches to religious education that spotlight themes and issues from womanist scholars, especially those in theology, history, and education. Womanist theology origins can be traced to Alice Walker's *In Search of Our Mothers' Gardens*.[35] She turned the spotlight on the uniqueness of Black women's lives as they continually struggle to maintain life and to make it better for themselves and their families.

The womanist tradition is identified with such notables as Harriet Tubman, Sojourner Truth, Anna Cooper, Mary McLeod Bethune, Rosa Parks, and countless other women who have shaped the womanist consciousness that now pervades the twenty-first century.

African American women have dominated Christian education leadership in the Black church. Black women have a long, successful track record as teachers and feel very comfortable in this ministry. During the

1920s, 1930s, 1940s, and 1950s many young Black women started their careers as Christian educators, including Dorothy I. Height, Matilda Mosley, Hattie R. Hagir, Dr. Mary McLeod Bethune, Pauli Murray, and Dr. Olivia Stokes. Most Sunday school teachers in the Black church have been women. While women may dominate the ranks of volunteer teachers, they have seldom numbered among the theorists who shape the future for religious education because of resistance by male clergy. Black women have found new places within and without the church to exercise their gifts of ministry. Some now hold full-time faculty positions in theological schools. They are bringing fresh scholarship and womanist perspectives to the academic disciplines that they teach. In their writing and teaching they are framing womanist approaches to religious education.

Prominent African American Catholic and Protestant womanists theologians involved in this writing and teaching include Shawn Copeland, Jamie Phelps, Diana L. Hayes, Jacquelyn Grant, Delores Williams, Kelly Brown Douglas, Renita Weems, Yolanda Smith, Evelyn Parker, and Lynne Westfield. Many of these female professors are ordained. Some have been or are presently serving as pastors. Within the past four decades it became more and more common to see and hear African American women theologians and clergy. Through its distinctive style of analysis and criticism, womanist theology has significantly influenced Christian religious education in recent years. It has also played a part in the theological education debate, in which womanist theologians themselves have even questioned Black women's experiences. How much influence has womanist theology had among African American clergywomen? Delores Carpenter, in her national survey of African American clergywomen, indicates that womanist theology has significant influence on African American clergywomen.[36] Black women continue to identify with theology from the perspective of Black women. Womanist theology has earned its rightful place in the theological curriculum. However, the same cannot be said about a place in the Christian education curriculum within the life of the church. This is the challenge of womanist theology: to find new places within the church.

How does womanist theology shape who we are and what we do as teachers? Womanist theologians seek to discover new ways of being and doing in teaching that increases one's love of God, neighbor, self, and all beings. Lynne Westfield's engaged pedagogy offers an educational process to increase love of God, neighbor, and self. Lynne Westfield has emerged as the pioneer of womanist religious education. Taking her cues from bell hooks and others, she developed womanist religious education pedagogy. For Westfield the "concealed gatherings" are points to begin and end for the learners and teachers of Christian education.[37] Womanist theology, in its methods and content, focuses on the deep relationality that strengthens life. Teaching then becomes less about techniques and methods, and more a way of being in relationship. Central to any womanist pedagogy must be attention to how the practice of teaching deepens authentic, just, and life-giving relationships. Womanist theologians and educators are committed to teaching that can transform the life of the church into a more responsive and faithful witness of the gospel in the twenty-first century.

What are some of the educational implications of womanist theology? Womanist theology creates awareness that male-oriented images–symbols, language, stories, and interpretations–have shaped our biblical and theological understandings of God, Christ, Holy Spirit, humanity, and church. Here the main task of religious education is a commitment to a new perspective on the Christian education ministry of the church, which understands God as a God of inclusion. Thus, any educational approach relevant to the contemporary Black church must take into account the reality of the womanist tradition. Hence there is a need for womanist ministry to be incorporated into Christian education curriculum so that congregations can be taught the value of female leadership, which could lead to a positive attitude toward women ministers. Womanist theology calls for a fresh look at pedagogy.

Womanist pedagogy emerges out of the experience of Black women challenging conventional and outmoded dominant theological resources that lead Black women into complicity with their oppression. Becoming partners in resistance furthers what Brita L. Gill-Austern has named "emancipatory praxis." Womanist pedagogy is engaged in the ongoing work of emancipatory praxis. "Such praxis approach names and struggles against the forces, the structures, the methods, and the content of subjects that have kept women from naming their own experience and the construction of knowledge. Pedagogy understood as emancipatory praxis must also help women see when and how they are instruments of their own and other people's oppression."[38]

Womanist theology sets forth that more emphasis ought to be placed on an experiential approach in religious education, an experiential approach that is rooted in spirituality; womanists "love the Spirit." In Carpenter's study, clergywomen were asked to check the image of God that they thought of "most of the time" and "much of the time"; Creator and Spirit were most frequently reported.[39] For many years Black women have fared better and gained far more acceptance in those churches that stress the free-flowing movement of the Holy Spirit.

Finally, womanist theology sets forth the educational implication that more emphasis ought to be placed on the development of a life-affirming, liberative curriculum. There is a need for a Christian religious education curriculum that integrates womanist theology and religious education into a holistic curriculum–a Christian education that focuses on the liberating message of Jesus, diversity, and inclusion; a Christian education that is affirming for Black women; a Christian education that does not teach patriarchy, Black men over Black women; and a Christian education curriculum filled with accurate data and history of Black women.

The womanist idea must be plowed into the Christian education curriculum in such a way that encourages dialogue with Black men and Black women, and each other. Womanist theology has been the hidden curriculum in the life of the Black church. The voices of those once invisible and unheard Black women can and do provide a needed stimulus for rethinking the meaning and relevancy of womanist theology and religious education in Black congregations today. Fortunately, womanist voices are growing stronger in the field of religious education and ministry; committed Black women are ensuring that gatherings, conferences, and meetings of clergywomen engage in womanist conversations. African American women as teachers of theology and religious educators have found virtue in necessity. Not being allowed to pastor, they have found new places to exercise their gifts in ministry. As a result, some of the best teaching and writing is now being done by African American clergywomen.

Spirituality and Religious Education

Black spiritual theology or spirituality is a search for meaning and significance by contemplation and reflection on the totality of human experiences. Spiritual theology is simply the act of reflecting on the mystery of God and God's relationship to humanity. African American spirituality is not pure piety or sanctification; it is also a cultural phenomenon. It is clear that contemporary interest in the spiritual tradition of the Black church or spirituality is increasing, not only for its own sake, but because Christian identity can be discovered in spiritual experiences.

The Black church expresses theology through biblical and doctrinal concepts, but also through spiritual sources and through the lived experience of faith in the church. The process of spiritual growth into Christ is known as sanctification, growth in holiness, and growth in the Spirit. It is an effort that enables us to grow into the likeness of God–to be Christlike. The history of African and African American Christianity is replete with examples of gifted people who helped others grow in holiness and wisdom. In the second century, the blood of martyrs such as Perpetua and Felicity blood became the seed of the church. Their lives are examples of commitment under persecution. From the desert tradition, St. Moses the Ethiopian and St. Basil the Great, pioneers in Christian monasticism, remind us that spirituality demands discipline. From the Americas (United States, Caribbean, and Brazil) the conjurers and obeah[40] tell us that sometimes we may feel like exiles in our search for African Gods.

The nineteenth century slave preachers counsel us that sometimes we feel like a motherless child, a long way from home. Richard Allen, James Varick, and William Miles remind us that grace abounds, that life is a pilgrimage, and that confession is good for the soul. William Seymour teaches us to worship continuously from the heart. Martin Luther King Jr. and others confront us with the need to relate prayer and social justice. Howard Thurman shares with us that suffering is an essential ingredient in the spiritual life. Womanists such as Jacquelyn Grant, Kelly Douglas, and Delores Williams speak of the need for ministry to include women—lay and ordained—in all levels of church life.

The relationship of spiritual theology to religious education in the African American church is both assumed and in the process of being discovered: assumed because everything within the life of the church is seen through the lens of spirituality, and being discovered because the task of Christian religious education in this postmodern era is a relatively new activity. Further, ancient African Christianity has been subject to a certain rediscovery during the late twentieth century as its spiritual-monastic-mystical roots are being recovered and its "Eurocentric captivity revealed." The critical theological work that has and is being done in African American spirituality, Black church history, and religious education has produced a corpus of writings that reflect upon ancient African sources from historical and contemporary perspectives, experiences and reflections of the founders of their traditions, and the lives of commanding religious educators who serve as spiritual mentors in our struggle for holiness.

Christian religious education and spiritual theology in the Black church generally are only at the beginning stage of this process. These areas of study, in many respects, are new. The process is one of discovering the continuity with the history and tradition of the Black church through the centuries. The impact of spirituality on Black theology and religious education has yet to be recognized. There has been no serious attempt to integrate the rich and varied spiritual expression of African Americans into African American theology and religious education. Flora Bridges states,

> the contemporary African-American theologian is not to create some new theory or express some old theological concept in a new way. It may be a more profoundly radical task of speaking about spirituality as it has always existed in the African American community in a way that, in and of itself, will integrate into Black theology that which has been neglected and left out by Black theologians doing theology.[41]

An African American spiritual theology of Christian religious education provides three basic foundations: one, spirituality and religious education are of the church; two, spirituality and religious education are grounded in worship; and three, spirituality and religious education must be lived out in their fullness.

The first premise, that both African American spirituality and religious education are of the church, means that they cannot be separated from the life of the church. Both seek God, desire to grow in the knowledge of God, and desire to experience the presence of God. Howard Thurman states it "[is] through experience that we come to know and understand God."[42]

The second premise focuses on Black worship as a spiritual lens through which education is understood, lived, and done. Black worship is a way of praying. Worship shapes and empowers persons in prayer. Worship shapes and gives utterance to life. Worship brings together the silent liturgy of the heart and visible liturgy of the church. Black worship is the work of the people of God, training themselves in the language of faith and using that language to address God. The gathering of the community in worship remains the fulcrum of the soul of Black folk.[43]

The third premise is the manner in which spirituality is communicated through education in its fullness. The ongoing interaction between meaning and experience creates education. When one addresses the life of faith, spirituality becomes the center of the curriculum. The focus of the educational process is the whole person in the community. Education of the whole person means engaging intuition as well as rational processes, body as well as mind, experience as well as theory.

The issues stressed in the preceding interpretation of spirituality have direct bearing on teaching. Here I sketch some of the implications for education. The signs of the times clearly point to an increased interest in spirituality. Dedicated Black church members have always acknowledged the importance of the spiritual life. There are many ways of nurturing and strengthening our relationship with God. Some of these resources can be found in the customs, rituals, and liturgies of our churches. Our great communal celebrations, especially baptism and the Lord's supper, and our hearing the gospel proclaimed can be opportunities for personal change and spiritual growth. Our churches, as places of renewal, may provide us with workshops, retreats, and small groups when we can come together for prayer, reflection, and support.

Consider educational emphases on spirituality and spiritual formation. Early Black theologians such as Daniel A. Payne, and most recently Howard Thurman and James Cone, repeatedly deal with piety-prayer-worship as a key emphasis in African American spirituality. But what are the educational implications of the wide responsiveness to devotional groups, study of spiritual disciplines, and other practices? We need to hear the longing expressed in this personal need for religious experience by Blacks at the same time we are called out of our practices into a more Afrocentric context. Certainly the context and content of our spiritual growth should be studied and taught.

Perhaps the primary implication for educators in the church is the sharing of spiritual experience that does not take place in the classroom. It is grounded in personal relationships in a communion so deep that separation from friends and family thousands of miles away, and those who have already departed this life, are only temporary physical inconveniences, for the love that binds us together in Christ keeps them as close as my thoughts and prayers. The models for growth in the spiritual life are the Black saints, monks, women, and men whose whole purpose and direction in life was to seek God and live.

The lives of saints and the remembrance of our spiritual ancestors in the faith provide models and inspiration for the struggles we face in the spiritual life. Their lives, writings, and their spiritual counsel help me reflect upon my own life. The images of the holy men and women stand together with me as I pray. With the help of experienced and spiritually wise people, I receive direction and guidance as I try to follow the way of love, forgiveness, truth, justice, peace, and joy. Spiritual experience continues to grow through the stories of the Black church's life in history.

The stories of struggles in the church, of women and laity, of bishops, and of conventions and conferences that met to reaffirm and clarify issues of faith and freedom are also part of the history of Black struggle that continues up to our day and beyond. The faith that Blacks confess today is the faith that others fought for and considered worthy of defending—even with their lives. The communions of saints are those that have gone on to glory. But there is also the communion of souls, the discovery of a saint, a book, an icon, and a teacher, which suddenly we find to be intimately linked with us. God speaks to us in our personal lives and in the relationships with mentors and friends.

Howard Thurman served as spiritual mentor and guide to many. Thurman certainly helped people encounter their deeper self. Beyond the theological understanding that can be gained from Howard Thurman's work, there is also a wealth of resources from which to draw implications for religious education. Thurman's work makes some of the gifts of the Black experience accessible to the practice of spiritual disciplines. The theology of Thurman is available to us from lectures, sermons, prayers, meditations, poems, and accounts of his life.[44] Thurman's work communicates a deep level of nurturing combined with spiritual guidance. His work, then, falls distinctly within the realm of spirituality as well as being an expression of his theology. Thurman's writings serve as a rich resource for living the spiritual life.

Teaching for Howard Thurman was not considered to be a pouring-out process but a leading-out, the development of the innate powers of the student's mind. His view of education was a process by which we learn to live with and for each other. His expressed aim was to provoke students to think. The object was to assist students to analyze the situations and activities in which they were engaged and to examine their purpose in the search for understanding and meaning. Thurman also speaks to those who teach theology, because he seems to consider theology itself not only as an intellectual journey but also as a journey of the heart, a search for wisdom and holy life.[45]

What are the implications of spirituality to liberation? Spirituality's contribution to liberation is that it treats the principalities and powers not as just institutions and systems. It comprehends their spiritual dimension. According to Walter Wink the spiritual powers are the inner aspect of material reality, the inner spiritual essence or ethos of an institution or system.[46] Liberation spirituality is reflection on the spiritual experience of Christians committed to affirming the human dignity of the poor and their status as people of God.

As to religious education, it affirms and encourages recognition of the gifts of Black folk of their pre-Christian existence, as gifts of the Holy Spirit. The contribution is strongest on the level of spirituality and liturgy, and not on the level of interpreting spirituality and theology. We therefore have to invent new forms of teaching if we want to learn from this spirituality and if we want to contribute with our own spiritual gifts.

Conclusions

In sum, each of these approaches can be found within most of the historic Black denominations. We should not think of these approaches as mutually exclusive. Each approach takes the teaching conversation in a different direction. It is likely that there will be a myriad of theologies at work in the local congregation, some more clearly articulated than others. All educators should be aware of their own theological assumptions and be capable of expressing these beliefs as they relate to educational practices.

The educator has to select a theological position as a basis for developing both theory and practice. Theology and education must be in conversation. A particular theology stands in the background for every educator. It may not be clearly articulated or at the forefront of one's consciousness. Theology may provide a background for Christian education theory and practice, but little has been done to apply it to educational theory. Theology stands in the background of any religious education theory, and sometimes it may take over the content. I see a variety of theologies as possibilities for the future of the theory of Christian religious education practice.

The theologies of the evangelicals and neo-Pentecostals have made strong gains in the past decades. The liberation theologies of the 1960s and 1970s also have value for today's church. The theological challenge mounted by womanist theology strove to place theology at the center of the educational enterprise. While evangelical theology has maintained a dominant role in the thinking and implementing of Christian religious education, a pluralism of theologies has emerged. Furthermore, African American spirituality maintains validity in any theory that is concerned with how Black Christians realize their potential.

The different theological views just presented are all current options on the contemporary theological scene. They all have adherents who perceive theology and religious education in the ways portrayed. While it may seem that such views can coexist together, there have been severe theological struggles between devotees of the different positions, especially liberation and womanist theologies of Christian religious education. On the academic theological scene, more so than in historic Black church denominations, professional Black theologians and biblical scholars continue to debate the issues.

While all of these theologies generate an understanding of religious education, none of them focus on the multicultural character of religious education. Next I discuss the implications of a Christian religious education that takes seriously the cultural diversity of the Black church.

The historic Black denominations have always recognized the presence more than the participation of various cultural and ethnic communities in and through the Black church. It is often reflected in the lack of Caribbean and African people in ecclesiastical decision-making positions. The twenty-first century is marked by the growing Hispanic presence in the United States and the communities that Black churches serve. The challenge, according to James Cone, is to reach out to non-Blacks. The growing Hispanic community has led some Black congregations in the United States to establish Hispanic ministries.[47] How does the Black church affirm cultural pluralism? Will the Black church participate in efforts to affirm and include previously excluded groups into the ecclesial mainstream? The inclusion of cultural groups on denominational boards and agencies has been slow.

During the nineteenth and twentieth centuries the historic Black denominations focused on the participation of cultural groups, not their identity. These cultural groups do not have representative influence on either the content of resources or the policies governing them. In addition, there is the lack of attention to the cultural content. We need new efforts to be inclusive in curriculum: pictures of people, places, and visibility of African and Hispanic cultural values and perspectives.

Historic Black denominational publishing houses have yet to publish culturally designated resources for African and Caribbean people. The early struggles for inclusion of laypeople and women persist. The agenda for inclusion, however, shifted from a concern for membership to a concern for the ability to influence. The agenda has to be with power—the power to recognize and affirm one's own cultural heritage.

The curricular implications of this perspective have only recently begun to be visible. This perspective may refocus Christian religious education discussions in the Black church to encompass the significance of the cultural heritages all people bring to the commonality they experience as the people of God. The issue of inclusion for the Black church becomes visible when the expectations of two or more ethnic/cultural communities collide over a specific ecclesiastical policy-political agenda. Historically, these clashes have often centered on inclusion in the political decision-making processes of the church rather than on religious education.

Recently, I had an encounter related to the use of language. It was during such an encounter that the cultural diversity in the religious education of the church became visible to me. A pastor serving in the Spanish-speaking Dominican Republic complained about the lack of resources for the people he served. He had often heard we prepared resources for the whole church. But since there are no Spanish language resources, he pointed out, "they are not prepared for us." This experience motivated me to develop Spanish language resources for the African Methodist Episcopal Church.

The historic Black denominations have experienced the persistent request for culturally sensitive resources and leadership. The temptation to respond as we have in the past will change. We need to make more visible the presence of the ethnic diversity of the Black church, developing bilingual and many-faceted theological resources. This calls for new images to fire the imagination of teachers, writers, education directors, and pastors. These efforts would break through the limitations of our present views of religious education theory and practice. Christian educators and theologians must find and develop ways to communicate and listen to what others say. To accomplish their responsibilities, they must consider dialogue, which is the topic of chapter 6.

CHAPTER SIX

Black Theologies in Dialogue

What I have taught and learned over the years is that "Christian education is a lifelong, ongoing dialogical process that seeks to discern God's truth" and to foster through praxis God's love and justice.[1] My identity as an African American person with the vocation of theological and church educator has meant that "I have worked on the borders of various communities of discourse. This position has provided a distinct perspective on the field that I have been privileged to share through this and other writings."[2] Several levels of conversation have emerged from my experience that I find compelling. I find conversation between theologians and church leaders regarding diverse Black theological traditions to be most interesting. Each perspective enriches our understanding of African American theology. African American Christian theologies have a significant contribution to make both to theology and the church. These theologies are ready and anxious for dialogue.

The twentieth century saw the development of various Black theologies. Although African American theologies emerged at various times, to date there has been relatively little dialogue between theologians and theologies. This chapter considers theology as dialogue. Theological conversations among Black theologians, religious scholars, church leaders, and educators have been rare and sometimes difficult to have. When we have talked to others across theological lines, the encounter is not likely to include the other perspective but to denounce it, and to define one's own position over against it. We talk a lot about the other. But we almost never talk *with* the other across theological lines. The conversations are not always easy and are often inconclusive.

For example, Tavis Smiley sponsored a cable C-SPAN program February 8, 2003, titled "The Role of the Church in Black America." Prominent Black clergy, scholars, and church leaders from across the country traveled to Detroit, Michigan to speak about the role of the church.[3] Substantive disagreement marked the dialogue around a variety of theological issues: the role of the Holy Spirit, the meaning of salvation, Christ and liberation, and gender justice. All of these arise out of differing understandings of scriptural authority and tradition. In particular, the conversations pointed out the wealth of different intellectual strands within Black communities. There is no single belief system for all Black people. All of these conversations aid in constructions of Black theology.

The confluence of cultures, faith traditions, and theological perspectives compel us to open the dialogue to diverse currents of religious thought. The unfolding of these theological traditions is based upon strivings to understand and serve life. Using the medium of theology, African American Christians provide enhancing personal and collective images that promote liberation and salvation for African Americans. Chapter 5 set up the defining parameters of Black theology. This chapter considers the dialogical process. Delores Williams, J. Deotis Roberts, and James Evans aptly termed this process the "dialogical intent" of Black theology. Roberts says one of the most difficult assignments for a theologian is to find a framework for discussion. Luis Pedraja points a way to consider the challenges of dialogue between theological perspectives.

Pedraja's essay, "Building Bridges Between Communities of Struggle: Similarities, Differences, Objectives, and Goals,"[4] provides a framework for discussing meaningful dialogue between theological perspectives. The dialogical intent here takes several forms. First, it is a dialogue between the theologians and the faith communities. Second, the theologians also engage in dialogue with other theologies from their community to clarify and refine their understanding of the community. Third, the dialogue extends beyond the particular community of faith, addressing other theological communities, and engaging them by either critiquing their theology or helping them to see new perspectives that might have been previously ignored. Fourth, the theologians also engage in a dialogue with their respective traditions, as well as the broader Christian tradition.[5] As a result, the dialogue occurs both internally within the community, and externally with other communities of faith and traditions. Even though Black theology is the most highly pluralized theology of recent times, most of the academic dialogue of African American theology has been largely conducted without substantive internal dialogue between academic and ecclesial theologies.

In this chapter I trace the development of Black theological dialogue in the African American community with some reference to the implications for religious education in the African American church.

The Practice of Dialogue

How then do we approach the challenge of theological diversity in the African American community? In the practice of dialogue, Christians are able to live out their faith in Christ in service of community with one's neighbors. In this sense, dialogue has a distinctive place within Christian life. In dialogue Christians seek to be "speaking the truth in love," not to be "tossed to and fro and be blown about by every wind of doctrine" (Eph. 4:14–15). Dialogue is an essential element of religious life. To live to some degree in community with others requires dialogue, not isolation. The practice of dialogue involves conversation between individuals and groups of persons. Here organized dialogue could be called "academic dialogues" in which exponents of different theological perspectives meet and discuss the theological bases of their traditions.

In African American theology the dialogue involves the following partners: theologians, educators, denominational/church leaders, and congregations. Theologians provide expert discourse. Educators provide practical discourse. Church leaders provide ecclesial discourse. Congregations provide communal discourse. The time is long overdue for theological conversation between Black theologians of diverse theological perspectives.

Kinds of Dialogue

As previously mentioned, Black liberation theology has held a privileged place in the academy. It has not found a prominent place in the life and ministry of the Black church. Therefore, the central question facing the Black church and the academy is to find ways to engage in dialogue. In working and teaching in the academy and the church, three levels of conversation have emerged: one, conversation between theologians and religious educators about the relationship between theology and religious education; two, conversation between Black theologians, church leaders, and educators within their respective religious traditions; and three, conversation between theologians and church leaders regarding diverse Black and other theological traditions. The first two I will discuss in this section, with the third treated in its own right in the next section.

Black Theologians and Religious Educators

In the late 1960s and early 1970s when Black theology of liberation was defining itself, similar developments began to arise among professional Christian educators. Olivia Pearl Stokes and Grant Shockley brought renewed insights to Black theology. In this process of dialoguing with Black theology, basic agreements and commonalities, as well as tensions, came to the surface. It is understandable that Black theology of liberation would extend its interests and influence into the education arena.

Stokes began the trend to put Black theology and Black religious scholarship into conversation with Christian religious education. Stokes argues for the necessity of Black theology to be the first point of departure for Black Christian education. She argues that such a discipline offers an important theory for all religious educators, providing new theological insights from which the Black perspective can be understood and interpreted. Dwight N. Hopkins's *Introducing Black Theology of Liberation* outlines four stages of Black theology. The fourth and present stage of Black theology developed under the pioneering leadership of the first generation of pastors and professors. The current stage involves a second generation of Black religious scholars, church leaders, and pastors. These thinkers emphasize an exploration of theology from any and all aspects of Black life and, most strikingly, the most exciting challenge of Christian educators (religious scholars and educators) who have pressed for a holistic Black theology that includes Christian education issues.

There needs to be a thorough conversation between Black theologians and religious educators. Black theologians must relate to the educative process. The involvement of Black theologians in the educative process should begin with Christian education in the local churches and should move through the denominational agencies of our churches. Dialogue between Black theologians should take place with professional educators and Christian education teachers. Most Christian education teachers are not professional educators. To make a living they sweep floors, sell real estate, work in a factory, work at home, or manage companies. Whatever they know about teaching likely comes from their own experience as a student or teacher. Theologians and Christian educators need one another. Educators need theological understanding of what they need to know. Theologians need ecclesial understanding of the education context of ministry.

Black theologians need to enter into conversation with Christian educators. In this process, theologians have much to receive, but they also have much to give. In recent years a number of Black scholars have pointed out how religious and theological communities have structured the life of faith and theological reflection in markedly different ways. There has been a widespread feeling that Black theologians are unnecessarily distant from the life of the church. This criticism of liberation theologians alike has taken on increased urgency and strength in light of the role of Black theology in religious education.

Since Black theologians are knowledgeable and committed, it will be their task to reach out to the churches. There also needs to be movement in the opposite direction. Black theologians and church leaders started out together in the late 1960s, but somewhere along the way they moved apart. African American church leadership and their theologians are now again getting closer. Now the same person can be both a church leader and a theologian. Christian Methodist Episcopal Bishop Thomas Hoyt and African Methodist Episcopal Church Bishops Vinton R. Anderson, Frederick H. Talbot, and Vashti M. McKenzie are prime examples.

At times, Black theology has appeared to be more theological than educational. In response, Grant Shockley, Olivia Pearl Stokes, Joseph Crockett, James Harris, Yolanda Smith, Lynne Westfield, and Anne Wimberly have offered an informative corrective to this tendency. These theologians have focused on the educational dimensions of Black theology more than any other contemporary thinkers. They argue for a Black theology of liberation with a cultural/educational thrust. They see theology as a mandate for cultural/prophetic education and praxis/vocation on the part of the Black church and community.

They believe one must first be in touch with the cultural context from which the call to teach arises. While arguing the importance of God/Christ on the side of the oppressed in their struggle for liberation, these theologians note that in order to fully understand and express that theology there must be education/instruction. Thus, African American theologians, religious scholars, and educators need to be engaged in sustained dialogue amongst themselves. Out of this ongoing dialogue, a Black theology of Christian religious education can be defined and developed.

Black Theologians, Church Leaders, and Educators

DIALOGUE WITHIN BLACK ECCLESIAL TRADITIONS

Black theologians, pastors, and Christian educators have received religious formation within denominations that express a particular confessional tradition (Baptists, Methodist, Pentecostal, and so on). Most of them address primarily issues that are essential in the life of their confessional heritage. They view their work as pastoral or church activity (practical theology). These religious educators have the self-understanding of being primarily Black Christian educators in addressing issues of church education. Here the church is the primary reference group for dialogue and practice. They view the task of religious education as primarily hanging on a faith that is re-interpreted and re-presented. Some of them have related to their traditions as loyal and critical defenders of institutional law and doctrine; others, have provided loyal, critical, and, at times, prophetic opposition.

These partners in dialogue need to have a good understanding of their own faith, which includes knowledge of one's particular confessional heritage, its history, and its strengths, as well as its limitations. Dialogue within confessional communities is a fundamental part of Christian identity and relationships. It is important for Black theologians, pastors, and Christian educators who confess a firm faith in a particular religious tradition to engage in dialogue. This is best thought of as an internal dialogue. Authentic dialogue between Black theologians, pastors, and Christian educators is at the heart of a confessional religious education. Confessional religious education is directed primarily at presenting an organized approach to religious education that is faithful to a particular religious tradition. Confessional thought is embodied in classic expressions or interpretations of a tradition, or one can point to certain classic expressions or near-classic expressions of religious education in the Black Christian tradition. All of those works have explicit connections with particular Black Christian theologies. Examples of such works include Richard Allen's *The Life and Gospel Labors of Rt. Rev. Richard Allen*; Anna Julia Cooper's *A Voice from the South: By a Black Woman*; Joseph H. Jackson's *A Story of Christian Activism: The History of the National Baptist Convention, U.S.A.*; Jarena Lee's *Religious Experience and Journal of Mrs. Jarena Lee*; Othal Hawthorne's *The History of the C.M.E. Church*; William Joseph Seymour's *The Apostolic Faith*; William J. Walls' *The African Methodist Episcopal Zion Church: Reality of the Church*; Daniel A. Payne's *History of the African Methodist Episcopal Church*; and James Patterson, German R. Ross, and Julia Mason Atkins' *History and Formative Years of the Church of God in Christ with Excerpts from the Life and Works of Its Founder–Bishop C.H. Mason.* In each of these works there is an expression of religious education in a particular faith and theological tradition. Christian education needs to keep such classics in print. Much is to be learned from these works and the theologies that they embody.

However, none of these works show that the sources of these expressions arise out of a communal dialogue among Black theologians, pastors, and Christian educators. They all need to engage in dialogue. They must find and develop ways in which to meet. This can be accomplished through the various denominational conferences, congresses, commissions, boards, leadership training convocations, and retreats. They offer an opportunity for theologians, pastors, and Christian educators to engage in conversation around religious education. If theologians, pastors, and Christian educators speak their own words in dialogue, they will experience their words as powerful expressions of their own faith and religious commitments.

Dialogue is a powerful tool for challenging and liberating a person from his or her own denominational biases. A dialogical religious education can help educators by forcing them to move a little out of their confessional role as teachers. Black theologians who are faithful to a particular religious tradition need careful exchanges with religious educators and pastors. What theologians would hear from pastors and educators may lead to a humbling realization that they have views and perspectives of which theologians have not thought. One should not be concerned that these conversations will undermine confessional identity; in fact, they may actually strengthen it for years to come. Black confessional traditions cannot and should not be ignored. They are an important part of the contexts within which Black Christians presently live. My argument is not that Black confessional traditions are irrelevant, but that dialogue is necessary to ensure their identity is not obscured in this postmodern era.

Diverse Theologies in Dialogue

Dialogue from and within Black religious traditions is critically important to the continuing development of Black theology. Black liberation theology has reached a state of maturity as a form of theological discourse. Black theology has come of age and is ready to participate in any theological conversation. New studies have opened a deep appreciation by Black theologians for the possibility of a two-way conversation between Black liberation theologians and believers of other traditions.

Historians of religion and sociologists of religion have made the most significant studies. They have written mostly nontheological interpretations of the Black religious experience. They provide a vital link to the present. I argue that Black liberation theology is ready to participate in a theological conversation with other theologies of the Black church. For too long Black liberation theology has not engaged in dialogue with other forms of Black systematic religious thought.

Here I discuss Black liberation theology as a serious dialogue partner with evangelical, Pentecostal, womanist, spiritual, and proclamation theologies. I explore how dialogue has taken place and the particularities of the dialogue. These Black Christian theologies reflect how Black belief interlaces the varied expressions of Black church and academic communities. None of these theologies represent a single denomination, but represent theological orientations cutting across an array of denominations, confessional traditions, and segments of denominations and independent churches.

This reaching out in interreligious dialogue is easier than an inter-confessional dialogue. These theologies can join in two-way conversation with less effort than theologians who interpret their faith/confessional tradition with absolute claims. These contemporary approaches to theology cut across the historic Black denominations and nondenominational churches. Each of these approaches can be found within most of the historic denominations. We should not think of these contemporary approaches as if they are mutually exclusive. Nonetheless, each approach takes the conversation in a different direction.

Black Liberation Theology and Evangelical Theology

In the late 1960s, when Black theology of liberation was defining itself, other theologies in the Black community began to arise. The dominance of Black liberation theology in the 1960s and 70s did not obscure other expressions of theology in the Black community. For instance, the National Black Evangelical Association (NBEA) predated the Black Power movement both in its founding and in its own embryonic formulations of Black theology. The Rev. Dr. William Bentley, who is regarded as the "Father" of NBEA, writes:

> There is and always has been a significant evangelical presence within mainline Black Christianity even from the first…Here was a strange thing! We were seeking to reach people, our people, but we had little awareness of the resources that had been forged in the fires of affliction and had not been exhausted by the mere

passage of time. We could not draw on these because we hardly recognized their existence.[6]

As the 1970s progressed, some of the members led by Dr. Bentley engaged in a Black consciousness-raising process. The struggle of NBEA had a parallel among Black evangelical theologians in embracing Blackness. The year 1978 proved crucial to the start of dialogue between Black liberation and evangelical theologies. In *Black Theology II: Essays in the Formation and Outreach of Contemporary Black Theology,* Calvin E. Bruce and William R. Jones assembled a group of essays bringing Black liberation theology and evangelical theology in conversation. In addition, the coeditors (William H. Becker, David T. Shannon, Clyde A. Holbrook, J. Deotis Roberts, Letty M. Russell, and Randolph C. Miller) examine Black liberation and evangelical theology by using feminist theological method, humanism, and process thought. The editors state in the introduction: "The writers consenting to address the question of where Black theology is headed share a belief that a decisive advancement is needed. Differing in background and ideology, these individuals are convinced that a number of crucial issues attend the task of Black theology making the next important step in its growth: that of critical expansion."[7]

This conversation/conference marked the first time in contemporary Black church history that African American Black liberation theologians and Black evangelical theologians had talked face-to-face. When Black liberation theology met evangelical theology, liberationists stressed race and culture while evangelicals cited the primacy of scripture and experience. Black liberation theologians accented the political "liberation" of the Black poor, and Black evangelical theologies underscored the importance of salvation–to be Black and Christian, to be spiritual and social. Herein lies the challenge of Black liberation theology to Black evangelical religious education.

Evangelicals have a predisposition to emphasize a biblical approach in education over one that exclusively highlights the Black church tradition or culture. Specifically, Black evangelicals, like their White counterparts, have tended to emphasize propositional approaches in their biblical interpretive and educative efforts. Black evangelicals' emphasis on scriptural distinctiveness has resulted in limited dialogue with those who identify the academic community of religious educators with a more diverse/liberation view. However, by the early 1990s, the progressive wing of Black evangelicalism theological orientation had gained legitimacy in evangelical circles.

Calvin Bruce has been the most consistent dialogue partner in the conversation between Black theology of liberation and evangelical theology. He argues, "[If] it is the constructive task of Black theology to foster genuine dialogue among Black persons of all religious persuasions, then it is needful for Black theologians to broaden their 'liberationist' appeals to attract the widest Black audience possible, including Blacks of strongly evangelical backgrounds."[8] In his reflection on the meaningfulness of Black dialogue, he writes: "Black evangelical Christianity offers a model for religious community growth, nurturance, and dialogical fellowship that the Black liberation community should prize and emulate."[9]

According to Bruce, writers in Black liberation theology need to attend to the spiritual needs of a religious community hungering and thirsting for more of God's righteousness, and for a closer relationship to the Lord of faith.[10] Evangelical theology offers and affirms the existential freedom for Blacks to be true to their religious and moral selves. In sum, the essence of Black liberation theologians in dialogue with evangelical theologians is that conversation rests on the conviction that religious, moral, and political freedom is one. Both must appreciate the concerns for freedom as the fulcrum for a balanced interchange of truth. Inasmuch as Blacks look to the Black church to meet fundamental spiritual and social needs, Black theology must be strongly evangelical as well as liberational.

Womanist Theology and Black Liberation Theology

Another voice historically absent from Black theology has been that of Black women. The past three decades Black women have become Black theologians and begun conversation with Black liberation theology. What does womanist theology have to do with Black liberation theology? Distinguished theologian Kelly Brown Douglas has summed it up that any attempt to understand what womanist and Black liberation theology have to do with each other must engage at least two issues: one, the role Black liberation theology played in the emergence of womanist theology, and two, the similarities and differences between the two theologies.[11] She further writes that the role of Black liberation theology in the emergence of womanist theology is two-fold. First, by linking God to the Black experience Black liberation theology gave access to systematic theological reflection. Second, by ignoring Black women's experience, Black liberation theology forced Black women to develop their own theological perspective.

What is womanist theology's distinctiveness in relation to Black liberation theology? The most obvious distinction between Black liberation and womanist theology is their respective points of departure. While Black liberation theology's starting point begins with the Black experience, womanist theology begins with Black women's story of struggle. Womanist theology grows out of Black liberation theology.

Womanist theology has emerged as a way for many women to affirm themselves as Black while simultaneously owning their connection with their African American brothers in the struggle against White supremacy and sexism in the church. In other words, the reality of oppression unites womanist and Black liberation theologies. The strongest affinity between womanist and Black liberation theology would appear to be how faith has enabled both to translate suffering into a vehicle of liberation.

The year 1987 proved crucial to the start of dialogue between Black liberation and womanist theologies. At that time, Katie G. Cannon produced the first written theological text to use the term *womanist*. However, the first text using the specific term "womanist theology" was Delores S. Williams' article "Womanist Theology: Black Women's Voices."[12] With the emergence of womanist theology, Black liberation theology discovered the importance of God's revelation for the full inclusion of men and women in a comprehensive fabric of decision-making, power, position, and pulpits. In other words, theologians and churches need to make a commitment to women and against those systems and structures of the church maintaining their subordination.

A theological exploration of these concerns then leads to a critical conversation with Black liberation theology (over method and interpretation) and womanist theology (accenting Black women's claim to embrace and affirm their cultural-religious traditions and their own embodiment). It was Delores Williams who set forth the critique of Cone's exodus model of liberation. Williams asserts the wilderness image as most representative of American Black women's reality and that survival and productive quality of life represent the central thread in womanist theology.[13]

Specifically, the Hagar and wilderness concepts gave Williams a biblically based Christian model, which deemphasized the authority of males and lifted up the roles of women. Clearly Williams' critique of the historical-critical method of interpreting the Bible has been a leveraging point for change in the interpretation of scripture. In sum, womanist theology affirms Black women's faith that God supports them in this fight for survival and liberation. Both theologies are concerned with the Black community's freedom and God's role in their freedom struggle. The current challenge is for both to raise critical questions and present them to the Black church and academy, demanding their inclusion in the ongoing religious dialogue.

Afro-Pentecostals and Black Liberation Theology

An emerging Black Pentecostal leadership has ushered in a new era within Black Pentecostalism. These leaders proposed a redefinition of Black Pentecostal denominations as Black churches with a Pentecostal perspective rather than being Black evangelicals with a Pentecostal experience.

As mentioned earlier, the lack of formal training in theology restricted the emergence of Black theologians equipped to present the Black perspective in the development of Pentecostal theology. Things are beginning to change, enabling Blacks to participate more fully in the construction of theology instead of simply learning theology from others.

Black Pentecostals are able to analyze church teachings, develop meaningful models of education, and challenge ecclesial structures.

One of the theological strands noticeably absent in theological discourse and dialogue is Pentecostal theology. Pentecostal commitment to dialogue with Black liberation theology is not easily accomplished, but some progress has been made. Vinson Synan observed that in the 1970s a number of Black Pentecostal theologians began conversation with Black liberation theology:

> Different writers began to engage Black theology from a Pentecostal perspective. William Bentley and Bennie Goodwin, Jr., sought to interject the liberationist agenda of Black theology with Pentecostal spirituality and evangelical themes. Leonard Lovett, James Forbes, and James Tinney sought to interject the liberationist agenda of Black theology in Black Pentecostalism. Within these quarters, Black Pentecostals participated in a serious dialogue with liberation theologians. During subsequent decades, Black Pentecostal and neo-Pentecostal theologians such as Robert Franklin, William Turner, Cheryl J. Sanders, Anthem Butler, Alone Johnson, and H. Dean Truer continued this dialogue from their posts as professors at colleges and theological seminaries.[14]

Liberationist theologians James Cone, James E. Evans, and James Harris have responded to the role of the Holy Spirit by interjecting the liberative dimension of Black liberation theology in the doctrine of the Holy Spirit. Black denominational leader, Bishop R.L. Speaks, provides a systematic theology of the doctrine of the Holy Spirit within the Black Methodist tradition. Bishop Speaks attempts to define the doctrine as core beliefs rather than experience and practice. He states, "The church is at its best when it is an instrument of the Holy Spirit. The Holy Spirit is the presence and power of Christ taking the initiative within the human heart, the church and the spiritual community."[15]

Dialogue between Black liberation and Pentecostal theologians has been hampered by their inability to fully listen to one another. Pentecostal theologians find it difficult to get a hearing. They publish in scholarly periodicals and hold scholarly conferences; these theologians deserve to be taken seriously. The trouble is that other scholars, Pentecostal leaders–let alone the rank and file–do not read their publications. Yet Pentecostal theologians have original contributions to make to theological discourse.

Preaching and Black Liberation Theology

The connection between Black liberation and proclamation theology began with Joseph A. Johnson's *Proclamation Theology*. Johnson's analysis of proclamation theology is both critical and complimentary of Black liberation theology. Johnson himself is firmly committed as a preacher-theologian to the idea of proclamation theology and, from this perspective, critiques the weaknesses of Black liberation theology. He states that there are flaws in James Cone's definition of "Black theology" because it constructs a universalized definition of Black theology, thereby creating an essentializing category.

Johnson's critique charges that Cone's definition utilizes outdated Black nationalist arguments of separatism and that it works against Black churches. On the other hand, Johnson identifies the positive perspectives in Black theology. He comments:

> It was the systematic theology of James Cone which forced me to develop the fundamentals of a preaching Christian theology, a Proclamation Theology, a theology which may be addressed not only to those which are oppressed but also to the oppressor; a theology which is both particular and universal, a theology which fully announces the sinfulness of men and the outgoing redeeming love and grace of God.[16]

Johnson's comments on Black liberation theology indicate the complex discussions among Black scholars and preachers who seek to shape the church's practice of Christian faith. Preaching is not a distinctive practice, but is part of the practice of worship. The sermon interprets Christian community as practice, and it interprets particular Christian practices. Dr. Olin Moyd has written an important book on preaching and theology in the African American church tradition, *The Sacred Art: Preaching and Theology in the African American Tradition.* Moyd reminds us that preaching is the centerpiece of worship in the Black church.[17] It brings Black spirituality and the strong oral tradition of Black folk together.

Proclamation theology can help the preacher interpret the significance of the gospel for the sake of the congregation. The dialogue between Black liberation and proclamation theology will continue. Both theologians and preachers benefit from this dialogue. This dialogue allows the theologian and the preacher to have a high degree of confidence that comes from critical thinking and understanding of Black churches' sense of ministry.

Black Liberation Theology and Spirituality

How does Black liberation theology link with spirituality? In recent years we have witnessed the development of Black liberation theology. Concurrent with this development there is now a renewed interest in forms of spirituality. It is not a totally new dialogue, but is heightened now as Black scholars write about it. Both terms—Black theology and spirituality—locate ways to identify important dimensions of Black Christian's lives. Many dynamics are at play in conversations between Black liberation theology and spirituality.

Today's Black liberation theologian cannot afford to ignore that Black liberation theology has a contemplative dimension. The works of Howard Thurman have enriched twentieth century studies in Black spirituality.

Howard Thurman, considered the forefather of contemporary Black liberation theologians, wrote extensively on spirituality. The conversation between Black liberation theology and spirituality is important because they are spiritual routes by which Black Christians discover their own identities. Howard Thurman was a modern-day contemplative in the tradition of Saint Francis. Contemplation for Thurman was self to God. Howard Thurman shared in the classroom, in the pulpit, and in print the oneness he felt with God and creation.

Black liberationists and contemplative scholars need to dialogue. I believe Howard Thurman made some progress in this direction. James Cone also has attempted a conversation, but in my judgment Calvin Bruce's effort goes beyond Cone to what he describes as "Black spirituality." Calvin Bruce writes that Black liberation theologians need to recognize the spiritual strength of Afro-American identity and the liberative qualities of Black spiritual striving.[18]

Black Catholic theology also is worthy of mention. The absence of the voice of Black Catholics from the dialogue is a serious one. In the past three decades, Black Catholics have begun to engage in theological reflection within the context of their marginalized status in the Roman Catholic Church.

Black Catholic theologians are now engaged in expanding the dialogue now taking place in Black theology, emphasizing their link with ancient African Christianity, especially its monastic, ascetic, and mystical spirituality.[19] Fr. Cyprian Davis has been in the forefront retrieving and interpreting the African American Catholic spiritual tradition.[20] African American Catholic spirituality and theology once invisible and unheard is now part of a vibrant dialogue regarding what it means to be truly and authentically Black.

J. Deotis Roberts' essay *Thurman's Contribution to Black Religious Thought* continues the dialogue between Black liberation theology and spirituality. Roberts' argues that Thurman's contribution in the area of spiritual disciplines should be lifted up again and again by each generation. It would be unfortunate if we uprooted ourselves from the taproots of Black spirituality in the pursuit of Black religious radicalism.[21] James Cone sought to educate the religious community regarding the spiritual relevance of liberation struggles. Cone writes, "[The] task of Black theology is to make Christianity really Christian by moving Black people with a spirit of Black dignity and self-determination so they can become what the creator intended."[22]

A formal conversation by Black liberation theologians on the works of James Cone and Howard Thurman took place in 1989 at the Howard University School of Divinity. The common thread that ties Black liberation theology and spirituality together exposed the racism of the White church and sought to make Black faith a powerful resource in the struggle against oppression. Black spirituality can be liberative and Black liberation theology has a spiritual component. Howard Thurman contributes the missing link in Black liberation theology.

These conversations point out in particular the wealth of different routes by which Blacks discuss and discover their spiritual identity. This conversation is heightened now as Blacks seek greater quest for meaning. Black spirituality offers a variety of theological constructions in which Blacks can experience and express their relationship to God.

The Significance of Black Theological Pluralism for AACRE

I have discussed Black liberation theology as a serious dialogue partner with womanist, evangelical, Pentecostal, proclamation, and spiritual theologies. Black Christian theology is not monolithic. Black Christian theologies differ in the manner in which they conceive a common tradition, and their intellectual and spiritual journeys are varied.

What is the significance of Black theological pluralism for religious education in the Black church? The pluralization of Black theology began almost with the Black theology movement itself and continues to the present. In relation to religious education in Black churches, several implications may be drawn from African American theology. How shall African American Christians face the new religious pluralism? Grant S. Shockley's approach is to learn how to live creatively with pluralism. The following suggestions contain potentially productive and innovative ways of how people can live creatively with religious pluralism.

First, religious and theological pluralism is here to stay and will remain an integral aspect of our social-religious environment. Second, religious and theological pluralism furthers understanding, teaching, and learning about other beliefs or faith tradition. Third, in the sense of influence and actual power, Black liberation is a minority perspective. Learning how to be partners in a dialogue with other theological perspectives is going to be challenging. Fourth, religious education in Black churches needs to intercommunicate and interrelate with persons of the faith who hold different perspectives, and with persons of other faiths. Fifth, African Americans need to understand and practice global/ecumenical education. It's not so much learning and sharing each other's knowledge, but becoming global/ecumenical in attitude and practice.

Thus far in discussing theology and religious education from a Black perspective it has been determined that such education should be theologically grounded, culturally sensitive to the Black experience, and educationally designed to maintain its integrity. To further educational tasks, the Black church it must continue pluralistic dialogue and remain open to the truly inclusive community. The pluralization of Black theology for religious education implies the need for several models of understanding the role of religious education in the Black community.

Conclusions

What will Christian religious education in the Black church look like in the year 2025? This analysis of Black theology demonstrates considerable diversity of theological perspectives. For theology to have an impact on the church's educational ministry it must enter a dialogue with religious education. Religious education is the vehicle/structure/process to bridge the gap between the academy and the church. Black theology has ignored oppression within the Black community. Black theology must look at the ways in which Blacks enslave themselves or perpetuate enslaving structures and systems. Black theology must challenge Black people to free themselves from the various forms of oppression within the Black community.

African American Christian educators must be trained to ask questions regarding power, culture, and race. We can model that skill in the way we discuss Christian education in our classes. By doing so we can add rigor to our thinking as well as discover pathways not yet considered. Black theologians and educators must be committed to teaching that can transform the life of the church into a more responsive and faithful witness of the gospel in the twenty-first century.

As Black professional educators, scholarly men and women began to explore their richly diverse history and tradition and to speak out of their own unique contexts. They are challenging and reformulating our understandings of the educational dimension of Black Christian theologies. In so doing they make the assertion that to be Black and Christian is not paradoxical, contradictory, or contrary to the Black struggle for freedom but is simply one of the many flowing streams that make up the river of the Black experience in the United States.

I am convinced that the texture of Black theology is undergoing change and reconstruction. What is emerging is a broadening and deepening of theological sensitivity attached to the movement of Black Christian religious education. The next chapter attempts to show how Black churches have committed themselves to achieve new forms and practices of religious education.

PART THREE

CHAPTER SEVEN

Educating in the
African American Church

The enterprise of Christian education in the African American church is a growing one. This judgment is attested to by a number of factors. There is an increasing awareness that Christian education extends beyond the needs of youth. Published books and articles have increased in the past decade. A number of prominent African American theologians and religious educators have devoted their attention to establishing a field of AACRE.

Many forms or models accompany this growth in religious education. From my personal experience with Christian education in African Methodist conferences, conventions, and congregations, I have been impressed with the rich variety of ways in which this education takes place. Creative ecclesial models, developed at both local and leadership levels, have emerged in many places. Models developed by scholars have presented additional ecclesial models of education.

The rich diversity of models being used in African American Christian education calls for some analysis. My intention in this chapter is to describe ecclesial models of African American Christian education that are presently in use and to explore their appropriateness. I make this attempt from the theological side, utilizing ecclesial models derived from the theory and practice of African American Christian education. My contention in this chapter is that the particular approach of religious education operative in the leadership and membership of a local church shapes the forms and models of religious education. In other words, there exists congruence between models of education, explicit or implicit, and the objectives and designs of religious education. Reflections upon theoretical models and my own experience as a Christian educator are the basis of this chapter. Since this experience comes from work in an African American religious community, my examples will pertain chiefly to this community.

As mentioned in the previous chapter, African American theologies are diverse. Each theology leads to its own distinctive theory and practice of religious education. I describe in this chapter six ways contemporary African American Christian educators approach the theory and practice of Christian education. While these approaches are not exclusive of one another and do not represent all the ways religious education can be defined, they do represent various frameworks used to understand the tasks of Christian education. The hope in exploring these models is filled with challenge. Among those challenges are the need to articulate the models so that they might be chosen and followed more self-consciously, and also the need to revise them so they might be even more helpful in the practice of teaching. The aim is to reflect upon, to interpret, and to understand them, but also to critically test and revise them. In this chapter, I provide a description and analysis of selected models of Christian religious education in the Black church. I examine and illustrate the characteristics and contribution of each approach.

Models of Religious Education in the Black Church

The following educational models have emerged as significant theologically and practically in the Black church: *kerygmatic, holiness, Afrocentric, contemplative, confessional,* and *liberation.* Each of these is a distinctive way of viewing the Christian education task. These models illume past practices and offer future possibilities.

Models

Kerygmatic education occurs through telling the gospel story in preaching and teaching.

Holiness education occurs through the indwelling of the Holy Spirit.

Afrocentric education occurs through affirming Black unity, cultural pride, and self-determination.

Contemplative education occurs through living a life of prayer.

Confessional education occurs through passing on the denomination's or church's beliefs, collective wisdom, values, and practices.

Liberation education occurs as people reflect on action and seek to transform society.

In this chapter I will present each model, including its view of teacher, method of instruction, aim, context, content, curriculum, and contribution. These educational models express various interpretative frameworks that are important in teaching and learning. In addition to describing these models of Black church education, I identify the theologies, forms of learning, and representative thinker associated with these models.

	KERYGMATIC	HOLINESS	CONFESSIONAL	CONTEMPLATIVE	LIBERATION	AFRO-CENTRIC
Aim	Salvation	Sanctification	Embrace faith tradition	Grow spirituality	Freedom	Centeredness
View of Teacher	Pastor as herald	Holy Spirit as teacher	Teacher as guardian	Teacher as guide	Teacher as change agent	Teacher as cultural voice and interpreter
Content	Bible	Experience of Holy Spirit, speaking in tongues, and healing	Church tradition	Nature, spiritual disciplines, and experience	Prophetic tradition and black religious experience	African religion, history, and culture
Context	Worship	Worship and life	Liturgical life and church school	Life and natural environment	Environment where people are oppressed	African person and community
Method of Instruction	Sermon and lecture	Prayer, praise, and worship	Lecture catechism	Practice of spiritual disciplines	Action-reflection	Lecture/storytelling, immersion
Curriculum	Preached word of God	Prayer, praise, and worship	Christian heritage, creeds, hymns, and liturgies	Experience, nature, and scripture	Social action, advocacy, and mobilization; critical reflection in action	African history, culture, religion, and Black experience
Contribution	The practice of preaching as educative	Increase awareness of the Holy Spirit as teacher	Continuity of Christian beliefs and practices	Teacher helps persons develop a relationship with God	Teacher helps develop critical consciousness/ Action for transformation	Teacher helps persons rediscover their identity
Theology	Evangelical/ Proclamation	Pentecostal/ Communal	Proclamation	Spiritual/ Womanist	Black/ Womanist	Black
Forms of Learning	Individual/ Communal	Individual	Individual	Individual/ Communal	Communal	Communal
Contemporary Thinkers	Joseph Johnson	Cheryl Sanders and David Daniels	J. Deotis Roberts and James Evans	Howard Thurman and Barbara Holmes	James Cone and Jacquelyn Grant	Yolanda Smith, J. Deotis Roberts, and Anne Wimberly

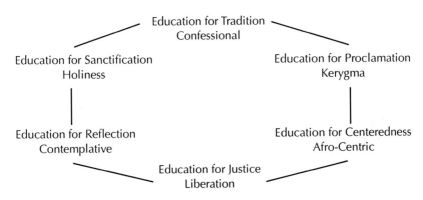

Education for Tradition
Confessional

Education for Sanctification
Holiness

Education for Proclamation
Kerygma

Education for Reflection
Contemplative

Education for Centeredness
Afro-Centric

Education for Justice
Liberation

KERYGMATIC

The kerygmatic model allies itself with evangelical theology. This model views theology as orthodox; at least historically it has been so, as Anthony Evans points out so well: "Historically, the Black church in America has held to the mainline assertions of conservative Protestant theology."[1] *Kerygma* has always been taken to mean both what is proclaimed and the act of proclaiming. For Christians, the proclamation is the life, death, and resurrection of Jesus, the Christ; of a saving God whose Word is with and for the people being fashioned. In the early twentieth century, the sermon continued to be the leading mode of learning of Christian education for the Black church. By the middle part of the twentieth century the Sunday school became the church's main vehicle of Christian education. Through the last decades of the twentieth century, the teaching sermon has surfaced as a major contributor to religious education.

The heart of the kerygmatic approach is an interpretation of the Bible that places emphasis on proclaiming the gospel as salvation history, initiating students into the presence of God through worship, engaging students intellectually in the study of Black Christian theology, and challenging students to witness to their Christian faith in their lives. Education for proclamation seeks to enable persons to consider their personal commitment to Jesus Christ. The task of proclamation involves teaching and preaching the gospel, along with the ministry of evangelism—sharing the basic content of the Christian faith, and teaching about the need for personal response and the need to make a decision regarding the new life offered in Jesus Christ. The educational ministry allows for persons to explore the dimensions of faith in response to the gospel.[2]

This concept borrowed heavily from Black Protestant evangelical theology that lay at the foundation of evangelical approaches to religious education. The analysis of the kerygmatic model is based primarily on the writings of Bishop Joseph A. Johnson and Black Protestants associated with the evangelical movement. Johnson's book *Proclamation Theology* is indicative of its theologically oriented, proclamatory posture. Johnson insists that the task of preaching is the primary means for the congregation to encounter the Bible, doctrine, and theology. Proclamation of the gospel message is central to his understanding of teaching practice. Johnson states:

> Every New Testament evangelist was inevitably a teacher. Every Christian teacher was seeking as were the evangelists to create faith and to awaken loyalty and acceptance to the message taught. The early Christian teachers were not impersonal and objective in their teachings. Their purpose in teaching was not to stimulate intellectual curiosity or to encourage the creation of an active inquisitive mind. The early Christian teacher's purpose was to win men to faith in Jesus Christ and promote Christian living. Therefore, the teacher was an evangelistic teacher and the preacher was a teaching evangelist.[3]

Johnson makes kerygma the central concept in his approach to religious education. He has infused kerygma with deeper meaning by utilizing concepts from the Black experience and systematic theology to explain the process of Christian learning. Johnson focused on education into the faith by participation in the worship life of the church. Religious education takes place in the interaction between the preacher and congregation. The preacher functions as the teacher, herald, announcer, and proclaimer of God's Word. The kerygma is experienced through preaching and celebration as well as an educational experience. Education occurs through "telling the story."

Theological influences exert a determining influence on aim. Johnson asserts that religious education's real purpose is to communicate the word of God with a view to spreading the faith. Transmission of salvation in Christ is the aim. The aim is to bring about an encounter with God that results in conversion. The goal of religious instruction is religious living. In most Black evangelical thinking a conversion experience is necessary for true growth as a Christian. The conversion experience in which the individual accepts Jesus as Savior and Lord is the means by which an individual enters the Christian life. Christian education for Bishop Joseph A. Johnson and other Black evangelical educators is the communication of biblical and theological truths in the classroom and from the pulpit. If faith comes by hearing, then students hearing these truths taught and preached well will live by these truths. The content of Christian education is God's revelation written in the scriptures. Most Black evangelical religious educators place a priority on the transmission of a biblical content as primary in Christian education.

From the kerygmatic perspective, content is an authoritative, biblically, and theologically founded message to be given to learners by teachers who, having received the message and experienced its benefits, are a witness to it.

The content of religious education is a revealed message of salvation. The centrality of Christ is the heart of the content of religious education. The Black church's educational ministry has been taught through preaching. The practice of preaching as educative and educating is the curriculum of kerygma. The curriculum of kerygma is to speak of the Word as that by which we are educated and to which we are educated. Christian education takes place when the congregation hears the Bible story and the story of the church during the sermon. The sermon teaches even when the Black preacher does not intend for it to do so. Consequently, the Black preacher needs to consider carefully the degree to which each sermon teaches the gospel.

In sum, Black evangelicals place a high premium on the teaching and preaching of the Bible. Some include preaching in the concept of Christian education. They see the pulpit as a viable source of teaching/learning. For example, the following Black evangelical leaders have built congregations on the teachings of scripture: E.K. Bailey, Concord Baptist Church, Dallas; William Bentley, Calvary Bible Church, Chicago; William Banks, Union Baptist Church, Philadelphia; and Anthony T. Evans, Oak Cliff Bible Church, Dallas.

HOLINESS

The Pentecostal model of Christian education seeks to combine both the kerygma and the Pentecostal spirit. As already noted, Pentecostal theology emerged among working class and marginalized Blacks in the context of their own holiness and Baptist backgrounds. The Pentecostal experience, which gained worldwide visibility at Azusa Street in 1906, remained the hallmark of the Pentecostal movement to the present day. This model advocates the abiding presence of the Holy Spirit as the guiding image for Christian education. The Pentecostal approach emphasizes individuals receiving Spirit baptism and speaking in tongues or *glossolalia* as evidence of the sanctified life. The theologians and educators identified with this model are Leonard Lovett, Iain MacRobert, James Tinney, James Forbes, Cheryl Sanders, and Robert Franklin. A fundamental presupposition of Pentecostal theology and practice is the central emphasis on the experience of the working of the Holy Spirit. The Pentecostal experience includes "gifts of the Spirit," especially healing, speaking in tongues, and prophesying.

Teaching is tied to the Holy Spirit. The Spirit is bound to the gospel content of scripture and its proclamation. The Holy Spirit is the primary teacher of the church. The written Word is its basic content. The aim is education for sanctification. Pentecostals relate the gospel directly to their troubles, and the process of understanding the gospel essentially begins in the context of felt needs. Education is primarily training in piety-education geared to the study of the Bible, literalist exposition of the text, and a practical concern for living by the Bible. The preacher functions not only as proclaimer of God's Word, but also as discerner of New Testament gifts. A theology grounded in the Bible and Holy Spirit is the central theme. The preacher is used by the Holy Spirit to help facilitate a direct, experiential, and continuing encounter with the Holy Spirit. The goal is to receive the gifts of the Spirit. The Spirit moves the preacher to anoint and heal.

Education occurs through the practice of a Pentecostal spirituality. In Pentecostal liturgy, education occurs by engaging in the forms of prayer, praise, and worship. The praise-and-worship tradition is found mainly among Pentecostal churches. Scripture teaches that praise prepares us for worship, or that praise is a prelude to worship. *The Church of God in Christ* and *Full Gospel Fellowship* are of Pentecostal origin. Worshipers bring their life experiences before God and open themselves to the power of the Spirit. The church encourages spontaneous expressions of praise such as speaking in tongues, raising hands, shouting, dancing, and clapping. The theological essence of Sunday morning worship is an affirmation of the moving power of God and the blessing received through giving God praise. Worship is a passionate activity. The whole body is actively engaged as giving service through worship. Music and expression of praise set the stage for the coming of the preached Word.

Pentecostal liturgy is mainly oral and narrative, with an emphasis on a direct experience of God, and results in the possibility of people being lifted out of their mundane daily experiences into a new realm of ecstasy. One of the central patterns and rhythms of Black Pentecostal churches is a communal life of prayer. Although prayer is often taught specifically as part of the worship experience, our focus here is prayer as a component of the curriculum of educational ministry.

A great form of religious life is worship. Black worship in general, and Pentecostal worship in particular, can be regarded as the corporate prayer of the church. We are educated to prayer, and prayer educates us. Worship shapes and empowers persons in prayer. Worship brings together the silent liturgy of the heart and visible liturgy of the church. The prayer of the heart structures the experience of worship, while worship shapes the content of personal prayer.

The church is living out its vocation to worship and to pray. Black Pentecostals place emphasis on corporate prayer. Corporate prayer is the form used to create identity as people at prayer. Forms of corporate prayer are the prayer meeting and the service of worship in which the entire community takes part. The life of prayer educates us most not when we read books but when we fall on our knees. The history and heritage of prayer, the lives of our saints in the faith, are taught better through worship than through classroom instruction. Although much still remains to be done, Black churches that embrace this model are beginning to do serious educational work of reshaping this particular ecclesial form. The contribution to educational ministry is its form of spirituality. This form enables one to live more or less consciously in the presence of God.

In sum, during the last decades of the twentieth century Black Pentecostalism found prominence as a religious preference and education approach. Across the United States, some of the largest churches are Black Pentecostal congregations. Black Pentecostalism counts within its ranks leaders that reflect a cross-section of perspectives on theology and education. Some of the leaders who have adopted a Pentecostal model of education and ministry include: T.D. Jakes, Potter's House, Dallas; Charles Blake, West Angeles Church of God in Christ, Los Angeles; Kirbyjon Caldwell, Windsor Village United Methodist Church, Houston; Grainger Browning, Ebenezer AME Church, Prince George County, Md.; and Paul Morton, Greater St. Stephen Full Gospel Baptist Church, New Orleans.

CONFESSIONAL

Confessional education presents an organized approach to religious education that is faithful to a particular religious tradition. The proponents of this approach usually emphasize that the teaching/learning experience consists of the transmission and preservation of Christian religious beliefs, practices, knowledge, and the context of the church's educational ministry. Tradition represents the social and cultural contexts in which we live, extended through time, space, and place. We are born into traditions and inherit them. To the extent that tradition helps inform our perspective and worldviews, tradition cannot help but shape the religious consciousness of African Americans. Tradition seeks to impose upon us normative views of how things should be. Mary E. Moore has called this religious education process the activity of "traditioning."

African American Christians must recognize the immense formative and normative power of tradition. For African American Christians, the one institution throughout the decades that has historically safeguarded the traditions of the faithful has been the Black church. African American Christians are believers who assemble in faith and freedom. Inevitably these communities of faith have developed traditions that form, inform, and transform African American Christians.

The confessional model of education has been a prominent one in the Black church. In this model the authority to teach comes from above, from those in authority. The religious educators (Christian education director, church school teacher, pastor, and others involved in the educational ministry), teach the faith heritage of the community. The role of theologians in this model is usually that of loyal but critical defenders of present teaching in the church. This model takes little account of charisms and ministries of teaching that might arise outside official structures. Christian education in the Black community must always deal with the Black Christian tradition and the contemporary attempts of the church to restate this tradition.

The heritage of faith, creed, the lives of our ancestors, sacraments, and church laws maintain and foster African American Christian identity and continuity.

A theology grounded in the Bible and story is the central theme. Knowledge of scripture and Christian faith heritage of Blacks is the aim. Christian education occurs through Bible study, teaching sermon, celebratory activities, custom, and law. The Bible or church tradition serves as the sources for doctrine or religious teachings. James H. Evans in *We Have Been Believers* was the first to give systematic expression to and rework the traditional Christian dogma of the church. For Evans, the African American church has served as the "keeper of the tradition." The heart of any Christian community is what it believes and practices, particularly through baptism and the Lord's supper. He writes, "The key to understanding the sacraments in the African American context is that they both derive their meaning in the concrete historical solidarity of the Christian and Christ with the community of faith in the Spirit of freedom."[4]

Confessional model of Christian education allies itself with traditional theologies that are based on specific biblical or church theologies. Traditional theologies look only to the tradition or one part of the tradition in developing their theologies. Theology in this model is an ordered understanding of beliefs within a theological system. The contribution of this model gives continuity in the Christian tradition, which is valuable since education in religion always entails dealing with the tradition and wisdom of the past. Traditional religious beliefs, practices, and liturgies entail elements that provide corporate identity for members of the church. Though confessional teaching is usually associated with didactic methods of instruction, other participative forms of teaching can be helpful. Confessional curriculum consists of the creeds, hymns, formal prayers, and liturgies that make it possible for African American Christians to identify with and to interpret its confessional heritage. The educator's task is to discover the confessional practices within the community of faith that transmit the faith, and to intentionally use them to call persons to identify with the faith tradition.

In sum, confessional approach to education is specific to orthodox and traditional church-oriented historic Black denominations such as Baptist and Methodist. They communicate confessional education primarily in and through liturgical experiences. Every liturgical service and season is an occasion to articulate the basic truths of the faith in order to lead persons into the life of the church. In addition, Black Catholics have long placed emphasis on the teaching and preaching of liturgical and sacramental spirituality.

CONTEMPLATIVE

Spiritual approach to AACRE emphasizes prayer, worship, and contemplative life in action. This model has a number of foundational sources:

biblical tradition, Black church history, and theology. The scriptures provide the ideals and norms that should characterize the lives of religious persons. The biblical tradition gives examples of many who lived lives of faith in response to God's call. African American spirituality's basic vision is faith in Jesus. This vision was first presented by ancient African monastics, forged in the crucible of slavery, and developed in the twentieth century by Howard Thurman.

Spiritual approach to Christian religious education looks at ancient and modern times. The past tradition is examined to show that this model has roots in African/African American religious experience. Black Catholics have published classic works in African American spirituality.[5] What these studies provide is a perspective of present forms of Black spirituality. Through such works we can get in touch with ancient African Christians and we are able to enter the cultural contexts in which they lived their lives. This approach examines contemporary experience, showing its relevance for present religious life. The theological views of Howard Thurman have enriched contemporary spirituality. For Thurman, the teacher is a guide who assists a person developing a relationship with God. The teacher as guide approach offers assistance to people who are developing a relationship with God. For Thurman the contemplative approach to such guidance emphasizes the act of contemplation, which is looking at or listening to something. His knowledge added to biblical tradition and history lays a firm foundation for understanding African American spirituality today.

The contemplative theme is consistent with the injunction heard in gospels and epistles to keep awake and watch. In this approach theologians state that spirituality must be the starting point for education. It is a spirituality that is born of moments of the African American sense of "conversion." Some of the qualities of an African American spirituality call particular attention to its contemplative, holistic, joyful, and communitarian nature. African American spirituality senses the immanence, transcendence, and intimacy of God. Spirituality has a contemplative dimension. Spirit-centered education occurs through living a life of prayer. Spiritual growth is the ultimate aim of religious education. African American spirituality involves the whole person: intellect and emotion, spirit and body, action and contemplation, individual and community, secular and sacred. At the same time, this approach to Christian education entails the persons desiring to become transparent to God, honestly giving full expression to all feelings and thoughts that are present.

African American spirituality explodes in the joy of movement, song, rhythm, feeling, color, and sensation. African American spirituality means community. Worship is always celebration of community. The content of spiritual education relates with curriculum and instruction. The content includes personal-communal theory-practice of spiritual disciplines.[6] It understands the meaning and nature of spiritual disciplines in parallel with how to teach the disciplines. Effective ways of teaching are well defined in terms of traditional methods such as mediation, contemplation, prayer, worship, action, and so on. The content of religious education pays close attention to the integration between curriculum and instruction. In this model not only the content, but also the adopted method should be viewed holistically.

Therefore, the spiritual approach of religious education emphasizes the importance of developing various methods in the process of planning the content of education. Finally, spiritual education forges a connection between prayer, worship, and action. African American Christians cannot remain committed to social action unless they are committed to a life of prayer. In sum, Black spirituality described here is not just a fact of history. It is still alive and well right now in many Black churches. To reiterate, it is the sacramental quality, the unremitting consciousness of divine presence in one's life, that is part and parcel of Black inspired worship and witness. One legacy of Black spirituality is that is has enabled Black worshipers to cultivate the "disciplines of the spirit." Our forefathers and mothers contended for the faith once delivered to the early saints. They inspired us to take hold of a way of living, a method, for greater spiritual excellence.

LIBERATION

A significant factor in AACRE has been the influence of Black liberation theology on religious education belief and practice. One theological model that arises out of contextual experiences in which people struggle to know the meaning of their humanity, Forrest Harris calls "liberating praxis." The model proposed here is one supported by Black liberation theology. In the Black church, liberation education emerges out of the Black Christian tradition and is expressed in various forms. A liberation model of education seeks to hold together the Black Christian story, reflection and action, and inner and outer liberation in the life of the church.[7] According to Forrest Harris, religious education in the Black church needs to embrace a "praxis model of ministry." The task of liberation Christian education is the continuing praxis of encouraging the development of critical consciousness and to be empowered to act for social transformation in line with the prophetic witness of the gospel.

Educators and theologians such as Grant Shockley, Olivia Stokes, James Harris, Anne Wimberly, and Forest Harris have identified with and utilized theology of liberation. Accordingly, they have argued for a more explicit social/cultural and political role for religious education. A liberation model of Christian education seeks to recover the Black church's historical relationship to social action. Drawing heavily on the work of Paulo Freire, Thomas Groome, and James Cone, the work of these Christian educators and theologians represent this tradition. The primary strategies of education are Afrocentric hermeneutic, critical action in reflection with the cultural context, and understanding of liberation in practice toward the reign of God.

Liberation education begins in deed. It thus provides a new understanding of the relationship between faith and action, and the content of beliefs and commitment. The key word is *praxis,* as the actual participation in the ongoing struggle for faith in freedom. It is an educational process, which involves living from and reflecting on the deeds of faith. Liberation educators begin with the biblical promise of freedom. This vision, combined with social analysis, inspires the vocation of liberation in the educational ministry activity of Black Christians. The action-reflection model proposed involves Black Christians bringing together the Black Christian story in dialectical tension with the biblical story of liberation and freedom under God.

Liberation Christian education becomes involvement for change, which critically and constructively shapes reality. Christian education becomes a prophetic task. Through liberation Christian education, persons are able to analyze their social context, to reflect on that context, and to engage in effective means of transforming social and political structures for freedom. The curriculum of liberation Christian education is multiple. The inclusion of advocacy, social action, and mobilization are essential curricular components of liberation Christian education. Their presence in the curriculum educates to ministries of liberation, and people who participate in them realize these ministries are educating them. Each of these components of curriculum has a prophetic dimension. The prophetic tradition suggests the need for Christian educators to grapple with the social-political implications of faith commitments. Liberation education promotes the search for education methods of action-reflection that will enable the Black church to be faithful to its liberating vision.

In sum, Christian religious education in Black churches has a social mandate. It is often difficult to see clearly the racial agenda in the struggle of African American against post–civil rights alienation. A liberation model of Christian religious education in both urban and suburban churches provides a means to restore relatedness and bring alienation to an end. Harold Trulear says that "religious educators must accept responsibility to help the number of Black middle-class church adherents understand that they are fully connected with those they have left behind."[8] In response to the widening gap between the social classes within the African American community, the congregation of Trinity United Church of Christ in Chicago, lead by their pastor Jeremiah Wright, voted to intentionally reconnect with those they have left behind through the establishment of relationships with the underclass. Churches that are both characterized by middle-class consciousness and located in urban impoverished areas need to seek ongoing opportunities for liberation religious education.

AFROCENTRIC

Afrocentric Christian religious education traces human origins to the continent of Africa. It acknowledges the importance of African civilizations in the ancient world, and their continuing influence in the modern world. Afrocentric approach to religious education rooted in cultural experience recognizes that our values, like our actions and emotions, are at least in part cultural products. Through identity formation, the church provides alternative constructs for self and group location. The Afrocentric dimension of the church developed around the thinking of Black nationalist religious leaders and educators. Black nationalism is a concept that provides an umbrella for discussing not only the historic movement by that name but also Afrocentrism. Harold Cruse and Maulana Ron Karenga helped lay the basis for the Afrocentric conception of reality. They believed that there could be no real liberation in the Black community without a cultural revolution. Cultural revolution implies and also means revitalizing, creating, and recreating culture.[9]

Afrocentricity is a concept coined by Molefi Kete Asante, who is perhaps the most recognized proponent of the Afrocentric idea.[10] The early Black nationalists perspective of race pride, cultural unity, racial identity, and Black self-determination offers an Afrocentric alternative for reversing the cultural and social destruction of Black heritage and life. The critique of race, culture, and religion by contemporary Afrocentrists challenges the Black church to reflect on the kind of Christian education theology and practice that does justice to the cultural realities of Black folk. Albert Cleage's *Black Christian Nationalism* represents the religious thrust of Afrocentrism's usefulness for ministry in Black churches. J. Deotis Roberts's work *Africentric Christianity: A Theological Appraisal for Ministry* provides theological reflection on Christian doctrine and Africentrism (or *Afrocentrism*). Thus, discussion is crucial to our understanding of the interplay between Christian creed and culture.

The Afrocentric educator's task is to help Blacks rediscover their identity through a dialogue of African heritage, culture, and contemporary experience. Christian education in this context is the process that allows for and fosters the transformation of the person, in a collective sense, to greater apprehension of self and humanity. Thus, a person reaches self-awareness through remembering historical and foundational experiences. Afrocentrism entails a serious attempt to understand the manner in which Africans viewed reality in their context of culture for thousands of years before they encountered the Western worldview.

As pedagogy, Afrocentricity offers a level of psychological well-being that most African Americans have yet to attain, especially given the fact that it has yet to become a broad-based orientation of the African American community. The Afrocentrists devote careful attention to the pedagogical issue of the importance of teaching centeredness. As a pedagogical principle, this means that as students, as teachers, as pastors, we have an African-centered self-understanding of life and ministry.

The aim of the Afrocentric curriculum is to teach what has been purposefully omitted. An Afrocentric curriculum focus is on the importance of Africa in the biblical world, the influence of African beliefs and culture on ancient Israel; Afro-American biblical hermeneutics, the color of Jesus, the transmission and preservation of Black history, culture, and Black church tradition. In addition, within an Afrocentric learning environment, the teacher is teaching students from a culturally relevant perspective. The teacher is a cultural interpreter. Teachers see themselves as part of the community and their role as giving something back to the community.

The Afrocentric idea has not found wide acceptance in the Black church yet, but a growing number of Black congregations, denominational publishing houses, and publications are seeking to implement it in their curriculum in an effort to increase motivation and enhance self-esteem among African American children. In some cases, Black religious leadership has effectively organized the educational life of the church in a way that addresses the cultural liberation of Black people. In Atlanta, Georgia, pastor Mark Akeita Lomax of First Afrikan Church crafted a liturgical calendar that reflects the multivalent rhythms of African spiritual life. He was convinced that it was the responsibility of the church to seek recovery, reclamation, preservation and pursuit of African spiritualities, histories, and cultures.

In sum, an Afro-centric approach to Christian religious education will endure because of its relevance to Black culture and realities, which define the lives of African Americans. A leadership posture that embraces Afrocentrism places the Christian education ministry in the position to train Black congregants to think theologically about Blackness and God's salvific concern for humanity. Black liberation grounds and supports the Afrocentric model of Christian religious education. Black churches must organize themselves to implement the Afrocentric curriculum. There are Black churches that have implemented an Afrocentric curriculum, but most African American congregations are not convinced that an Afrocentric curriculum is the solution.

Educational Implications

In conducting this research I have had the opportunity to teach "Christian Education in the African American Experience" to pastors, educators, and teachers of different racial backgrounds in both the church and academy. At the end of the class session I asked each person to fill out an evaluation. In these evaluations I asked them to identify the major approaches used by their congregations (more than one approach could be chosen) and what approach they wished was emphasized more. The tables on page 136 show their responses.

These approaches suggest some ways the Black church can develop Christian education goals and objectives. The differences highlight the need for intentional planning, so that the mission and goals are clear. Then specific curriculum, aims, and ministries can be developed based on the selected approach.

The most emphasized models of Christian religious education are kerygmatic and confessional. The least emphasized models are holiness and liberation. The models respondents wished would be emphasized more are Afrocentric and contemplative. A number of respondents desired no change in Kerygma, Holiness, and Confessional models of Christian religious education used in their churches.

It seems worthwhile asking whether or not any one model may prove especially hopeful for the long-term future of the theory and practice of Christian religious education. I have looked at a number of models of religious education. I am not convinced that there needs to be a unified model. I recognize that African American Christians must be spiritual, liberational, communal, and confessional, but I do not see clearly how it can be this in all contexts. I recognize that different contexts call for different models. For example, an exclusive emphasis upon content in confessional orthodoxy can ignore the essential dimension of the Holy Spirit. Likewise, an exclusive emphasis upon the experience of oppression in praxis can ignore the essential experience of the Christian tradition. An effective curriculum weds Christian heritage, identity, and action. No simple formula to accomplish an adequate blending exists, but certain guidelines can be shared.

APPROACH EMPHASIZED	
EDUCATIONAL APPROACH	% OF RESPONDENTS
Kerygmatic	88%
Holiness	7%
Confessional	88%
Contemplative	37%
Afrocentric	25%
Liberation	7%

APPROACH THEY WISHED WAS EMPHASIZED MORE	
EDUCATIONAL APPROACH	% OF RESPONDENTS
Kerygmatic	40%
Holiness	37%
Confessional	40%
Contemplative	48%
Afrocentric	51%
Liberation	33%

DESIRED NO CHANGE	
EDUCATIONAL APPROACH	% OF RESPONDENTS
Kerygmatic	14%
Holiness	7%
Confessional	7%
Contemplative	1%
Afrocentric	1%
Liberation	1%

Conclusions

Models for "Christian education are multiple, but can be woven together to provide an impressive tapestry of ministry."[11] The fashioning of an approach provides the occasion to integrate insights from various foundations in a connective way and link together practices in earlier centuries.

All of these models affirm that the decisions Christian educators make directly affect the practice of education. Christian educators must care for the content they are sharing and the context in which their students live. The teacher must be knowledgeable of the historical, cultural, and religious content and context of the African American Christians they teach.

I conclude with the conviction that there is need for African American theologically oriented Christian instruction in the area of religious education. I am also confident that today an African American theology is developing that may form the basis for the type of Christian religious education needed in Black Christian communities.

Will these historic models of religious education communicate well to the current generation of Black believers? New models of religious education rooted in the theological bedrock of the historic Black church, responding to the new realities of the twenty-first century, are emerging. It is critical that we think about new models, the theological grounding that will sustain them, and the cultural realities that must also shape them. Finally, it must be noted that these models of Christian religious education put the pastor in differing roles as educator. The following chapter emphasis is on the pastor's key role in Christian education.

CHAPTER EIGHT

Teaching Roles of African American Clergy

I teach because I have been commanded to. Jesus commanded his followers to go and teach. As one to whom the gospel has been entrusted by the church, there is no question about my mandate to teach. In my thirty-one years in ministry, I have traveled a great distance. During this time, I also traveled a great distance in my understanding of the pastor's role in Christian education ministry.

To this point in the book, I have concentrated on the vocation of teaching in the African American church. I have argued that the central task of ministry is teaching the Christian faith. In this chapter I suggest that clergy teach in everything they do. Everything that happens in ministry and in the church offers an opportunity for teaching and learning. In this chapter I explore the vocation of pastor as teacher.

Black religious leadership is a unique phenomenon in the history of the Black church. There is great need for a realistic assessment of what Black church leaders have been doing and are doing to educate the Black community. The Black pastor as teacher is the most important leader in the educational ministry of the Black church. How Black churches have developed and engaged educational ministry cannot be understood without an assessment of the relationship between the pastor and the Black church.

What can Black pastors do to enrich the educational practice in the Black church? What is the Black pastor's central role? Historically, the "cultural womb" of the Black church has nurtured the most effective Black community leaders.[1] Most literature written about Black religion either is historical in nature or deals with the singular facet of the Black preaching tradition. Scant attention, however, is given to Black religious leaders as educators. This lack of emphasis has produced a poverty in knowledge regarding teaching leadership strategies employed by Black pastors for designing and structuring educational ministry. J. Deotis Roberts's assessment of the teaching ministry is that in "the Black church tradition we have majored in preaching. Nevertheless, in many large Black churches, the educational ministry is not present or is inadequate for the needs of the people."[2]

This chapter is the result of the recognition of a genuine need for a major stimulus to and guide for pastoral leadership in the religious education of the African American church. With appreciation for those who have made significant contributions in the past to the discussion of the importance of the pastor's role as religious educator, I provide a fresh interpretation of this vital concern. In this chapter I discuss the pastor as teacher and pastors' teaching role in the African American church.

Pastor as Teacher

The very nature of the pastor's role is that of a teacher. One of the ministerial functions of the pastor is teacher. The role of pastor is one who protects and instructs the flock under his or her care. Many Black pastors tend to identify more with the ministries of preaching, leading, and evangelizing than they do with the title of teacher. The church has segmented its work into pastoral ministry and Christian education. Pastors should not look down upon their biblical title of teacher. Jesus called himself a teacher and he said to his disciples, "You call me Teacher and Lord—and you are right, for that is what I am" (Jn. 13:13).

Jesus demonstrated that he was the master teacher. He mastered the art of teaching. His knowledge of scriptures and ability to extend the teaching of scriptures to their deeper meanings enabled him to connect with people. Jesus' appropriate use of varied teaching styles and his living of the spiritual and moral precepts he taught made a great difference in the lives of his disciples.

In the context of the educational ministry of the Black church, teaching and learning must be of vital concern to advance its mission. The pastor is expected not only to proclaim the gospel but to teach. Many years of working in the area of Christian education have convinced me that no Christian education program will be effective without the active involvement of the pastor in the process. This involvement must exceed the normal duties of appointing the superintendent, approving the faculty, etc., and must include involvement in setting the philosophy of education and assisting in charting the course of action.

The pastor is not only the administrative head of the local church, but also the leader of its educational work. By virtue of position, the pastor is chiefly responsible for the total program of Christian education. As spiritual leader and theological advisor, the pastor sets the outlook for the types of programs that are planned and the types of curricula that are used. As a developer and nurturer of leaders, the pastor plays a large part in helping individuals discover the gifts God has given them. Years ago, when I was a pastor, a bishop visited my Sunday/church school class. He then called the next day to compliment me on the fine job I was doing. I didn't realize I was doing anything special until he called my attention to it. From that moment on, I knew that God had called me to be in the classroom.

In many ways the pastor is a teacher. The pastor as teacher stands at the intersection of three centers of teaching in the church: the congregation, the denomination, and the seminary:

> Because of their [pastors] special relationship to the denomination, they are uniquely qualified to facilitate dialogue between various centers of teaching authority in the church. Similarly, they often are the persons in their congregations most knowledgeable of denominational policies, programs, and teachings. In short, they occupy a critical position amid the three centers of teaching authority.[3]

Some pastors take their role as teachers more seriously than others and are willing to take time from other duties to read, prepare lectures, and write. Some Black pastors fulfill their teaching role at seminaries and at local colleges and universities. Some do this primarily for economic reasons. They serve as pastors and associates in low-paid or unpaid positions. They continue to work as teachers out of necessity. Others teach as adjunct or visiting scholars to fulfill their calling. Still others exercise their teaching role through their writings. Some have become nationally recognized as teaching pastors through articles, books, audiotapes, and videotapes. Still others have been published in their denominational publications: *African Methodist Episcopal, Christian Recorder, Journal of Christian Education, Christian Methodist Episcopal, Christian Index, African Methodist Episcopal Zion, Star of Zion, National Baptist Convention,* and *Christian Informer.* The center of teaching and learning in the Black church is the local congregation. Pastors make a special contribution to the interpretative task of the teaching ministry. They are to teach all members of the congregation how to reflect upon their lives theologically. They fulfill this role predominately through the church school.

The ministry of Bible teaching is the first of the basic components of the educational ministry of the Black church. The Bible is the foundation for the Christian education ministry of the Black church. Black folk regard the Bible as sacred, holy, and the revelation of God's presence in historical situations with and on behalf of a chosen people for the welfare of humankind. The

Bible has always stood at the center of teaching and preaching. Although it has never been the sole textbook of the Black church, it was and is the chief source of all teaching. The Bible is valuable as a teaching source in the Black church because it teaches, it moves the heart, and it stirs the soul. The most important structure for most Black churches for Bible teaching is the Sunday/church school.

This remains true even in the face of serious problems that some Black churches have experienced in recent years with Sunday/church school. Overall enrollments in church schools in general have declined in recent decades. Some experts feel that the Sunday/church school is in a struggle for its very existence. The church school is certainly an arena of crucial importance. Black pastors tend to spend more time conducting weekday Bible study than teaching Sunday/church school classes. Laypersons believe that the Black pastor needs to pay greater attention to the church school. I believe that some pastors have neglected the church school because some consider the church school as trivial, second-rate ministry, busy work, or carry negative baggage from youth experiences with a lack of understanding and training.

The members of the congregation observe the ways in which the pastor teaches, or leads, a Bible study. The pastor shows them how to tell the story of their faith. Sometimes the pastor has to be involved in the details of carrying out Christian education. Pastors as educators represent the gospel. The purpose of their teaching is to enable others to read the Bible for themselves and to carry out practical theological reflection in their lives. They teach so that others might minister with greater understanding. Their task is to ensure that the gospel is heard in their congregations.

The pastor plays an important role in passing on the core convictions by which the denomination is constituted as a community. At key points in the congregation's life, clergy have the opportunity to be directly involved in teaching in order to make sure that a firm foundation in scripture and church tradition is laid. Officer training, new member classes, Bible studies, and teacher training are all opportunities for ministers to pass on the normative beliefs and practices of the church. In addition, the pastor plays a key role in the promotion of the church's educational ministry. Promotion of the educational ministry takes place through church bulletin boards, church publications, direct mail, electronic media, and press releases to newspapers. At the congregational level, unless pastors give their support to this ministry in terms of administrative commitment, financial allocations, and the creation of an overall ethos in which Christian education is considered important, the church's teaching ministry is likely to languish.

The Teaching Role of the Pastor

The pastor has a significant role as the chief educator in the local church, especially in equipping the saints for works of service. In the dual capacity of pastor-teacher, the pastor is also a member of an education team in the local church. In most churches, Christian education directors, church school superintendents, and teachers share the daily management of the educational ministry. Thus, while clergy may well have important administrative responsibilities in the church, clergy's most important role is to encourage the congregation and its leaders to know and to love God. In this section I explore the teaching role of the pastor. How we educate as pastors depends on our skills, abilities, and gifts.

Clergy who preach in a teaching mode use different forms of teaching. However, all share one common purpose: to teach the gospel. The form of teaching flows out of our giftedness. Pastors teach and practice what they learn. As Parker J. Palmer states, "We teach who we are."[4] In other words, nothing I do as a teacher will make any difference to anyone if it is not rooted in my nature; one needs to be authentic to one's self. To understand the pastor as teacher one must understand the teaching roles of congregational life. The teaching roles include the following: love of scripture on the part of the pastor; ability of the pastor to discover the gifts of people who receive the Holy Spirit; the way pastors help people experience sacramental encounters; the capacity of the pastor to live in the presence of God and to promote the spiritual development of the congregation; the pastor's leading the congregation in criticizing and resisting the principalities and powers that oppress; the pastor's preaching and the worshipers' hearing the stories that build community; and the pastor's helping the congregation affirm African/African American cultural practices, their continuing significance, and their benefits.

THE TEACHING ROLES OF THE PASTOR
Pastor as biblical interpreter
Pastor as discerner of gifts
Pastor as cultural teacher
Pastor as prophetic agent
Pastor as storyteller
Pastor as spiritual educator
Pastor as sacramental educator

Pastor as Biblical Interpreter

Who interprets the Bible? What is the place of the clergy as interpreter? For the most part, in the Black church tradition the Black pastor has determined the boundaries of interpretation. However, in recent years Black theologians and scholars from around the world have expanded the boundaries of interpretation. In most Black denominations the clergy mirrors the interpretations of the denomination that ordains them and the congregations in which they find themselves. The pastor has a special responsibility to teach scripture. What happens when Black pastors teach the Bible?

Historically Black pastors' approaches to teaching scripture have focused on content-oriented Bible study. What is the content to be communicated and explored? There are two kinds of content—the biblical and the African

American–used in matters of interpretation. Biblical interpretation involves the weighing of scripture in relation to African Americans' personal and communal beliefs and practices. The processes of interpretation regarding scripture and African American culture focus clearly on what content is to be passed on. In his book *The Bible and African Americans,* Vincent L. Wimbush outlines what, when, and how biblical and African American content has/is used to interpret scripture. Wimbush believes the work of biblical hermeneutic today is not the original meaning of the text but to explore how meaning and text are at issue. He writes, "It is the more complex phenomenon of engagement–the collective consciousness being threaded through changing, and being changed by the Bible over time."[5]

Pastors need to clarify what the purpose of their Bible teaching will be. Pastors need to define their task as religious educators by making a clear distinction between the devotional use of scripture and content-oriented Bible study. Robert Mulholland calls this a distinction between an informational and formational approach to scripture.[6] More than a need to know something about God is a thirst for God and a yearning to be known by God. Through the Word we discover a way to respond to God's invitation to an intimate relationship.

The pastor's role as religious educator in relation to scripture depends on one's devotion to scripture. The average church member expects the pastor to have a thorough knowledge of scripture. The pastor, as biblical interpreter, is to help create and sustain in the laity a deep hunger for God. Along with the responsibility to increase the hunger comes the requirement that this hunger be fed. How does one acquire that lean and hungry look? The more we feed on God's Word, the hungrier we get. The pastor must begin with a personal practice of disciplines. An actual encounter with Christ in the Word moves the individual to repentance, and a humbled hungry heart is the necessary prerequisite for effective study. Only a humble heart is teachable. Typically, it is the converted that long to study scripture. The laity is hungry for knowledge. Black pastors need to teach those who will teach.

For Christian education to be effective, it must have cultural integrity with the African American experience and tradition. Christian education for the Black church involves a process of teaching scripture in light of the experiences and traditions of African Americans. Focusing on this understanding of Christian education for Black pastors has several implications. First, there is a shift from informative to formative approaches to scripture. Second, teaching scripture with cultural integrity upholds respect for the traditions and experiences of African Americans while allowing for new interpretations of meaning. A third implication is that teaching scripture with cultural integrity provides the opportunity for future generations to learn the cultural/historical/biblical context through which faith and identity emerge.[7] Fourth, we have not done enough to teach persons a deep hunger for God. We need to teach persons how to receive the transforming power of God into their lives or how to live their lives within the transforming presence of God. Matters of interpretation affect all who are involved in the educational work of the church: teachers, parents, pastors, and professionals. They need to think through their personal understanding of how they interpret scripture and how this relates to their work as teachers. When pastors have come to an understanding of the authority of the Bible and African American culture, they will be able to teach authoritatively.

Pastor as Spiritual Educator

Pastors are called to reflect on their image as spiritual leaders and to promote the spiritual development of their congregation. The spiritual education of God's people offers the most fertile opportunity for pastors to shape their lives in God's image and among the people in their congregations. To be formed in Christ and to have Christ formed within us are clearly gifts from God. Spiritual education of God's people is a unique opportunity for personal and congregational growth. Here the pastor teaches people how to receive the transforming power of God into their lives within the transforming presence of God. The difference in views turns on the way one conceives spirituality and spiritual leadership.

Black spirituality is not a dimension of our life; it *is* our life. Black Christian spiritual formation addresses how to share this life. Black Christian spirituality has its roots in traditional African religion, ancient African Christianity, and the writings of African American theologians. It involves awareness that to be alive is to be in God. Howard Thurman and others deepen our understanding of God's activity in all of life and in all creation. His view sees spirituality as profoundly integral to life in all dimensions. To him, all pastoral activities are moments of speaking to God, learning about God, and living in the presence of God. To be in God in the Black religious tradition is to be in the presence of God through prayer and a hunger and thirst to know God through study.

Spiritual education in the Black church does not take place over and above the tasks, ministries, and progress that already define the pastor's work. Spiritual education of God's people already calls for classes that address the spiritual disciplines of prayer, fasting, Bible study, and so on. Obviously, such disciples led or encouraged by the pastor with a deep commitment to the spiritual development of the congregation can lead them toward a Spirit-led life. These approaches can be taught to members of the congregation either through modeling/mentoring or through natural extensions of the pastor's teaching ministry. For example, the Black Christian tradition is rich with images of the mentor: the pastor who counsels the person of faith, or the elder who helps the younger over the rough road. The pastor functions in all these ways for people. Church members attend classes because of their trust and confidence in their pastor. The core of good biblical teaching grows out of relationships even more than content.

Prayer and study disciplines are essential for pastors as persons in their prayer life. Again, we look at the prayer life of Jesus, and note only one class on prayer is recorded. The disciples asked Jesus to teach them to pray. The disciple's request for a prayer class was inspired by their yearning to experience God. The challenge for Black pastors today is more than a need to know something about God; it is thirst for God and yearning to be known by God, especially to create a spiritual learning environment that creates a hunger, a thirst for the knowledge of God among Black believers.

Black pastors who have a thorough knowledge of the Bible are more skillful and effective. For Black pastors to have a thorough knowledge of the Bible requires understanding the nature of the biblical texts, their history and shape, and the ways in which they have been interpreted. The pastors use their skill to help create a spiritual learning environment that guides believers to find connections between the scriptures and their lives, connections that will enable them to live more faithfully as disciples of Jesus Christ. This teaching process becomes an art as it evolves beyond skills, growing out of the pastor/teacher's love for the Bible and believers, and enlivened by the inspiration of God's Spirit. Through the Word we discover a way to respond to God's invitation to an intimate relationship. Today Black believers also hunger and thirst for God's presence. In sum, every pastor should live a life of prayer and teach prayer, which can nourish the lives of members of the church. That is to say that every meeting at which the pastor presides, every class that is taught, every visitation made, and every worship service conducted should evidence a life of prayer. Every aspect of a pastor-led education work can have the character of prayer, always recognizing that the ground on which we are standing is holy.

Pastor as Discerner of Gifts

The pastor as discerner of gifts understands how the church works as a spiritual force through the extraordinary powers God gives people who receive the Holy Spirit. Spiritual gifts are special, extraordinary abilities God gives to build up the body of Christ, the church, for ministry to its members and, through its members, the world. Paul declared, "Now there are varieties of gifts, but the same Spirit" (1 Cor. 12:4–5). There are varieties of gifts of service. The Corinthian text names a total of twelve: wisdom, knowledge, faith, healing, miracles, prophecy, discernment, tongues, interpretation, apostleship, helps, and administration (1 Cor. 12:8–11, 27–31). Romans 12:6–8 and Ephesians 4:6–8 list seven: prophecy, service, teaching, exhortation, giving, leadership, and mercy.

The primary source of spiritual gifts is God, who creates a special relationship between the faithful members of the body of Christ. The basis for this special relationship is the common good. Once these abilities, as spiritual gifts, are acknowledged and properly used, certain basic religious activities become powerful resources for aiding the church to fulfill its divine purpose. Some of the activities are worship, Bible study, prayer, and praise.

The pastor must be more than a manager. He or she must emphasize the role of the Holy Spirit. The Pentecostal approach to the religious education of all members of the body of Christ is designed to present specific ways for the Holy Spirit to operate in the life of the pastor and the church. The Pentecostal approach describes the revolution in education and ministry understanding and practice that is taking place. This revolution makes possible a widening of the ability of the pastor to discern the gifts of people who receive the Holy Spirit.

Pastors who are perceived as effective are good at helping laypersons identify, sharpen, and focus their gifts. Effective Black clergy as discerners of gifts are called to function interdependently with laity, acknowledging and supporting their gifts and calling them to ministry. These powers are manifestly present in the discovery, development, and deployment of spiritual gifts by which we are able to be more (in the Spirit) than what we are (in the flesh) and to do more (in the Spirit) than what we can (in the flesh).

Black Christians are more open and eager to discover and claim ministries that are designed by God for them. Today in the Black church pastors are beginning to study the manifestations of the Holy Spirit and charismatic structuring of church ministries. The explosive force of "new wine" has resulted in new church and ministries coming to birth. When people open themselves to God, they find that an experience of the Spirit of God is inseparable from the discovery and exercise of the *charismata,* the gifts.

As with all gifts (charismata), all Black Christians express some measure of praise, but certain denominations, congregations, and pastors receive the spiritual gift of prayer-praise. This gift is the extraordinary ability to pray to and to praise God. They praise God with such a joy-filled intimacy with Christ that faith is strengthened and ministries become effective. This gift has been controversial and confusing for some Black mainline denominations and pastors. Black pastors who engage in charismatic teaching radiate an enthusiastic devotion to Christ as a personal Lord that permeates all they do. They delight in reading the Bible for personal devotions as well as the primary source of teaching material, and discover the Bible is full of relevant measures for today.

Charismatic pastor/teachers are more inclined to search out the meaning of scripture. This anointed teaching is a reciprocal companionship that helps pastors and believers as they move together toward perfection in Christ. The bond is a spiritual partnership, each giving to the other a way to experience God. Black pastors are engaged in this charismatic renewal; new vigor and growth are taking place. This movement is not going away.

Pastor as Sacramental Educator

One of the chief priestly responsibilities of the pastor is teaching the sacraments of the church. Starting with baptism, and to the Lord's supper, the pastor can initiate powerful educational and liturgical life for the entire congregation. This image is a religious education grounded in a sacramental approach to the preparation of the whole people of God. The church ordains and empowers the pastor to administer the sacraments and to teach the faithful the correct doctrines, which support the sacramental approach.

The greatest gift of all, without question, is God's grace, which we have received through Jesus Christ. The gift of grace has continued to speak to Black Christians in formative ways. The sacraments are instruments of God's grace to be given to the faithful. The sacraments point to and participate in the grace of God. They are living symbols of the story of God's actions through Christ and the church. From birth to death, the visible symbols of baptism, communion, confirmation, marriage, consecration, and ordination make possible God's presence and action in our lives.

What do Black pastors do in terms of the integration of religious education and liturgical life? Black pastors are involved in the preparation of persons for sacramental life, but may not perceive these preparations to be religious education. For example, education of the total congregation concerning the meaning and power of the sacraments takes place during public worship. The entire service is integrated with baptismal and eucharist scriptures, liturgical richness, imaginative preaching, and drama around the sacrament itself.

The key to understanding the sacraments in the African American context is that they derive their meaning in the concrete historical solidarity of the Christian and Christ with the Black church in the spirit of freedom.[8] Pastors and the church as a whole invite persons to be involved in the Christian faith through the proclamation of the gospel. Through the act of baptism, membership in the community of faith is confirmed. In the Black church, the pastor usually instructs the new convert in a new membership class on the meaning of the sacraments. In the Black church there are two sacraments: baptism and holy communion.

First baptism is an initiation rite. In certain churches baptism is administered to children as a sign of their inclusion in the church community. The second way of seeing baptism is an adult confession of faith. Here the person joins the church as the result of an inner personal conversion. The Black church is made up of those who have been converted to Christ's liberating work. Baptism is administered with water. Since baptism is intimately connected with the corporate life and worship of the church, it is usually administered during the public worship so that members of the congregation may be reminded of their own baptisms and may welcome into their fellowship those who are baptized and whom they are committed to nurture in the Christian faith.

Pastors have a special responsibility for the education of the people of God concerning the meaning of the communion meal. The Lord's supper, or eucharist, is basic in the life of the Black church. Holy communion is essentially the sacrament of the gift, which God makes to us in Christ through the power of the Holy Spirit. Holy communion, which always includes both Word and sacrament, is a proclamation and a celebration of the work of God. Christian faith is deepened by the celebration of the Lord's supper.

Here the pastor instructs the new convert that holy communion is the celebration of the sacrifice and promise of Jesus Christ. Thus, the elements of the bread and wine are symbols of the death and resurrection of Jesus Christ. Pastors educate as they bring persons into participation at the table through sharing the bread and wine and by using liturgies that reenact the image of the Lord's supper, buttressed with preaching and teaching during communion that proclaim the death and resurrection of Christ.

Pastor as Prophetic Agent

The pastor leads the congregation in criticizing and resisting the principalities and powers that oppress. Some Black pastors approach the religious education of their people by educating them to deal with the difficult issues of racism, sexism, and social justice. Part of the gift of the Black church is a long legacy of continually challenging injustice and championing social reform. Social concern, though less active at times, has never disappeared among Blacks. Black pastors have been politically involved on behalf of the Black community from the inception of African American history. The pastor, as prophetic model of leadership, seeks to reveal the contradictions in the dominant culture and to clarify the vision and action of justice. The emphasis on prophetic leadership assists people in identifying and opposing social evil that affects them.

Prophetic leadership in the Black church tradition began with Richard Allen, the first Black bishop and founder of the African Methodist Episcopal Church in Philadelphia in the ninetieth century, and continued in the twentieth century with Adam Clayton Powell, pastor of the historic Abyssinian Baptist Church in New York, and on to Martin Luther King Jr. Black pastors, in light of history, have sometimes been mistaken. But they continue to teach and preach that the gospel is social as well as personal and that the "spiritual" cannot be detached from the sociopolitical conditions of Blacks.

The goal of the prophetic agent is to help us see the injustices within contemporary society and to inspire us to work as God's partners to transform society and bring about God's Kingdom. Here the goal is not simply to instill knowledge in power but to teach the right use of knowledge and to transform society. The educational emphasis is on living out our Christian faith in faithful action. Pastors as prophetic agents believe that a key image in the Bible is that of the righteous God of justice and freedom. The exodus story, a story of God's liberation of slaves who became a chosen people, is seen as the central story, the model for Black freedom. The pastor educator should always keep before the congregation the idea that the goal of the Christian life includes concern for the liberation of the oppressed.

Grant Shockley has correctly indicated the need for religious education for social justice. Shockley writes: "Pastors have an exciting opportunity to model and stimulate others to become engaged in social justice ministries... Such a social ministry must be undertaken in community with the laity who are involved in the very structures of society where they can make a difference."[9] The strength of this approach is the emphasis on social analysis and action.

It begins with action, building a house for the homeless, serving the helpless, lobbying for policy change, mobilizing for church reform, and linking their experience and stories with the call for justice as revealed in the Bible. When the church is willing to deal with reform within its own life, it has greater integrity to its social witness in the wider society. In sum, to meet the challenge of social justice, the Black pastor's role is to reawaken a prophetic social conscience that brings with it the potential for liberation.

Pastor as Storyteller

The Black pastor has been the primary storyteller of the Black community. The history of the Black pulpit is a history of utterance that has been highly conditioned by the storytelling tradition derived from African tradition. Story is integral to the Black Christian tradition. Through preaching the Black pastor connects everyday life stories with the Christian faith story found in scripture. Pastors also connect their personal stories with Christian faith heritage stories of African Americans found outside scripture. The intent is for African Americans to be encouraged by the lives of persons who faced life circumstances with which they can identify.

For example, the Bible depicts experiences that many Blacks can identify with: Egyptian bondage and oppression of the Israelites, deportation into Babylonian captivity, the request of their captors to sing "their songs" in a strange land, and a mocked and crucified Jesus.

Professor Vincent Wimbush reminds us of the importance of the stories of the biblical word: "Since most of the earliest African American Christians had been denied, from the beginning of their experience in the Americas, the opportunity to be fully human...What became important were the telling and retelling, the hearing and re-hearing of biblical stories..."[10]

The pastor as a member of the community is set aside to tell the Christian story to others. The pastor helps the congregation hear the story through the Bible and through Black history with an eye and ear toward interpreting how the Bible and Black history are significant for the church and world today. Through the sermon, the pastor can help the congregation become a community of faith. The sermon is part of a teaching and learning environment when it helps the congregation learn or recall the stories of the Bible and Black history. What we remember and the way we remember, we do in narrative (story). The past is a story we tell and retell. Through storytelling we make connections with our community's past. Stories help create our sense of self, others, community, and world. They tell us who we are and point us to what we are to do.

One of the most critical tasks facing the church has to do with the effectiveness with which each successive generation appropriates the story of its heritage and internalizes the promises inherent in the story. Ann Wimberly calls this religious education process the activity of story linking. As Wimberly says, its intent "is to place us in touch with our African American forebears' faith and their experience of God's action in their liberation and vocation; links with our forebears' story helps to inspire and to foster our commitment to continue on the Christian faith walk."[11] It is a process of narrative or story. The story functions in the community both to give it a historical origin and a future or destiny.

The challenge of binding generations is not simply the imparting of the wisdom of the saints of our community's past, but is how we keep faith with our identity. Black oratory and worship serves as a repository of the community past. The stories of faith are linked to the ritual and liturgical life of the congregation. The most obvious of these associations are made through the liturgies, creeds, doctrines, sacraments, symbols, songs, dances, and practices of piety of congregational life. If we do not know the sounds of joy and sorrow, we cannot sing the hymns of praise and spirituals distinguishing the faith of our ancestors.

The repository continues to illustrate the persistence of how the Bible, experience, and the Black church tradition have shaped the life and mission of a community. Through storytelling Black worshipers have maintained and renewed a sense of community and identity through subsequent generations. There is no discontinuity. Story establishes in us memory and we live as brothers and sisters with Miriam, Moses, the prophets, Peter, Paul, Dorcas, Charles Wesley, Richard Allen, Frederick Douglass, Marcus Garvey, Harriet Tubman, Martin Luther King Jr., Malcolm X, and others. The task of building community requires constant attention to nurturing these historical relationships.

In sum, pastoral leadership has a primary investment in the conscious continuity of the story. The continuity of the story is dependent upon the commitment of the pastor, educators, and members to participate in the story-linking process.

Pastor as Cultural Teacher

A central way that Black pastoral leadership influences religious education is by affirming African/African American cultural practices. Here the pastor is to lead Black believers to esteem their "Africanness" as a gift of

God. There is a cultural context that the pastor should know. This requires cultural knowledge of the African background of African Americans. Black pastoral leaders who consider themselves Afrocentric in the Black cultural tradition affirm the importance of Black consciousness, unity, self-determination, and identity. While many traditional Black pastors find aspects of Afrocentrism theologically unacceptable, one notes that many of them still admire the call of Black cultural nationalists for restoring and recovering what has been lost in the cultural destruction of Black heritage and life. Afrocentrism challenges the Black church to reflect on the kind of religious education theory and practice that reflect the cultural reality of the people served.

As Asante proclaims, this education must be an Afrocentric/African-centered education, which means "locating Blacks" within the context of their culture. African American Christians must be educated within a context and under a well-defined pedagogy that affirms, supports, and perpetuates their culture. Afrocentric education reacquaints African American Christians with the religious and cultural traditions of their ancestors, from ancient Egypt to modern Harlem. African American Christian education is called upon to reeducate us about the African presence and participation in Christian faith and history.

Afrocentric pastors call for a fundamental shift in the development of Christian education. Their task has to do with the process of shaping African American Christians within the confines of their own cultural reality. The pastor teaches and preaches from a worldview wherein Black people are located in the center. The pastor's task is to create an Afrocentric teaching/learning environment. The goal of Afrocentricity is to restore an appreciation for our culture and reclaim our history. African American Christians must receive an education that places them at the center of reality, interpreting and empowering a culturally affirming curriculum. Yolanda Y. Smith calls this a triple-heritage curriculum: African, African American, and Christian.

To keep Christian education relevant to the African American church, pastors must know the African background of the congregations they serve. An African-centered Christian is one who governs his or her understanding of Christ within the context of a history that includes Africans in the Bible. For example, African Americans benefit greatly from learning about Africans in the Bible who have shaped our faith. Africans in the Old Testament include Asenath (Gen. 41 and 46), Shiphrah (Ex. 1), Jethro (Ex. 3, 4, and 8), and Ebedmelech (Jer. 38). Those in the New Testament are Jesus, Peter, Paul, and the Ethiopian eunuch (Acts 8). The stories of Africans who have shaped our faith force us to focus on the history and culture of the Bible.

In addition, Afrocentric pastors' philosophy of Christian religious education actively supports and infuses traditional African principles and practices into Christian education; for example, the incorporation of the principles of Nguzo Saba found in the Kwanzaa celebration and rites of passage (initiation of youth into adulthood). These two Afrocentric cultural practices help to recapture the communal life for African American Christians. Effective Afrocentric teaching/preaching does not languish in cultural captivity. It is effective when it is anchored deeply in Black history and culture. In sum, there is a need for the development of African-centered churches to bear witness to the cultural dimension of ministry. Some Black pastors are taking the lead in educating their people, including Rev. Jeremiah Wright, Trinity United Church of Christ in Chicago; Carlyle Stewart, Hope United Methodist Church in Southfield, Michigan; and Rev. Frank Reid, Bethel AME in Maryland. But there are not enough Afrocentric pastor-teachers in the Black churches.

Conclusions

In conclusion, pastors are Christian educators. Pastoral leadership is key to all programs in Black churches; the pastor must intervene in the educational ministry of the church if it is to be significant. Pastors must insist that religious education is at the heart of the church's ministry. Our people are too often confused and unaware of the full gospel message for life and suffer from lack of teaching in our churches. Our sermons are often inspiring and uplifting, but without a vital teaching content.

The Black pastor is integral to the educational and spiritual life of the Black church. When Black pastors assume their responsibility as religious educators, they become biblical interpreters, cultural teachers, and discerner of gifts; prophetic agents, storytellers, and spiritual and sacramental educators. All of these pastoral roles provide opportunities for Christian education. Each of these roles is central to African American Christian education. Each reinforces the religious education of the pastor in the total work of the church. While the church must teach what Christ expects of us, pastors as educators must also create an accepting environment that encourages new members to remain involved with their new congregation, and that also teaches, through example, that God is love. In these efforts, the pastor's role remains a crucial one.

CHAPTER NINE

Reshaping the Future of African American Christian Religious Education

What is the role of Christian educational ministry as we look forward to the uncertainty of the future? What will AACRE in the United States look like in the year 2025? What will be the state and theology of African American Christian education? What will Black Christians contribute to the future church? Black Christian educators, pastors, and theologians must reflect more on their mission and ministry in the new millennium. The educational ministry of the church can make a difference in the twenty-first century.

A new century, a new commitment, provides a new challenge. Life will be different in the decades to come. The challenge for educational ministry to give direction to anticipated changes has never been greater. The work of Christian religious education involves many dimensions, each of which will encounter new challenges as the African American community moves into the twenty-first century. Here I imagine the possible future of religious education in the African American church. As African American Christians set their gaze on the start of the third millennium, certain issues seem to be particularly urgent. Three aspects of this challenge are worth examining: the challenge of ministry, the challenge of culture, and the challenge of theology.

Challenge of Ministry: Teaching and Training

One of the major challenges facing African American Christians in the twenty-first century is to redefine ministry. We must expand our understanding of the meaning of ministry and ordination. We must raise awareness of persons to a critical stage so that ministry takes on a new significance beyond the pastoral ministry. This section includes a brief overview of some of the issues and questions that ministry generates for religious education.

Ordination and Christian Education Ministry

One of the challenges facing the Black church in the twenty-first century is pertaining to the role and status of education in the church, including call to ministry, accountability, empowerment, educational requirements, and justice for those who serve in this capacity, especially in nonordained positions. The present is a time of evaluating ministry as it has been shaped and formed by the eighteenth, nineteenth, and twentieth centuries of African American Christianity. The twenty-first century must be different. For a revival of hope to take place, Black churches must accept the value/call of the educational ministry of the church on par with pastoral/preaching ministry. The Black church needs to consider ordaining Christian educators.

Many Christian education directors, superintendents, and teachers begin their journey to ministry in the church school of the local congregation. They believe that their ministry and identification with the laity are definitive in living out their call as educator. Other educators (missionary, lay, or youth) are called to serve within the ordered life of the church. Ordination is one way by which God's people—the church—explicitly authorize critical acts of ministry and by which they request accountability.

Ordination ought to be an authentic personal commitment to God, to offer the gifts that God bestows for service. When men and women feel a call to the ministry of teaching they should be ordained. For example, I was ordained a deacon and an elder in the African Methodist Episcopal Church, though I expected to make teaching my life work. I asked for ordination because I believe that the church should be alerted to the possibility of equal status for educators. We are indeed commanded to love God with our minds.

The ordination of Christian men and women should not be limited to preaching. We have a right to exercise the full instrumental manifestation of God. For too long the Black church has only ordained preachers. In the twenty-first century it must extend the opportunity to participate fully and in all forms of religious expression and ordination. I believe that the ministry of the gospel can take different forms—all with the common purpose of proclaiming the gospel and offering the means of grace through teaching. I am not suggesting that all educators are called to or will ultimately seek ordination. I believe that appropriate policy changes can clarify and enhance the relationships between educators and the churches they serve, and can address various justice concerns of which we are aware.

Clergy Education

There is a critical need for effective Christian education today. The Black church calls for an urgent response in the realm of leadership and clergy development. The proliferation of mega-churches has caused traditional Black denominational churches to reflect on the effectiveness (or lack thereof) of their teaching and educational ministries. In the twenty-first century more and more clergy understand the necessity of formal religious training and are heading toward Bible schools and seminaries in order to be equipped with the tools to assist them in their charge for ministry. Retired professor of Christian education Jonathan Jackson says that Christian education is that ministry that supports and undergirds all the other ministries in the church. If Dr. Jackson is accurate, then that poses several questions for institutions that train clergy: First, are Christian education courses offered as core classes or electives? Second, are students trained in developing effective Christian education ministries in their local churches? How extensive is the training? Third, what sources and resources are students required to use in Christian education courses? Fourth, are the literary sources recent and do they have an interdisciplinary concentration? Fifth, is the curriculum designed to help clergy develop Christian education ministries that have a social and cultural focus? And sixth, do the Christian education classes help students synthesize the other areas of study so as to make them applicable to practical ministry? These are just some of the questions that deserve attention if the church is to assist clergy in growing educationally and spiritually.

The Profession of Christian Education

Today, African American Christian education associations provide their members with the most current information and trends in Christian education through its resources, publications, and networking system. Membership guarantees that one can find fellowship with other Christian educators and discuss a variety of ways to grow both personally and professionally. Tomorrow's challenge for these Christian education ministry organizations is for them to develop and mature as full-fledged ministry organizations for Christian educators, organizations that can review church personnel policies that exclude Christian educators, encourage congregations to elect Christian educators as elders, and recommend to strengthen the certification process, thus encouraging the ministry of the educator within the local congregation.

Every Black denomination maintains, under one name or another, a national board of Christian education that is ordinarily charged with responsibility for devising and recommending programs and producing the leadership development and curriculum materials needed for their implementation in the churches. In addition, some Christian education departments offer a wide variety of services and publications. In response to the calls for trained, certified, and professional Christian educators, a few denominational boards of Christian education have established Christian education ministry organizations or associations. In the ministry of Christian education, one of the most significant recent achievements has been the establishment of Christian education associations. Both the African Methodist Episcopal Church (Fellowship of Church Educators) and African Methodist Episcopal Zion Church (Association of Christian Educators) organized associations. Since Christian religious education must take place at the local level if it is to be significant at all, the associations' work in certifying, training, and assisting in spiritual growth and fellowship is a valuable asset to the current education efforts of churches.

The Holy Spirit and Teaching

Another challenge facing the Black church is the rise of neo-Pentecostalism/Charismatic renewal. Black theologians, pastors, and educators are alerting persons to realize that God is working in a variety of ways to usher in the reign of God. A spiritual renewal is under way and will not go away. A spiritual renewal is being called for. The goal is clear. The methods of achieving that goal will be varied. God's spirit is at work. Christians experience the indwelling presence of the Holy Spirit in their lives. The work of the Holy Spirit transforms all dimensions of life, including the ministry of teaching.

According to Robert W. Pazmiño, the Holy Spirit undergirds the ministry of teaching. As a spiritual gift, teaching is a ministry of instructing and clarifying God's will and our response to God under the influence of the Holy Spirit. In Pazmiño's work *God Our Teacher*, he proposes an educational framework for considering the person and work of the Spirit of God in three phases of preparation, instruction, and evaluation.[1] Using this model enables Christian educators to see the work of the Holy Spirit in their own teaching ministry. There is a great need today for anointed teaching. Teaching requires partnership with the Holy Spirit if conversion, sanctification, and spiritual growth are ever to be possible.

Women, Ministry, and Education

We come now to the most controversial question in regard to the place of women in the Black church. Black pastors and churches have differences of opinion on this subject. The term *ministry* here refers to all its aspects—in the volunteer and professional activities of men and women in the church. Some Black pastors agree that it ought to be done; however, more disagree with the idea that women should be ordained to pastor. The Black Pentecostal and Baptist church have been hampered by theological objections to ordination. The Black Methodist Church has not been hampered by theological objections to ordination, but by aspects of its connectional system, especially placement of clergywomen in major pulpits, which until recently prevented full annual conference participation that would assure full inclusion of women in decision-making positions.

Ironically, the church accepts Black women in educational ministry and views them as equal partners with Black men in the teaching ministry. God indeed calls all people, male and female, to ministry. God's salvation is for the entire community. Black men and women together have gifts that are vital for what Jacquelyn Grant calls a "holistic liberation" of the Black church and community. As Delores C. Carpenter says, this is a "Time of Honor." More and more women are enrolled in seminary, graduating, being ordained, and setting their sights on full-time ministry.

There are stirrings toward greater acceptance of clergywomen in many churches today. As Delores C. Carpenter has stated, "For African American clergy women, the ultimate honor comes whenever they can use their gifts and graces to the fullest and in the service of God's people."[2] We must wait and see.

Challenge of Culture: Curriculum and Technology

Another challenge facing African American Christians is cultural diversity and technology. The concern is to make certain that the content of curriculum be relevant to the global experience of Blacks and to bridge the digital divide among religious educators and the church.

The Struggle for Cultural Inclusion

AACRE involves the awareness of the cultural diversity. What are the prospects for African American Christians in the twenty-first century, when the United States will be actually a demographic multiracial/multicultural society? How will these forthcoming demographic changes affect our thinking about culture and ministry? What will the changes mean for African American Christian education? The cultural milieu in the United States at this time of the millennium includes a conspicuously new ethnic and racial identity. Based on the Middle Series Census Bureau projections, by about 2050, Whites will represent only a slight majority (53 percent) of the population. According to the projections, that population of three hundred ninety-four million will be almost 24 percent Hispanic, 14 percent Black, 8 percent Asian, and 1 percent Native American. The demographic and social realities of life among racial and ethnic groups suggest a new vision of a possible future society.

The goal is a multiracial/multicultural civil society in which pluralistic coexistence is the hallmark. A future of multicultural harmony in the United States depends strongly on the extent to which church and society include different ethnicities and races. Religion can contribute to harmony by viewing ethnicity as a gift to the church. The challenge of cultural diversity confronts us with the question of the need for a multicultural religious education. Black pastors and educators increasingly experience the persistent request for culturally sensitive resources and leadership. The future calls for new images and metaphors to fire the imagination of teachers and writers. It also involves the inclusion of cultural experiences in the church that have been previously excluded.

Here a major agenda for the future would involve development of a multicultural view of Christian education and evangelism. The goal would be to make more visible the presence of the cultural diversity of the Black church in curricular resources and the hiring, appointing, and electing of African, Caribbean, and South America representatives to denominational and regional agency staffs. It also involves evangelization to new non-Black communities, especially Hispanics who are now the largest minority in the United States. To draw upon the educational experience of the variety of cultural experience in the church would require the training of teachers to recognize and incorporate various cultural traditions into their own teaching. These efforts would break through our present view of African American religious education.

Integrating Technology into Christian Education

African Americans exist in a world in which rapid technological change can frustrate and challenge those seeking to stay abreast of the latest innovations in computer and communication technology. An emerging question for African American Christians is how to harness the holy use of technology on behalf of religious values. A new learning context is now being created through the interest in long-distance and lifelong learning, greatly facilitated by current information technology development. The information superhighway widens every day, and technological advances emerge with dizzying speed. These innovations, however, present new challenges and opportunities for Christian educators. Cyberspace communities can now form and speak to one another via the Internet.

As former executive director of Christian education for the African Methodist Episcopal Church, I challenged the church to be concerned about technology and ministry. I led the way with computers and Internet use for the educational ministry of the church. I was first in using video projection in making my departmental report to the 45th Quadrennial Session of the General Conference. In addition, I helped to develop and provide worship and Christian education software for pastors, musicians, and Christian educators. The challenge to pastors, educators, and leaders is to help the local congregation use the new technology for equipping their members for ministry in the present age.

What is clear is that without an African American Christian presence on the Internet, major cultural conversations will move forward without the African American voice as partner. The development of online Black religious education literature is crucial to bridging the digital divide between religious educators and the church. African American Christian education will also need to include technologies as part of the curriculum and content for the sake of having a voice in forming and shaping the technologies as they develop. This does not mean that all Christian educators must become experts in science and technology, although they need to become better informed and more widely read.

Challenge of Theology

One the most important issues of African American life concerns the struggle of Black people to define and embrace their Blackness or Africanness. Can I be Black and Christian? Without such awareness there is, I believe, limited scope for a clear understanding of the necessity for a theology for Black Christian education. The discovery of Black selfhood is primarily a theological task. Black theology has served as the essential theological tool and first point of departure in the creation of a new paradigm for the Christian education of Black people. Black Christians hope to contribute a Black perspective to the developing theology of Christian education. If Black Christians want to contribute to a present and future theology of Christian education in the Black church, they must be well-informed of the traditions that have gone before them in the history of Africans, African Americans, and Christians. A vanguard of dedicated African American seminarians, laypeople, educators, pastors, and theologians are moving forward in the church in the United States. In our midst there are new visions of the meaning of God, Jesus, the Spirit, church, human experience, and the cross–born of a history of enslavement, oppression, and struggle for liberation.

Constructing a Black Theology of Christian Education

Several years ago Ronald F. Thiemann challenged theological educators to develop a constructive theology for the public square. Drawing on Thiemann categories, we can establish a framework for what such a theology might look like for Christian education. Theology of Christian education emerging out of critical reflection and faith can help to overcome the gap between the academy and church, between the scholarly and pastoral that so bedevils theological education.[3] Here I offer a conception of a theology of Christian education as critical, formative, communal, and liberation activity that can serve as the integrative factor in both the local church and seminary teaching.

Black theology of Christian education is a critical activity. Black and womanist theologies offer critical reflection and new standards to which theologians and educators make their critical judgments. Critical theorists like Cornell West and Anthony Pinn have provided an important body of scholarship analyzing the role of critique as a form of reflection that combines theory and practice. I believe we need to engage in serious conversation with the Afro-humanist tradition as a source of theological reflection.

Black theology of Christian education is a formative activity. Here theology seeks to assist in the formation of religious identity and character. Black theological educators must be engaged in reflection upon religious practices. Scholars like Ann Wimberly and Barbara Holmes in their works attend to the practices of worship in African American churches. In analyzing the structures and language of the practices, they identify the basic convictions and value commitments that shape the way Blacks actually live their lives.

Black theology of Christian education is a communal activity. Theology as communal activity does its work in the midst of Black communities and their traditions. Such a theology acknowledges the strength inherent in historic Black values, which place a premium on the good of the community rather than the good of the individual. This perspective emphasizes a communal understanding of God and humanity. Theology as "communal deliberation" enhances a sense of spiritual and social belonging. Black theologians and educators must recapture the sense of community and make a concerted effort to help African Americans resist tendencies toward individualism.

Black theology of Christian education is a liberational activity. Theology as liberation is the development of critical consciousness and empowerment to act for social advocacy, action, and mobilization in line with the prophetic witness of the gospel. In African American theology the emphasis is on "faith in freedom." Freedom is essential to God's character. For African American Christians the focus is what that freedom means in relation to the struggle of Black people for liberation. The process used to discern meaning calls for critical reflection on their experience of injustice.

Teaching and Forming Youth

Another major challenge for tomorrow's African American Christian educators is teaching and forming youth. African Americans need to broaden the struggle for human freedom to embrace the concerns of Black youth. The challenge to church and theological education is preparing men and women for youth ministry. Youth ministry remains an overlooked and/or ignored arena of service. Leadership training in youth ministry for clergy has been limited. Clergy tend to view their congregations as adult-oriented. More attention is paid to programs for youth than ministries to youth. In addition, Black seminary education curriculums rarely offer courses in youth ministry. Full-time youth pastors are desperately needed in this present age. By placing a greater emphasis on the vocation, youth ministry offers the holistic connection that Jesus embraced when he received youth in his arms and blessed them. In other words, when we receive God's creative word in the flesh–God the Son (or Child)–we receive God the Child incarnate.[4]

Formation issues challenge us to develop more liberative models of theology and youth ministry. Jacquelyn Grant believes that the problems with Black youth ministry are essentially theological.[5] Jacquelyn Grant and Janet Pais articulate a theology of liberation for all humankind that includes children and youth. This is the theology of God the "Child," Christ the child incarnate and liberator, and the Holy Spirit the transformer. A liberation theology in this context must be a theology that acknowledges youth value and values their feelings and perceptions of reality. Among Black youth their understanding of contemporary hip-hop culture is crucial. Therefore, a theological understanding of Black youth ministry will enhance the prospects of a change in adult attitudes toward relationships with Black youth. In sum, the focus must be squarely on youth–their expectations, needs, and hopes. New alternatives and practices concerning youth ministry in the church must be established.

Concluding Reflections

In the concluding days of writing this final chapter, I pause to reflect on my search for a better understanding of the process of how we educate. Attention to remembering the voices of our ancestors, the stories of faith, the theologies, and approaches of religious education has enhanced my understanding and contributed to my becoming a better teacher. The learnings that I have adopted from our scholars, pastors, theologians, and lay leaders have often provided resources for making sense of those educational and spiritual experiences that make all of life an adventure.

Such experiences contribute to my firm conviction that careful attention to Christian education is a powerful gift of God. I believe my task, as educator, is to call to our attention the need for Christian education; to be the first among equals in enabling the African American church to pride itself on having an intellectual life. This means that the value of being a thinking church must be elevated, not as a superior reality to that of feeling, but equally as rich and rewarding. So, it is a challenge.

After almost thirty-five years of teaching and researching in Christian education, I realize that the future of this exciting field cannot be a simple continuation of the past. We are standing at a new threshold where the critical searchlight of womanist and gender questions, as well as spiritual and cultural concerns, compel us to rethink our knowledge positions and practical commitments. To have a viable future, AACRE will depend on whether it has sufficient flexibility to respond to different ideas, to a different context of study, and to the need for a different purpose. Ideas from the past will have to make room for new paradigms, for new theoretical models and approaches in understanding the study of African American religious education, but also for new practical considerations.

AACRE will continue to make a contribution to the life of the academy and the church. Besides its contribution to the ongoing growth and knowledge, this discipline also possesses tremendous resources for helping people to develop a holistic way of life. Studying Black religion and religious education can become a means for feeding the zest for life and for enabling people to live better and fuller lives. Religious education can free people's minds and hearts. It can link the academic endeavors of religious scholars within seminaries to the practical concerns of ministry.

The teaching of Christian education in the African American experience enriches our understanding of African American religion. Perhaps the greatest challenge is to find some wisdom to live by, as well as some wise ways in which to study AACRE. Given all these challenges, the future looks exciting. African American Christian educators should play an ever-increasing role in calling the Black church to a deeper awareness of its gifts, especially teaching. African American Christians must not lose sight of their deeply spiritual vision. In sum, our task as religious educators continues to be that of helping people of faith mature in faith, to be educated by faith, and to live by faith.

Notes

Chapter 1: Understanding the Discipline

[1]Grant Shockley, "The Black Experience and Black Religion," *The Black Church* (1974): 94–97; "Christian Education and the Black Church: A Contextual Approach," *Journal of the Interdenominational Theological Center* 2 (1974): 75–85.

[2]Gromes Eannes De Azurara, *The Chronicle of the Discovery and Conquest of Guinea* (London: Hakluyt Society, 1896), 150–51.

[3]Charles C. Jones, *The Religious Instruction of the Negroes in the United States* (New York: Oxford University Press, 1842), 127.

[4]Grant Shockley, "Christian Education and the Black Religious Experience," in *Ethnicity in the Education of the Church,* ed. Charles R. Foster (Nashville: Scarritt, 1987).

[5]This section relies on philosopher-historian of Black culture Maulana Karenga's categories of analysis that characterized the Black student movement. Maulana Karenga, *Introduction to Black Studies* (Inglewood, Calif.: Kawaida Publications, 1982).

[6]Shockley, "Christian Education and the Black Religious Experience," 75.

[7]Charles C. Jones, *The Religious Instruction of the Negroes in the United States;* Carter G. Woodson, *The Education of the Negro Prior to 1861* (New York: G.O. Putnam, 1915); Benjamin E. Mays and Joseph Washington, *The Negro's Church* (New York: Russell and Russell, 1933); E. Franklin Frazier, *The Negro Church in America* (New York: Schocken Books, 1964); James D. Tyms, *The Rise of Religious Education Among Negro Baptists* (New York: Exposition Press, 1966); Olli Alho, *The Religion of the Slaves* (Helsinki: Academia Scientarium Fennica, 1976); Olivia P. Stokes, *The Educational Role of Black Churches in the 70's and 80's* (Philadelphia: United Church Press, 1973); Charles R. Foster, Ethel R. Johnson, and Grant S. Shockley, *Christian Education Journey of Black Americans: Past, Present, Future* (Nashville: Discipleship Resources, 1985).

[8]Shockley, "Christian Education and the Black Church," 75.

[9]Stokes, *Educational Role of Black Churches,* 65.

[10]C. Eric Lincoln and Lawrence H. Mamiya, *The Black Church in the African American Experience* (Durham, N.C.: Duke University Press, 1990).

[11]Joseph V. Crockett, *Teaching Scripture from an African American Perspective* (Nashville: Discipleship Resources, 1990); Anne S. Wimberly, *Soul Stories: African American Christian Education* (Nashville: Abingdon Press, 1994).

[12]Yolanda Smith, *Reclaiming the Spirituals: New Possibilities for African American Christian Education* (Cleveland: Pilgrim Press, 2004); Anne Wimberly, *Nurturing Faith and Hope: Black Worship as a Model for Christian Education* (Cleveland: Pilgrim Press, 2004); Barbara A. Holmes, *Joy Unspeakable: Contemplative Practices of the Black Church* (Minneapolis: Fortress Press, 2004

Chapter 2: Reconnecting with Our History

[1]C. Eric Lincoln and Lawrence H. Mamiya, *The Black Church in the African American Experience* (Durham, N.C.: Duke University Press, 1990), 52–53.

[2]E. Franklin Frazier, *The Negro Church in America* (New York: Schocken Books, 1964), 16.

[3]Dwight N. Hopkins, *Shoes That Fit Our Feet: Sources for a Constructive Black Theology* (Maryknoll, N.Y.: Orbis Books, 1993), 3.

[4]Norman Yetman, *Life Under the "Peculiar Institution," Selections from the Slave Narrative Collection* (New York: Holt, Rinehert and Winston, 1970), 53.

[5]Howard Thurman, *The Inward Journey* (Richmond, Ind.: Friends United Press, 1961), 7.

[6]Gayraud Wilmore, *Black Religion and Black Radicalism* (Maryknoll, N.Y.: Orbis Books, 1998), 6.

[7]Yosef Ben-Jochannan, *African Origins of the Major Western Religions* (New York: Alkebulan Books, 1970), 164.

[8]John Jackson, *Man, God, and Civilization* (New Hyde Park, N.Y.: University Books, 1972), 123.

⁹John S. Mbiti, *African Religions and Philosophy* (New York: Praeger, 1969), 275.
¹⁰Ibid.,141.

¹¹John Blassingame, *The Slave Community* (New York: Oxford University Press, 1972), and Andrew Billingsley, *Climbing Jacob's Ladder: The Enduring Legacy of African American Families* (New York: Simon & Schuster, 1992).

¹²Yolanda Smith, "Preserving Faith and Culture in the African American Church: A Tri-Collaborative Model for Teaching the Triple-Heritage Through the African American Spirituals" (Ph.D. diss., Claremont School of Theology, 1998), 117.

¹³Ibid., 119.

¹⁴W.E.B. Dubois, ed., *The Negro Church* (Atlanta: Atlanta University Press, 1903), 8.

¹⁵Olli Alho, *The Religion of the Slaves: study of the religious tradition and behaviour of plantation slaves in the United States, 1830-1865* (Helsinki: Academia Scientiarum Fennica, 1976), 52–53.

¹⁶Norman B. Harlan, *Encyclopedia of World Methodism*, vol.1, (Nashville: United Methodist Publishing House, 1974), 67.

¹⁷Anne Boylan, *Sunday School: The Formation of an American Institution 1790–1880* (New Haven, Conn.: Yale University, 1988), 23.

¹⁸Carter G. Woodson, *The Education of the Negro Prior to 1861* (New York: Arno Press, 1968), 124.

¹⁹Boylan, *Sunday School,* 29.

²⁰Information from Wilberforce University Web site, http://www.wilberforce.edu/student_life/library_archives_timeline.html.

²¹Charles S. Smith, as quoted in Kenneth Hill, *Charles S. Smith, a Portrait: Sable Son of God* (Nashville: AMEC Publishing, 1993), 11–12.

²²Ohal H. Lakey, *The History of the CME Church* (Memphis: CME Publishing, 1996), 397.

²³William J. Walls, *The African Methodist Episcopal Zion Church: Reality of the Black Church* (Charlotte, N.C.: AME Zion Publishing House, 1974), 288.

²⁴Mark L. Chapman, *Christianity on Trial: African American Religious Thought Before and After Black Power* (Maryknoll, N.Y.: Orbis Books, 1996), 100.

²⁵Albert Cleage, *Black Christian Nationalism* (New York: William Morrow and Co., 1972), 213.

²⁶Therion E. Cobb, *Adult Teacher Quarterly* (Nashville,: AMEC Publishing, 1975), 33.
²⁷Ibid.

Chapter 3: Reading, Interpreting, and Teaching the Bible in the African American Church

¹Stephen Beck Reid, *Experience and Tradition: A Primer in Black Biblical Hermeneutics* (Nashville: Abingdon Press, 1990), 11.

²Anne Wimberly, *Soul Stories: African American Christian Education* (Nashville: Abingdon Press, 1994), 116.

³Oneal Sandidge, *A Manual for Teacher Training in the African American Church* (Evanston, Ill.: Chicago Spectrum Press, 1996); Keith A. Chism, *Christian Education for the African American Community* (Nashville: Discipleship Resources, 1995); and Sid Smith, *Reaching the Black Community Through the Sunday School* (Nashville: Convention Press, 1984).

⁴Joseph Crockett, *Teaching Scripture from an African American Perspective* (Nashville: Discipleship Resources, 1989) and Wimberly, *Soul Stories.*

⁵Vincent Wimbush, *The Bible and African Americans* (Minneapolis: Fortress Press, 2003).

⁶Flora Bridges, *Resurrection Song: African American Spirituality* (New York: Orbis Books, 2001).

⁷Albert J. Raboteau, *Slave Religion: The 'Invisible Institution' in the Antebellum South* (New York: Oxford University Press, 1978), 99.

⁸Wimbush, *The Bible and African Americans,* 36.

⁹Benjamin Quarles, ed., *Frederick Douglass,* Great Lives Observed (Englewood Cliffs, N.J.: Prentice Hall, 1968), 108.

¹⁰Peter J. Parris, *The Social Teaching of the Black Churches* (Philadelphia: Fortress Press, 1985), 93.

[11]Wimbush, *The Bible and African Americans*, 36.

[12]David Walker, "David Walker's Appeal," in *Witness for Freedom: African American Voices on Race, Slavery and Emancipation*, ed. C. Peter Ripley (Chapel Hill, N.C.: University of North Carolina Press, 1993), 44.

[13]Wimbush, *The Bible and African Americans*, 37.

[14]James D. Tyms, *The Rise of Religious Education Among Negro Baptists* (New York: Exposition Press, 1965), 89.

[15]Charles B. Copher, *Black Biblical Studies: An Anthology of Charles B. Copher* (Chicago: Black Light Fellowship, 1993), 134.

[16]Ibid., 134.

[17]Iris V. Cully, *The Bible on Christianity Education* (Minneapolis: Fortress Press, 1985), 1.

[18]Wimberly, *Soul Stories*, 38.

[19]Thomas Hoyt, "Biblical Scholarship for the Black Church Tradition," in *Stony the Road We Trod: African American Biblical Interpretation*, ed. Cain Hope Felder (Minneapolis: Fortress Press, 1991), 24.

[20]Ibid., 25.

[21]Crockett, *Teaching Scripture from an African American Perspective.*

[22]Wimberly, *Soul Stories*, 33.

[23]Delores S. Williams, *Sisters in the Wilderness: The Challenge of Womanist God-Talk* (New York: Orbis Books, 1993).

[24]Bishop Joseph A. Johnson, *A Proclamation Theology* (Shreveport, La.: Fourth District Press, 1977).

[25]Ibid., 44.

[26]Michael Brown, *Blackening of the Bible: Aims of African American Biblical Scholarship* (Harrisburg, Pa.: Trinity Press International, 2004), 20.

[27]James Cone, *A Black Theology of Liberation* (Philadelphia: Lippincott, 1970), 18.

[28]James Evans, *We Have Been Believers: An African-American Systematic Theology* (Minneapolis: Fortress Press, 1992), 51.

[29]J. Deotis Roberts, *Liberation and Reconciliation* (Maryknoll, N.Y.: Orbis Books, 1994), 11.

[30]Reid, *Experience and Tradition.*

[31]Thomas Hoyt, "Biblical Scholarship for the Black Church Tradition," in *Stony the Road We Trod*, 24.

[32]Brown, *Blackening of the Bible*, and Wimbush, *The Bible and African Americans.*

[33]Alice Walker, *In Search of Our Mother's Gardens* (San Diego, Calif.: Harcourt Brace Jovanovich, 1983), xi–xii.

[34]Renita Weems, *Just a Sister Away: A Womanist Vision of Women's Revelation in the Bible* (San Diego, Calif.: Lura Media Press, 1988).

[35]Thomas Hoyt, "Biblical Scholarship for the Black Church Tradition," in *Stony the Road We Trod*, 24.

[36]Reid, *Experience and Tradition*, 18.

[37]Wimbush, *The Bible and African Americans*, 12.

[38]H. Edward Everding Jr., "A Hermeneutical Approach to Educational Theory," in *Christian Education in an Era of Change*, ed. Marvin Taylor (Nashville: Abingdon Press), 41.

[39]James D. Smart, *Teaching Ministry of the Church* (Philadelphia: Westminster Press, 1964), 19.

[40]Christine Eaton Blair, *The Art of Teaching the Bible: A Practical Guide for Adults* (Louisville: Geneva Press, 2001), 3.

[41]Reid, *Experience and Tradition*, 13.

[42]Walter McCray, *The Black Presence in the Bible* (Chicago: Black Light Fellowship, 1990), xi.

Chapter 4: Hearing and Understanding Contemporary African American Theological Voices

[1]This is a reference to Gustavo Gutiérrez, *We Drink from Our Own Wells: The Spiritual Journey of a People* (Maryknoll, N.Y.: Orbis Books, 2003).

[2]Patricia O'Connell Killen and John DeBeer, as quoted in Richard Quebedeaux, *The Young Evangelicals: Revolution in Orthodoxy* (New York: Harper and Row, 1974).

[3]William H. Bentley, "Bible Believers in the Black Community," in *The Evangelicals,* ed. David F. Wells and John D. Woodbridge (Grand Rapids, Mich.: Baker Book House, 1975).

[4]Ibid.

[5]Ronald E. Roberts, "Leadership Studies in Black Evangelicalism" (Unpublished D.Min. diss., Dallas Theological Seminary, 1985), 17.

[6]Anthony T. Evans, *Biblical Theology and the Black Experience* (Dallas: Black Evangelistic Enterprise, 1977), 3.

[7]Anthony P. Pinn, *Making the Gospel Plain: The Writings of Bishop Reverdy C. Ransom* (Harrisburg, Pa.: Trinity Press International, 1999).

[8]Stephen W. Angell and Anthony B. Pinn, *Social Protest Thought in the African Methodist Episcopal Church, 1862–1939* (Knoxville, Tenn.: University of Tennessee Press, 2000), 310.

[9]James H. Evans, *We Have Been Believers: An African American Systematic Theology* (Minneapolis: Fortress Press, 1992), 7.

[10]Henry H. Mitchell, *Black Preaching* (Philadelphia: J.B. Lippincott Company, 1970), 196.

[11]Bishop Joseph A. Johnson, *Proclamation Theology* (Shreveport, La.: Fourth District Press, 1977).

[12]Ibid., 30.

[13]Ibid., 152.

[14]Ibid., 132.

[15]Mitchell, *Black Preaching,* 196.

[16]Edward P. Wimberly, *Pastoral Care in the Black Church* (Nashville: Abingdon Press, 1979).

[17]James Forbes, *The Holy Spirit and Preaching* (Nashville: Abingdon Press, 1989), 9.

[18]Carlyle F. Stewart, *African American Church Growth* (Nashville: Abingdon Press, 1994).

[19]James H. Harris, *Preaching Liberation* (Minneapolis: Fortress Press, 1995), 21–32.

[20]Cleophus J. LaRue, *The Heart of Black Preaching* (Louisville: Westminster John Knox Press, 2000), 123.

[21]Dwight N. Hopkins, *Introducing Black Theology of Liberation* (Maryknoll, N.Y.: Orbis Books, 1999). Chapters 2 and 3 of this work give an excellent overview of the major Black theologians. Much of my discussion will be based on his analysis.

[22]Joseph R. Washington Jr., *Black Religion: The Negro and Christianity in the United States* (Boston: Beacon Press, 1964.)

[23]James Cone, *A Black Theology of Liberation* (Philadelphia: J.B. Lippincott, 1970).

[24]James Cone, *God of the Oppressed* (New York: Seabury Press, 1975), 18.

[25]Albert Cleage, *The Black Messiah* (New York: Sheed and Ward, 1968).

[26]J. Deotis Roberts, *Liberation and Reconciliation: A Black Theology* (Philadelphia: Westminster Press, 1971).

[27]Major Jones, *Black Awareness: A Theology of Hope* (Nashville: Abingdon Press, 1971).

[28]Gayraud S. Wilmore, *Black Religion and Black Radicalism* (Garden City, N.J.: Doubleday, 1972).

[29]Grant Shockley, "Black Theology and Religious Education," in *Theologies of Religious Education,* ed. Randolph Crump Miller (Birmingham, Ala.: Religious Education Press, 1995); and Olivia Pearl Stokes, "Black Theology: A Challenge to Religious Education," in *Religious Education and Theology,* ed. Norma Thompson (Birmingham, Ala.: Religious Education Press, 1982).

[30]Diana L. Hayes, *And Still We Rise: An Introduction to Black Liberation Theology* (New York: Paulist Press, 1996).

[31]Earl R. Riggins Jr., *Dark Symbols, Obscure Signs: God, Self, and Community in the Slave Mind* (Maryknoll, N.Y.: Orbis Books, 1993).

[32]Dwight Hopkins and George Cummings, eds., *Cut Loose Your Stammering Tongues: Black Theology and the Slave Narratives* (Maryknoll, N.Y.: Orbis Books, 1989).

[33]Cain Hope Felder, *Troubling Biblical Waters: Race, Class and Family* (Maryknoll, N.Y.: Orbis Books, 1969).

[34]James Evans Jr., *We Have Been Believers: An African American Systematic Theology* (Minneapolis: Fortress Press, 1991).

[35]Will Coleman, *Tribal Talk: Black Theology, Hermeneutics, and African/American Ways of "Telling the Story"* (University Park, Pa.: Penn State Press, 2000).

[36]Kelly Brown Douglas, *The Black Christ* (Maryknoll, N.Y.: Orbis Books, 1994).

[37]Anne Wimberly, *Soul Stories: African American Christian Education* (Nashville: Abingdon Press, 1994).

[38]Hopkins, *Introducing Black Theology of Liberation,* 52.

[39]Ibid., 65.

[40]Molefi Kete Asante, *The Afrocentric Idea* (Philadelphia: Temple University Press, 1987).

[41]James H. Cone and Gayraud Wilmore, *Black Theology: A Documentary History, Volume II 1980–1992* (Maryknoll, N.Y.: Orbis Books, 1993).

[42]As cited in James S. Tinney, "William J. Seymour: Father of Modern-Day Pentecostalism," *Journal of the ITC* (1972): 34–44.

[43]Cheryl J. Sanders, *Saints in Exile: The Holiness-Pentecostal Experience in African American Religion and Culture* (New York: Oxford University Press, 1996), 15.

[44]James Tinney "The Blackness of Pentecostalism," *Spirit* 3, no. 2 (1979): 27–36.

[45]Robert Beckford, "Black Pentecostals and Black Politics" in *Pentecostals After a Century: Global Perspectives on a Movement in Transition,* ed. Allan H. Anderson and Walter J. Hollenweger (Sheffield, U.K.: Sheffield Academic Press, 1999), 48–49.

[46]The speech was the keynote address of the conference titled "Into the World: Black Pentecostalism in Global Contexts," It took place on March 18, 2005, at Harvard Divinity School. For further information on this event, see the *Harvard University Gazette,* March 24, 2005.

[47]James Forbes, "Shall We Call This Dream Progressive Pentecostalism," *Spirit* 1, no.1 (1977): 31–35.

[48]Sanders, *Saints in Exile,* 15.

[49]C. Eric Lincoln and Lawrence Mamiya, *The Black Church in African American Experience* (Durham, N.C.: Duke University Press, 1990).

[50]Walter J. Hollenweger, "The Black Roots of Pentecostalism," in Beckford, *Pentecostals After a Century: Global Perspectives on a Movement in Transition,* 36–41.

[51]Vashti M. McKenzie, *Not Without a Struggle: Leadership Development for African American Women In Ministry* (Cleveland: United Church Press, 1996).

[52]Jacquelyn Grant, "Black Theology and the Black Woman," in Cone and Wilmore, *Black Theology: A Documentary History,* 418–43.

[53]Delores Williams, *Sisters in the Wilderness* (Maryknoll, N.Y.: Orbis Books, 1993).

[54]Delores Williams, Jacquelyn Grant, Katie Cannon, Emile Townes, Renita Weems, Cheryl Saunders, Kelly Brown Douglas, Jamie Phelps, and Diana L. Hayes.

[55]Jacquelyn Grant, *White Women's Christ and Black Women's Jesus* (Atlanta: Scholars Press, 1989), 209.

[56]Lynn Westfield, *Dear Sisters: A Womanist Practice of Hospitality* (Cleveland: Pilgrim Press, 2001), 2.

[57]Yolanda Smith, *Reclaiming the Spirituals: New Possibilities for African American Christian Education* (Cleveland: Pilgrim Press, 2004).

[58]McKenzie, *Not Without a Struggle,* 54.

[59]Robin Maas and Gabriel O'Donnell, *Spiritual Traditions for the Contemporary Church* (Nashville: Abingdon Press, 1990).

[60]Jamie Phelps, "Black Spirituality," in *Spiritual Traditions for the Contemporary Church,* ed. Robin Maas and Gabriel O'Donnell (Nashville, Abingdon Press, 1990), 333.

[61]Flora Wilson Bridges, *Resurrection Song: African American Spirituality* (Maryknoll, N.Y.: Orbis Books, 2001).

[62]Calvin E. Bruce, "Black Spirituality, Language, and Faith," in *Religious Education* 4 (July/August, 1976): 63–76.

[63]Ibid.

[64]Bridges, *Resurrection Song,* 3.

[65]Father Paisius Altschul, *An Unbroken Circle: Linking Ancient African Christianity to the African American Experience* (St. Louis: Brotherhood of St. Louis, 1997).

[66]Carlyle F. Stewart, III, *Soul Survivors: An African American Spirituality* (Louisville: Westminster John Knox Press, 1997).

[67]Bridges, *Resurrection Song,* 43.

[68]Phelps, "Black Spirituality," 333.

[69]Howard Thurman, *Deep River and the Negro Spiritual Speaks of Life and Death* (Richmond, Ind.: Friends United Press, 1975).

[70]Calvin E. Bruce, "Black Spirituality and Theological Method," *The Journal of the Interdenominational Theological Center* 1 (Spring 1976): 63–76.

[71]Luther E. Smith and Howard Thurman, *The Mystic as Prophet* (Richmond, Ind.: Friends United Press, 1991).

[72]Howard Thurman, *Luminous Darkness* (New York: Harper and Row, 1965).

[73]Howard Thurman, *Meditations of the Heart* (Richmond, Ind.: Friends United Press, 1953), 29.

Chapter 5: Understanding the Relationship between Theology and the Dynamics of Educating African American Christians

[1]James H. Harris, *Pastoral Theology: A Black Church Perspective* (Minneapolis: Augsburg Fortress Press, 1991), 58.

[2]Cheryl J. Sanders, *Saints in Exile: Holiness-Pentecostal Experience in African American Religion and Culture* (New York: Oxford University Press, 1996), 123.

[3]Padraic O'Hare, "Religious Education: Neo-Orthodox Influence and Empirical Corrective," *Religious Education* 73 (November-December 1978): 627.

[4]Sara Little, "Theology and Religious Education," in *Foundations for Christian Education,* ed. Marvin Taylor (Nashville: Abingdon Press, 1976), 31–33.

[5]Norma Thompson, "Current Issues in Religious Education," *Religious Education* 73, no. 6 (1978): 613–18.

[6]Richard R. Osmer, *A Teachable Spirit: Recovering the Teaching Office in the Church* (Louisville: Westminster/John Knox Press, 1990), 144.

[7]James Cone, *For My People: Black Theology and the Black Church* (Maryknoll, N.Y.: Orbis Books, 1984), 118.

[8]J. Deotis Roberts, *Black Theology in Dialogue* (Philadelphia: Westminster Press, 1987), 117.

[9]Harris, *Pastoral Theology,* 113.

[10]Grant Shockley, "Black Theology and Religious Education," in *Theology of Religious Education,* ed. Randolph Crump Miller (Birmingham, Ala.: Religious Education Press, 1995), 321.

[11]Olivia Pearl Stokes, "Black Theology: A Challenge to Religious Education," in *Religious Education and Theology,* ed. Norman H. Thompson (Birmingham, Ala.: Religious Education Press, 1982), 97.

[12]N. Lynne Westfield, *Dear Sisters: A Womanist Practice of Hospitality* (Cleveland: Pilgrim Press, 2001) and Yolanda Y. Smith, *Reclaiming the Spiritualists: New Possibilities for the African American Christian Education* (Cleveland: Pilgrim Press, 2004).

[13]Anne Wimberly, *Nurturing Faith and Hope: Black Worship as a Model for Christian Education* (Cleveland: Pilgrim Press, 2004), 17.

[14]Little, "Theology and Religious Education," 39.

[15]Calvin E. Bruce, "Black Evangelical Christianity and Black Theology," in *Black Theology II: Essays on the Formation and Outreach of Contemporary Black Theology,* ed. Calvin E. Bruce and William R. Jones (Lewisburg, Pa.: Bucknell University Press, 1978), 176.

[16]Ronald E. Roberts, "Leadership Studies in Black Evangelicalism," (unpublished D.Min. diss., Dallas Theological Seminary, 1985), 17.

[17]Harris, *Pastoral Theology,* 7.

[18]Joseph A. Johnson, *A Proclamation Theology* (Shreveport, La.: Fourth Episcopal District, 1977), 155.

[19]Wimberly, *Nurturing Faith and Hope,* 131.

[20]Harris, *Pastoral Theology,* 103.

[21]Ronald J. Allen, *Preaching and Practical Ministry* (St. Louis: Chalice Press, 2001), 42.

[22]Henry Mitchell, *Black Preaching* (Philadelphia: J.B. Lippincott, 1970), 162.

[23]J. Deotis Roberts, *Liberation and Reconciliation: A Black Theology* (Philadelphia: Westminster Press, 1971).

[24]Major Jones, *Black Awareness: A Theology of Hope* (Nashville: Abingdon Press, 1971).

[25]Lawrence H. Mamiya and E. Eric Lincoln, *The Black Church in the African American Experience* (Durham and London: Duke University Press, 1990), 179.

[26]Gayraud Wilmore, "Pastoral Ministry in the Origin and Development of Black Theology," *The Journal of the Interdenominational Theological Center* (Fall 1974): 216.

[27]Forrest E. Harris, *Ministry for Social Crisis: A Theology and Praxis in the Black Church Tradition* (Macon, Ga.: Mercer University Press, 1993) and Shockley, "Black Theology and Religious Education."

[28]See, for example, Grant Shockley "Liberation Theology, Black Theology, and Religious Education," in *Foundations for Christian Education in an Era of Change,* ed. Marvin J. Taylor (Nashville: Abingdon Press, 1976), 80–95.

[29]Olivia Pearl Stokes, "Education in the Black Church: Design for Change," *Religious Education* 69, no. 4 (1974): 440.

[30]Ibid.

[31]Michael Dyson, *Between God and Gangsta Rap* (Oxford, Miss.: Oxford University Press, 1996).

[32]J. Deotis Roberts, *Africentric Christianity: A Theological Appraisal for Ministry* (Valley Forge, Pa.: Judson Press, 2000).

[33]Cheryl Townsend Gilkes, "We Have a Beautiful Mother: Womanist Musings on the Afrocentric Idea," in *Living the Intersection: Womanism and Afrocentrism in Theology,* ed. Cheryl Sanders (Philadelphia: Fortress Press, 1995), 21–22.

[34]Osmer, *A Teachable Spirit,* 71.

[35]Alice Walker, *In Search of Our Mothers' Gardens* (San Diego: Harcourt Brace Jovanovich, 1983).

[36]Delores C. Carpenter, *A Time For Honor: A Portrait of African American Clergywomen* (St. Louis: Chalice Press, 2001), 140.

[37]Westfield, *Dear Sisters,* 32.

[38]Brita L. Gill-Austern, "Pedagogy Under the Influence of Feminism and Womanism,"in *Feminist and Womanist Pastoral Theology,* ed. Bonnie J. Miller-McLemore (Nashville: Abingdon Press, 1999), 151.

[39]Carpenter, *A Time for Honor,* 140.

[40]Obeah is a religion that involves witchcraft, originally practiced in Africa and surviving mostly in the English-speaking Caribbean.

[41]Flora Bridges, *Resurrection Song: African American Spirituality* (Maryknoll, N.Y.: Orbis Books, 2001), 3.

[42]Howard Thurman, *Creative Encounter: An Interpretation of Religion and Social Witness* (New York: Harper & Brothers, 1954), 20.

[43]Kenneth Hill, *Reflections on Black Worship: Expressing a Way of Prayer* (Nashville: AMEC Publishing House, 1998).

[44]Howard Thurman, *With Head and Heart: The Autobiography of Howard Thurman* (New York: Harcourt Brace Jovanovich, 1979).

[45]Ibid.

[46]Walter Wink, *Unmasking the Powers: The Invisible Forces That Determine Human Existence* (Philadelphia: Fortress Press, 1986), 4.

[47]The U.S. Census Bureau estimates that 1.4 million Hispanics are African American and that another 0.3 million are biracial. See the press release titled "Young, Diverse, Urban: Hispanic Population Reaches All-Time High of 38.8 Million, New Census Bureau Estimates Show." Available on the Internet at: http://www.census.gov/Press-Release/www/2003/cb03-100.html.

Chapter 6: Black Theologies in Dialogue

[1]Drawn from Robert Pazmiño, *Foundational Issues in Christian Education* (Grand Rapids: Baker Books, 1997), 254.

[2]Ibid., 255.

[3]List of participants: Wendell Anthony–President, NAACP, Detroit; James Cone–Professor, Union Theological Seminary; Michael Eric Dyson–Professor, University of Pennsylvania; James Forbes–Senior Minister, Riverside Church; Jacquelyn Grant–Professor, Interdenominational Theological Center; Noel Jones–Minister, Greater Bethany Community Church; Tom Joyner–Talk Show Host, ABC Radio; Vashti Murphy McKenzie–Bishop, African Methodist Episcopal Church; Paul Morton–Bishop, Full Gospel Baptist Church Fellowship; Eugene Rivers–Minister, Azusa Christian Community; Tavis Smiley–

Talk Show Host, NPR (National Public Radio); Gardner Taylor–Senior Pastor Emeritus, Concord Baptist Church; Marvin Winans–Minister, Perfecting Church; Jeremiah Wright–Minister, Trinity United Church of Christ; Charles Adams–Minister, Hartford Memorial Baptist Church; Jamal-Harrison Bryant–Minister, Empowerment Temple; Carlton Pearson–Minister, Oklahoma City; Cynthia Hale–Pastor, Ray of Hope Christian Church; Floyd Flake–Minister, Greater Allen A.M.E. Cathedral; Cain Hope Felder–Professor, Howard University, Divinity School; Kwame Kilpatrick–Mayor of Detroit; Cheryl Townsend Gilkes–Minister, Union Baptist Church; and Carolyn Ann Knight–Professor, Interdenominational Theological Center.

⁴Luis Pedraja, "Building Bridges Between Communities of Struggle: Similarities, Differences, Objectives, and Goals," in *The Ties That Bind,* ed. Anthony B. Pinn and Benjamin Valentin (New York: Continuum, 2002) 205–19.

⁵Ibid., 207.

⁶William H. Bentley, *National Black Evangelical Association: Evolution of a Concept of Ministry,* rev. ed. (Chicago: Wm. H. Bentley, 1979), 12.

⁷Calvin E. Bruce, *Black Theology: Essays on the Formation and Outreach of Contemporary Black Theology,* ed. William R. Jones (Lewisburg, Pa.: Bucknell University Press, 1978), 20.

⁸Ibid., 163.

⁹Ibid., 165.

¹⁰Ibid., 172.

¹¹Kelly Brown Douglas, *The Black Christ* (Maryknoll, N.Y.: Orbis Books, 1984), 114.

¹²Delores S. Williams, "Womanist Theology: Black Women's Voices," in *Weaving the Visions: New Patterns in Feminist Spirituality,* ed. Judith Plaskow and Carol P. Christ (San Francisco: HarperCollins, 1989), 183.

¹³Delores S. Williams, *Sisters in the Wilderness: The Challenge of Womanist God-Talk* (Maryknoll, N.Y.: Orbis Books, 1993), 167.

¹⁴Vinson Synan, *The Century of the Holy Spirit: 100 Years of Pentecostal and Charismatic Renewal 1901–2001* (Nashville: Thomas Nelson, 2001), 285.

¹⁵R.L. Speaks, *The Prelude to Pentecost: A Theology of the Holy Spirit* (Charlotte, N.C.: A.M.E. Zion Publishing House, 1985), xii.

¹⁶Bishop Joseph A. Johnson, *Proclamation Theology* (Shreveport, La.: Fourth Episcopal District Press, 1977), 152.

¹⁷Olin P. Moyd, *The Sacred Art: Preaching and Theology in the African American Tradition* (Valley Forge, Pa.: Judson Press, 1995).

¹⁸Calvin E. Bruce, "Black Spirituality and Theological Method," *The Journal of Interdenominational Theological Center* 1 (Spring 1976): 65.

¹⁹Father Paisius Altschul, *An Unbroken Circle: Linking Ancient African Christianity to the African-American Experience* (St. Louis: Brotherhood of St. Moses the Black, 1997).

²⁰Cyprian Davis, "Black Spirituality: A Catholic Perspective," in *One Faith, One Lord, One Baptism: The Hopes and Experiences of the Black Community in the Archdiocese of New York,* vol. 2 (New York: Archdiocese of New York, 1988).

²¹J. Deotis Roberts, "Thurman's Contribution to Black Religious Thought," in *God and Human Freedom: A Festschrift in Honor of Howard Thurman,* ed. Henry James Young (Richmond, Ind.: Friends United Press, 1963), 143.

²²James H. Cone, *Black Theology and Black Power* (New York: Seabury Press, 1969), 130.

Chapter 7: Educating in the African American Church

¹Anthony T. Evans, *Biblical Theology and the Black Experience* (Dallas: Black Evangelistic Enterprise, Inc., 1977), 3.

²Drawn from Robert Pazmiño, *Foundational Issues in Christian Education* (Grand Rapids: Baker Books, 1997), 45.

³Bishop Joseph A. Johnson, *Proclamation Theology* (Shreveport, La.: Fourth District Press, 1977), 107.

⁴James Evans, *We Have Been Believers: An African American Systematic Theology* (Minneapolis: Fortress Press, 1992), 140.

⁵Cyprian Davis, *The History of Black Catholics in the United States* (New York: Crossroad, 1990); and Jamie T. Phelps, ed., *Black Catholic: The Challenge and Gift of Black Folk Contributions of African American Experience and Thought to Catholic Theology* (Milwaukee: Marquette University Press, 1997).

[6]Richard Foster, *Celebration of Discipline* (New York: Harper & Row, 1978).

[7]Forrest Harris, *Ministry for Social Crisis: Theology and Praxis in the Black Church Tradition* (Macon, Ga.: Mercer University Press, 1993), 63.

[8]Harold Dean Trulear, "African American Religious Education," in *Multi-cultural Religious Education*, ed. Barbara Wilkerson (Birmingham, Ala.: Religious Education Press, 1997), 180.

[9]Harold Cruse, *The Crisis of the Negro Intellectual* (New York: William Morrow, 1967); and Maulana Ron Karenga, *Introduction to Black Studies* (Inglewood, Calif.: Kawaida Publications, 1982).

[10]Molefi Kete Asante, *Afrocentricity* (New Jersey: Africa World Press, 1988).

[11]Pazmiño, *Foundational Issues*, 45.

Chapter 8: Teaching Roles of African American Clergy

[1]Eric C. Lincoln and Lawrence H. Mamiya, *The Black Church in the African American Experience* (Durham, N.C.: Duke University Press, 1990), 8.

[2]J. Deotis Roberts, *The Prophethood of Black Believers: An African American Political Theology for Ministry* (Louisville: Westminster John Knox Press, 1994), 41.

[3]Richard Osmer, *A Teachable Spirit: Recovering the Teaching Office in the Church* (Louisville: Westminster/John Knox Press, 1990), 205.

[4]Parker J. Palmer, *The Courage to Teach: Exploring the Inner Landscape of a Teacher's Life* (San Francisco: Jossey-Bass, 1998), 1.

[5]Vincent L. Wimbush, *The Bible and African Americans* (Minneapolis: Fortress Press, 2003), 85.

[6]Robert M. Mulholland, *The Power of Scripture in Spiritual Formation* (Nashville: The Upper Room, 1985).

[7]Joseph V. Crockett, *Teaching Scripture: From an Africa American Perspective* (Nashville: Disciplines Resources, 1991).

[8]James H. Evans, *We Have Been Believers: An African-American Systematic Theology* (Minneapolis: Fortress Press, 1992).

[9]Grant S. Shockley, "Black Pastoral Leadership in Religious Education: Social Justice Correlates," in *The Pastor as Religious Educator*, ed. Robert L. Browning (Birmingham, Ala: Religious Education Press), 206.

[10]Vincent Wimbush, "Biblical Historical Study as Liberation: Toward an Afro-Christian Hermeneutic," in *The Journal of Religious Thought* 42, no.2 (Fall-Winter, 1984–85): 10.

[11]Anne Wimberly, *Soul Stories: African American Christian Education* (Nashville: Abingdon Press, 1994), 33.

Chapter 9: Reshaping the Future of African American Christian Religious Education

[1]Robert W. Pazmiño, *God Our Teacher: Theological Basics in Christian Education* (Grand Rapids, Mich.: Baker Academic, 2001), 87.

[2]Delores C. Carpenter, *A Time for Honor: A Portrait of African American Clergywomen* (St. Louis: Chalice Press, 2001), 180.

[3]Ronald F. Theimann, *Constructing a Public Theology: The Church in a Pluralistic Culture* (Louisville: Westminster/John Knox Press, 1991), 167–68.

[4]Janet Pais, *Suffer the Children: A Theology of Liberation by a Victim of Child Abuse* (Mahwah, N.J.: Paulist Press, 1991).

[5]Jacquelyn Grant, "A Theological Framework," in *Working with Black Youth: Opportunities for Christian Ministry*, ed. Charles R. Foster and Grant Shockley (Nashville: Abingdon Press, 1989), 55.

Bibliography

Alho, Olli. *The Religion of the Slaves.* Helsinki: Academia Scientarium Fennica, 1976.

Allen, Norm R. *African American Humanism.* New York: Prometheus Books, 1991.

Allen, Richard. *The Life, Experience, and Gospel Labors.* Nashville: AME Publishing, 1990.

Allen, Ronald J. *Interpreting the Gospel: An Introduction to Preaching.* St. Louis: Chalice Press, 1998.

_____. *Preaching and Practical Ministry.* St. Louis: Chalice Press, 2001.

Altschul, Father Paisuis. *An Unbroken Circle: Linking Ancient African American Christianity to the African-American Experience.* St. Louis: BSMD, 1977.

Angell, Stephen W., and Anthony B. Pinn. *Social Protest Thought in the African Methodist Episcopal Church, 1862–1939.* Knoxville: University of Tennessee Press, 2000.

Asante, Molefi Kete. *The Afrocentric Idea.* Philadelphia: Temple University Press, 1987.

Atlantic Monthly. September 1902.

Baker-Fletcher, Karen. *A Singing Something: Womanist Reflections on Anna Julia Cooper.* New York: Crossroads, 1994.

Beck, Stephen. *Experience and Tradition: A Primer in Black Biblical Hermeneutics.* Nashville: Abingdon Press, 1990.

Beckford, Robert. "Black Pentecostals and Black Politics." In *Pentecostals After a Century: Global Perspectives on a Movement in Transition,* edited by Allan H. Anderson and Walter J. Hollenweger, 48–59. Sheffield, U.K.: Sheffield Academic Press, 1999.

Ben-Jochannan, Yosef. *African Origins of the Major Western Religions.* New York: Alkebu-lan Books, 1970.

Bentley, William H. "Bible Believers in the Black Community." In *The Evangelicals,* edited by David F. Wells and John D. Woodbridge, 128–41. Grand Rapids, Mich.: Baker Book House, 1975.

_____. *National Black Evangelical Association: Evolution of a Concept of Ministry,* rev. ed. Chicago: Wm. H. Bentley, 1979.

Bethune, Mary McLeod. "Girding for Peace." Bethune papers at Bethune Cookman College, Daytona Beach, Fla.

_____. "What I Believe About Jesus Christ." Bethune papers at Bethune Cookman College, Daytona Beach, Fla.

Billingsley, Andrew. *Climbing Jacob's Ladder: The Enduring Legacy of African American Families.* New York: Simon & Schuster, 1992.

Birchett, Colleen. *Urban Church Education.* Birmingham, Ala.: Religious Education Press, 1989.

Blair, Christine Eaton. *The Art of Teaching the Bible: A Practical Guide for Adults.* Louisville: Geneva Press, 2001.

Blassingame, John. *The Slave Community.* New York: Oxford University Press, 1972.

Boylan, Anne. *Sunday School: The Formation of an American Institution 1790–1880.* New Haven: Yale University, 1988.

Bridges, Flora Wilson. *Resurrection Song: African American Spirituality.* New York: Orbis Books, 2001.

Brown, Michael. *Blackening of the Bible: Aims of African American Biblical Scholarship.* Harrisburg, Pa.: Trinity Press International, 2004.

Bruce, Calvin E. "Black Evangelical Christianity and Black Theology." In *Black Theology II: Essays on the Formation and Outreach of Contemporary Black Theology,* edited by Calvin E. Bruce and William R. Jones, 163–87. Lewisburg, Pa.: Bucknell University Press, 1978.

_____. "Black Spirituality, Language, and Faith," in *Religious Education* 4 (July/ August 1976): 363–76.

_____. "Black Spirituality and Theological Method," in *The Journal of the Interdenominational Theological Center* 1 (Spring 1976): 65–76.

Bruce, Calvin E., and William R. Jones. *Black Theology: Essays on the Foundation and Outreach of Contemporary Black Theology.* Lewisburg: Bucknell University Press, 1978.

Brueggemann, Walter. *The Creative Word: Canon as Model for Biblical Foundation.* Philadelphia: Fortress Press, 1982.

Carpenter, Delores C. *A Time for Honor: A Portrait of African American Clergywomen.* St. Louis: Chalice Press, 2001.

Carter, J.L. "The Negro Vacation Church School," in *International Journal of Religious Education* (March 1931): 17:22.

Chapman, Mark L. *Christianity on Trial: African American Religious Thought Before and After Black Power.* New York: Orbis Books, 1996.

Chism, Keith. *African American Christian Education for the African American Community.* Nashville: Discipleship Resources, 1995.

Christian Recorder, August 11, 1866.

Cleage, Albert Jr. *The Black Messiah.* New York: Sheed and Ward, 1996.

_____. *Black Christian Nationalism.* New York: William Morrow and Co., 1972.

Cobb, Therion E. *Adult Teacher Quarterly.* Nashville: AMEC Publishing, 1975.

Coleman, Will. *Tribal Talk: Black Theology, Hermeneutics, and African/American Ways of Telling the Story.* University Park, Pa.: Penn. State University Press, 2000.

Cone, James. *A Black Theology of Liberation.* Philadelphia: Lippincott, 1970.

_____. *Black Theology and Black Power.* New York: Seabury, 1969.

_____. *For My People: Black Theology and the Black Church.* New York: Orbis Books, 1984.

_____. *God of the Oppressed.* New York: Seabury, 1975.

Cone, James H., and Gayraud Wilmore. *Black Theology: A Documentary History, Volume II 1980–1992.* Maryknoll, N.Y.: Orbis Books, 1993.

Cooper, Anna J. "Negro Students Questionnaire," courtesy of Moorland Springarn Research Center.

Copher, Charles B. *Black Biblical Studies: An Anthology of Charles B. Copher.* Chicago: Black Light Fellowship, 1993.

Crockett, Joseph V. *Teaching Scripture from an African American Perspective.* Nashville: Discipleship Resources, 1991.

Cruse, Harold. *The Crisis of the Negro Intellectual.* New York: William Morrow, 1967.

Cully, Iris V. *The Bible on Christianity Education.* Minneapolis: Fortress Press, 1985.

Davis, Cyprian. "Black Spirituality: A Catholic Perspective," in *Review & Expositor* 80 (Winter 1983): 97–108.

De Azurara, Gromes Eannes. *The Chronicle of the Discovery and Conquest of Guinea.* London: Hakluyt Society, 1896.

Douglas, Kelly Brown. *The Black Christ.* New York: Orbis Books, 1984.

Dubois, W.E.B. *The Negro Church.* Atlanta: Atlanta University Press, 1903.

_____. *Souls of Black Folk.* New York: Bantam Books, 1903.

_____. *The Autobiography of W.E.B. Dubious: A Soliloquy on Viewing My Life from the Last of Its First Century.* New York: International Publishers Co, 1968.

_____. *W.E.B. Dubois Speaks 1890–1919,* ed. Philip S. Foner. New York: Pathfinder Press, 1970.

Dyson, Michael. *Between God and Gangsta Rap.* Oxford: Oxford University Press, 1996.

Edwards, Lonzy. "Religious Education by Blacks During Reconstruction," in *Religious Education* 69 (July-August 1974): 412–21.

Eldridge, Daryl. *The Teaching Ministry of the Church.* Nashville: Broadman & Holman, 1995.

Evans, Anthony T. *Biblical Theology and the Black Experience.* Dallas: Black Evangelistic Enterprise, 1977.

Evans, James. *We Have Been Believers: An African-American Systematic Theology.* Minneapolis: Fortress Press, 1992.

Everding, H. Edward, Jr. "Hermeneutical Approach to Educational Theory." In *Foundations for Christian Education in an Age of Change,* edited by Marvin Taylor, 41–53. Nashville: Abingdon Press, 1976.

Felder, Cain Hope. *Stony the Road We Trod.* Minneapolis: Fortress Press, 1991.

_____. *Troubling Biblical Waters: Race, Class and Family.* Maryknoll, N.Y.: Orbis Books, 1969.

Fletcher-Baker, Karen. *A Singing Something: Womanist Reflections on Anna Julia Cooper.* New York: Crossroads, 1994.

Forbes, James. "Shall We Call This Dream Progressive Pentecostalism," in *Spirit* 1, no. 1 (1977): 12–15.

_____. *The Holy Spirit and Preaching.* Nashville: Abingdon Press, 1989.

Foster, Charles R., Ethel R. Johnson, and Grant S. Shockley. *Christian Education Journey of Black Americans: Past, Present, Future.* Nashville: Discipleship Resources, 1985.

Foster, Richard. *Celebration of Discipline.* New York: Harper & Row, 1978.

Franklin, Robert M. *Liberating Visions: Human Fulfillment and Social Justice in African American Thought.* Minneapolis: Fortress Press, 1990.

_____. *Another Day's Journey.* Minneapolis: Fortress Press, 1997.

Frazier, E. Franklin. *The Negro Church in America.* New York: Schocken Books, 1964.

Gilkes, Cheryl Townsend. "We Have a Beautiful Mother: Womanist Musings on the Afrocentric Idea." In *Living the Intersection: Womanism and Afrocentrism in Theology,* edited by Cheryl Sanders, 21–42. Philadelphia: Fortress Press, 1995.

Grant, Jacquelyn. "Black Theology and the Black Woman." In *Black Theology: A Documentary History,* edited by James H. Cone and Gayraud Wilmore, 418–33. Maryknoll, N.Y.: Orbis Books, 1993.

_____. *White Women's Christ and Black Women's Jesus.* Atlanta: Scholars Press, 1989.

_____. "A Theological Framework." In *Working with Black Youth: Opportunities for Christian Ministry,* edited by Charles R. Foster and Grant Shockley, 55–76. Nashville: Abingdon Press, 1989.

Griffin, Paul R. *The Struggle for a Black Theology of Education.* Atlanta: ITC Press, 1993.

Groome, Thomas H. *Christian Religious Education.* San Francisco: Harper Row, 1980.

Harlan, Louis R. *Booker T. Washington: The Wizard of Tuskegee, 1901–1915.* New York: Oxford University Press, 1983.

Harlan, Norman B. *Encyclopedia of Work of Methodism.* Nashville: United Methodist Publishing House, 1974.

Harris, Forrest E. *Ministry for Social Crisis: A Theology and Praxis in the Black Church Tradition.* Macon, Ga.: Mercer University Press, 1993.

Harris, James H. *Pastoral Theology: A Black Church Perspective.* Minneapolis: Fortress Press, 1991.

_____. *Preaching Liberation.* Minneapolis: Fortress Press, 1995.

Hayes, Diana L. *And Still We Rise: An Introduction to Black Liberation Theology.* New York: Paulist Press, 1996.

Hill, Kenneth H. *Charles S. Smith, A Portrait: Sale Son of God.* Nashville: AMEC Publishing, 1993.

_____. *Drinking from Our Well: Foundations for the Ministry of Christian Education in the African American Methodist Episcopal Church.* Nashville: AMEC Publishing House, 1994.

_____. *Reflections on Black Worship: Expressing a Way of Prayer.* Nashville: AMEC Publishing House, 1998.

Hill, Ruth Edmonds, and Patricia Miller King, eds. "Interview with Olivia Pearl Stokes." In *The Black Women Oral History Project,* vol. 9. Westport, Conn.: Meckler Publishing, 1991.

Hollenweger, Walter J. "The Black Roots of Pentecostalism." In *Pentecostals After a Century: Global Perspectives on a Movement in Transition,* edited by Alan Anderson and Walter J. Hollenweger, 33–44. Sheffield, U.K.: Sheffield Academic Press, 1999.

Holmes, Barbara A. *Joy Unspeakable: Contemplative Practices of the Black Church.* Minneapolis: Fortress Press, 2004.

Hopkins, Dwight N. *Introducing Black Theology of Liberation.* Maryknoll, N.Y.: Orbis Books, 1999.

_____. *Shoes That Fit Our Feet: Sources for Constructive Black Theology.* New York: Orbis Books, 1993.

Hopkins, Dwight N., and George Cummings, eds. *Cut Loose Your Stammering Tongues: Black Theology and the Slave Narratives.* Maryknoll, N.Y.: Orbis Books, 1989.

Hoyt, Thomas. "Interpreting Biblical Scholarship for the Black Church Tradition." In *Stony the Road We Trod,* edited by Cain Hope Felder, 17–39. Minneapolis: Fortress Press, 1991.

Hufford, Don. "The Religious Thought of W. E. B. Dubois," in *The Journal of Religious Thought* 53, no. 2 (1997): 73–94.

Jackson, John. *Man, God, and Civilization.* New Hyde Park, N.Y.: University Books, 1972.

Johnson, Bishop Joseph A. *Proclamation Theology.* Shreveport, La.: Fourth District Press, 1977.